T0205192

"This book is the first to recognize that 'Consulting is about experiences,' as Scott Mason puts it. Those who seek to excel must have the skills to make their experiences authentic. And that is just one gem among the many this book offers. Anyone who is thinking about getting into the profession or who is already a consultant—in any industry, not just healthcare—should read it to glean insights from decades of successful engagements. With this book, Scott ascends to being a consultant's consultant. Let him be your guide to a fascinating, rewarding, and fulfilling profession, with your eyes wide open to the risk involved and the effort required."

—B. Joseph Pine II
International speaker, management advisor, and author of
The Experience Economy: Competing for Customer Time, Attention, and Money

"Consulting is a fulfilling career. Not only do you get to meet lots of great people, but you also get to change lives and experience amazing transformations. Because you see lots of different perspectives and innovations in action, you have the pleasure of sharing best practices and watching organizations learn and grow. Yet, being a great consultant is more than having good content. Running the business side can be tricky. Scott Mason does a wonderful job of giving you the foundation you need to succeed. I wish there had been a book like this when I was starting out."

—Quint Studer
Founder of the Studer Group and Studer Community Institute and
author of multiple books, including *The Busy Leader's Handbook*

"I found Scott Mason's book fascinating. Both thought provoking and interesting, it brought back a lot of memories! I really liked the observation, 'To do well in consulting is to understand the client's perspective.' Right on! With nearly one-fifth of the nation's gross domestic product devoted to healthcare, there are virtually unlimited opportunities for knowledgeable, independent individuals to introduce improvements. At a time when healthcare is being reimagined, this book will ensure that the aspiring consultant is prepared to avoid common mistakes and able to venture closer to exceptionalism."

—Norman R. Augustine
Retired chairman and CEO of Lockheed Martin and prolific writer,
speaker, and international consultant

"I cannot think of anyone better qualified to write this book than Scott Mason. He has an impressive track record and reputation for thought leadership in healthcare strategy. His insights are born of a wide variety of experiences, with many different organizations, where he has been a valued counselor to top healthcare leaders. This one-of-a-kind book covers all aspects of healthcare consulting. It is detailed, but not laborious; insightful, offering great tips; and very well written. Everyone who reads this book will benefit from it."

—Carson F. Dye, FACHE
Search consultant, author, and speaker on healthcare and physician leadership

The
Healthcare
Consultant's
Handbook

The
Healthcare
Consultant's
Handbook

Career Opportunities and Best Practices

Scott A. Mason

ACHE Management Series

Library of Congress Cataloging-in-Publication Data

Names: Mason, Scott A., author.
Title: The healthcare consultant's handbook : career opportunities and best practices / Scott A. Mason.
Other titles: Management series (Ann Arbor, Mich.)
Description: Chicago, IL : Health Administration Press, a division of the Foundation of the American College of Healthcare Executives, [2021] | Series: HAP/ACHE management series | Includes bibliographical references and index. | Summary: "In an era of increasing complexity in healthcare, consultants can help organizations address inefficiencies, improve patient experiences, and set overall strategy. This book explains what it takes to be an exceptional consultant"—Provided by publisher.
Identifiers: LCCN 2020045807 (print) | LCCN 2020045808 (ebook) | ISBN 9781640552067 (paperback) | ISBN 9781640552081 (epub) | ISBN 9781640552098 (mobi)
Subjects: MESH: Health Services Administration | Consultants | Career Choice | Vocational Guidance | Practice Guideline
Classification: LCC RA440.9 (print) | LCC RA440.9 (ebook) | NLM W 64 | DDC 362.1023—dc23
LC record available at https://lccn.loc.gov/2020045807
LC ebook record available at https://lccn.loc.gov/2020045808

The paper used in this publication meets the minimum requirements of American National Standard for Information Sciences—Permanence of Paper for Printed Library Materials, ANSI Z39.48-1984. ⊚™

Acquisitions editor: Jennette McClain; Manuscript editors: Roger Eichorn and Robert Shannon; Cover designer: James Slate; Layout: Integra

Found an error or a typo? We want to know! Please e-mail it to hapbooks@ache.org, mentioning the book's title and putting "Book Error" in the subject line.

For photocopying and copyright information, please contact Copyright Clearance Center at www.copyright.com or at (978) 750-8400.

Health Administration Press
A division of the Foundation of the American
   College of Healthcare Executives
300 S. Riverside Plaza, Suite 1900
Chicago, IL 60606-6698
(312) 424-2800

*This book is dedicated to Vaughan A. Smith (1943–2014), president
of the American Association of Healthcare Consultants from 1971 to 1998,
who approached his craft with selfless devotion to its members and to
the profession of healthcare consulting.*

Contents

List of Exhibits

Preface

I SET OUT TO WRITE this book in order to describe my experience serving as a strategy consultant to healthcare organizations. Many years ago, a colleague, Roger Witalis, shared with me a story about his father, who had run a successful medical practice. When his father retired, all the confidential notes and medical records of his patients ended up in a garbage bag in his garage. I became determined to capture some of what I've learned as a management consultant in a different way.

Early in my career, I faced a choice: I could go the established direction of anyone who had earned a master's degree in hospital administration, or I could take a more unusual path and become a career consultant. I knew I could live a comfortable life as a healthcare executive, yet for some reason—and to the surprise of more than a few people—something drove me to take "the road less traveled." On reflection, I think my decision was, in part, motivated by my firsthand experience with some of the pervasive political challenges that permeate healthcare at virtually all levels.

What followed was a career in strategy consulting to healthcare organizations. I moved 2,300 miles from Phoenix, Arizona, back to Washington, DC, where I had gone to graduate school and had a support group, to launch my solo consulting practice—National Health Advisors, Inc. With that, the adventure began, and I never looked back—until now.

This is not intended as a how-to book, though I do describe many best practices in some detail.[1] In *Flawless Consulting*, his well-known how-to book on consulting, Peter Block writes, "An authentic consultant is not an oxymoron, but a compelling competitive advantage, if unfortunately, a rare one." My intent is to write about the *experience* of management consulting, with an emphasis on

---

1. There are various ways to acquire the requisite skills or learn how to start a consulting practice. See, for example, Consulting.com and the extensive resources available at One Page Business Plan (www.onepagebusinessplan.com), which was founded by the late Jim Horan. I have not tried to replicate these resources.

authenticity. My understanding of the nature of authenticity relies in part on Jim Gilmore and Joe Pine's *Authenticity: What Consumers Really Want*. Whereas Gilmore and Pine (2007) focus on authenticity in the business context of an economic offering (e.g., a product or service), I focus instead on authenticity as an individual or interpersonal trait. Authenticity is essential to becoming an exceptional consultant.

In consulting, there is the formal, didactic portion that most people might identify, and then there is the less formal "stuff" that really matters. This is an attempt to focus more on the stuff. Specifically, I set out to

- dispel some of the myths about consulting,
- address the intense demands of consulting,
- focus on the some of the nuances specific to management consulting,
- examine the all-important client–consultant relationship from different perspectives,
- help to separate what is important from what is less so,
- discuss some practices common to the best management consultants,
- profile aspects of the healthcare industry that tend to be the focus of consulting services,
- share some of the interesting history of consulting to a relatively young industry like healthcare, and
- analyze some of the learnings from my experiences as a career strategy consultant.

I have divided the book into three parts. The first focuses on the individual experience of consulting, the second on the experience of working at a consulting firm, and the third on best practices for both individuals and firms:

1. **Part I: The Individual Experience.** What is important to know about consulting and how it works? Consulting has both allure and problems associated with it. The value proposition of consulting is critical to understand, notably as it applies to healthcare. Consulting takes different forms and approaches. It is important to understand motivations for becoming a consultant and how these might be positioned from a career perspective. Consultants require a basic set of tools. It is not easy being a consultant, and there is a difference between one who has received formal training and one who has not. Among the requirements to do consulting well is the ability to understand the client perspective. Consultants must also be able to differentiate between a client's perspective and their own.

2. **Part II: The Firm Experience.** How are firms similar or different? Firms take on different forms, which have important implications. There are some interesting surveys of the "best consulting firms." Any consulting firm, regardless of size, must perform an array of basic functions if it is to be sustainable. A few firms are described in each key category to illustrate how they differ. Which firm is right for you is an individual choice that can be based on a variety of relevant criteria.

3. **Part III: Exceptional Consulting.** What are the best practices of the best consultants and firms? Exceptional consulting involves numerous critical success factors, some of which are common sense and others that are quite nuanced. Among the most important is managing the client relationship and the details in such an effective way that it might lead to additional work or a solid referral. Some of the most valued lessons are shared from more than 40 years of healthcare strategy consulting. Consulting to healthcare organizations has a rich history and offers both a fascinating area of focus and a great opportunity for future growth. Residual emotions always seem to be involved in moving on from an existing client, and they need to be carefully managed.

Although this book is meant to be read front-to-back, it is written in such a way that each chapter can stand on its own. I invite readers to begin anywhere and jump around as desired.

REFERENCE

Gilmore, J. H., and B. J. Pine II. 2007. *Authenticity: What Consumers Really Want.* Boston: Harvard Business School Press.

Acknowledgments

I MUST BEGIN BY ACKNOWLEDGING how much I have learned about effective consulting from my clients. In this regard, I have truly been blessed. Professionalism demands that I maintain client confidentiality, but you know who you are and how grateful I am.

Leon Gintzig, PhD, was a professor and second chairman of the Department of Healthcare Administration at George Washington University for more than 20 years, beginning in 1967. He served as my faculty sponsor when I was a doctoral student and spent many hours with me in one-on-one conversations, giving me direction. I continue to be inspired by the memory of his spirit and his energy.

I spent a few years with the American Hospital Association (AHA) in its Washington, DC, office, which was focused mainly on health-policy advocacy. I helped staff in what is now the Center for Health Systems, founded by Dr. Robert Toomey, former CEO of Greenville Hospital System and one of the pioneers of the regional system. Working at the AHA also allowed me to get to know the organization's leadership, including Alex McMahon, at the time the CEO, and Dr. Leo Gehrig, then senior vice president in charge of the Washington office, which oversaw all of the government-relations functions of the AHA. From them I learned some of the nuances of being an internal, as opposed to an external, consultant. In addition, I was exposed to the politics of healthcare and the dynamics of this highly diversified industry.

Through the AHA and my next assignment at Samaritan Health System (now Banner Health) in Phoenix, Arizona, I was able play a supporting role in the dramatic consolidation of the hospital industry into regional health systems that has been taking place ever since. Steve Morris, a CEO pioneer who formed Samaritan, gave me full access to the C-suite of an evolving health system, including to the board of trustees, as the youngest member of his executive team. He had an aggressive leadership style that, while controversial, created a unique culture that enabled considerable innovation during this critical time in the evolution of the US healthcare system.

While I was with Samaritan, half my time was allocated to Associated Hospital Systems (now Premier). There, I was fortunate to report to Roger Larson, who took me under his wing as the first person in that organization to focus on government relations (a precursor to what is now Premier's advocacy arm). The annual guest lecture of the AHA Section on Health Care Systems that bears his name memorializes his courageous leadership as the head of Legacy Health in Portland, Oregon.

My introduction to consulting was with the global consulting firm of Booz Allen Hamilton (hereafter Booz Allen), before I joined the AHA. Bob Tschetter was the leader of the Health and Medical Practice at the time. His kindness of spirit and collaborative leadership style made a lasting impression on me. James Reynolds, who hired me at Booz, instilled in me greater discipline and perhaps a sharper edge. Caro E. Luhrs, MD, also of Booz Allen, was an ex-White House Fellow with extraordinary vision and energy. A Swarthmore graduate and one of only seven women to graduate from Harvard Medical School in 1960 (Harvard Medical School 2020), she brought joy to the profession with her deep intellect and her caring heart.

I must thank Gary Adamson, founder of Starizon Studio, and his team for exposing me to the power and energy of redesigning healthcare to be more of an experience-based business. I took a health system client team through their learning lab for a five-day immersion experience at his Keystone, Colorado, studio. It truly helped me lead a change process for that client and changed my outlook on the future. Through Gary I was also introduced to Joe Pine and Jim Gilmore, who introduced us to and taught us valuable lessons about the experience economy (Pine and Gilmore 2020). Their concepts have guided both my practice and the advice that I have given clients in the latter part of my consulting career.

John Blank, MD, former chief medical officer for United HealthCare, helped me understand some of the nuances of managed care as we collaborated on one of the first seminars on this topic for the American College of Healthcare Executives in the 1990s. He is a board-certified pediatric hematologist who, like many of his colleagues, burned out early in his challenging clinical career. John gave me a genuine appreciation for the healthcare experience that is now embodied in the concept of social determinants of health.

Russ Coile was a pioneering consultant and futurist. A prolific writer and speaker, Russ saw what others missed and was fearless in attempting to communicate his insights. Easily the most collaborative colleague with whom I ever worked, Russ was taken from us way too soon, passing away in 2003 at the age of 60. His legacy is honored in numerous ways, including by an endowed chair and an annual Coile Lectureship at my alma mater, the public health program at George Washington University's Milken Graduate School.

Sister Irene Krause was an early client of mine with whom I spent many hours in pursuit of favorable healthcare strategies. She taught me what it meant to care for the people you work with and that leadership carries with it certain burdens.

I am indebted to many of my colleagues who were part of the now-defunct American Association of Healthcare Consultants (AAHC),[1] including Howard Gershon, Jim Lifton, James Morell, Ed Parkhurst, Larry Tyler, and Jeff Frommelt.

AAHC thrived for almost 30 years under the leadership of Vaughan Smith, to whom this book is dedicated. It was a great honor to serve for many years on the AAHC board of directors and to have served as chairman in 1996–1997. Vaughan Smith, with help from Carolyn Friedman, did a remarkable job in his capacity as president of the association. I will always regret that, despite the efforts of many good people, including James Morrell, Don Wegmiller, and one of my partners, Don Seymour, we were unable to find a softer landing for Vaughan as he approached retirement and that we failed in our efforts to sustain the operations of the association going forward. My 20 years of AAHC experience were made richer by Chet Minkalis (Herman Smith),[2] Larry Tyler (Tyler & Company), Ken Kaufman (KaufmanHall), Dick Johnson (TriBrook), Chuck Heineman (Herman Smith), Earle Wivle (MEDCO), Karl Bartscht (Chi Systems), Larry Lammers (Lammers and Gershon), Hans Tronnes (Hans Tronnes Associates), and Carl Thieme (Cambridge Associates), to name a few. These people taught me much about consulting and about life.

Through AAHC I was also exposed to David Maister of the Harvard Business School, who was considered one of the leading thinkers on managing professional service firms. His highly regarded book, *Managing the Professional Service Firm* (Maister 1993), was published around the time a group of us made a pilgrimage to seek his advice, visiting him at his impressive home office in Cambridge in 1992.

I also wish to acknowledge Deborah J. Bowen, FACHE, CAE, president and CEO of ACHE. She and her predecessor, Tom Dolan, PhD, FACHE, stepped up after the demise of AAHC in an attempt to make a home for consulting members. ACHE plays a unique role as the premier credentialing body for healthcare professionals. I am grateful for her leadership and the support her superb staff have given to this effort over the years. David L. Woodrum, an independent consultant, formerly with the AHA, and Jack Schlosser of Spencer Stuart have done much to give voice to healthcare consulting, having devoted many hours to the ACHE

---

1. See Appendix A for a brief history of AAHC.

2. Chet was an inspirational leader whom we lost at an early age. AAHC created a service award for consulting excellence in his name. Larry Tyler was one of the recipients of this award in 1989.

Healthcare Consultants Forum. Their efforts have done much to inspire me to write this book. I hope to build on their past leadership.

Thanks also to Vicki Gaudette, Rob Shannon, and Jennette McClain (Health Administration Press) for their editorial support.

Finally, I am grateful to my friend and mentor Ron Schram, former leader of Ropes and Gray health law practice in Boston. Ron is a strategic lawyer with whom I worked closely, completing many of the hospital mergers in the late 1990s and early 2000s throughout New England as the hospital industry was consolidating. A true renaissance man, Ron titled his first book, written after retirement, *Nonbillable Hours*. The reflections in my book on some of the times we spent together are a small way of expressing my appreciation for his friendship, heart, and intellect.

REFERENCES

Harvard Medical School. 2020. "Caro Luhrs, MD." Accessed July 27. https://primarycare.hms.harvard.edu/faculty-staff/caro-luhrs.

Maister, D. 1993. *Managing the Professional Service Firm*. New York: Free Press.

Pine, B. J., II, and J. H. Gilmore. 2020. *The Experience Economy: Competing for Customer Time, Attention, and Money*. Boston: Harvard Review Press.

Introduction

Healthcare organizations are challenged like never before to become more responsive to criticisms of complexity, lack of access, and being too costly. Thus, the healthcare industry is undergoing significant disruption, and consultants are playing an important role in its transformation. Indeed, while many people are satisfied with their own doctors and hospitals, most agree that there remains significant inefficiency (waste), healthcare costs more than it should, and there is too much variation in clinical outcomes. The demand for change has never been clearer.

As a result, we healthcare consultants often find ourselves in a unique position as disruptors to help organizations that are attempting to improve the healthcare experience. While the best at our craft can make such engagements seem easy, this is deceiving because many of these engagements are anything but easy. Earning trust as a consultant is hard. Keeping it is perhaps harder.

As society continues to demand a better, less costly healthcare experience, consultants have an essential role to play in helping organizations meet these evolving demands. However, having no real authority or power to demand change, independent consultants can only advise, offering experienced insights and focused communication to influence key changes that can be implemented by their clients. The clarion call for disruption in healthcare involves a broader reach beyond healthcare. According to a recent survey of consultants from *Forbes* (Valet 2019):

> At a time when disruption is seemingly the only constant in the corporate world, business leaders have increasingly enlisted management consultants to develop the digital solutions, employee experiences, and financial strategies they need to remain competitive.

Not all consulting is disruptive. Some consulting is more refined and less dramatic, and some might be more focused on research, innovation, and technology transfer. By sharing observations and experiences from a career of consulting to healthcare organizations, I intend to help you, the reader, better understand what all of this entails, and hope it will improve your ability to manage expectations and aspirations if consulting is in your future.

Much of the book is focused on practical insights into the business of *management consulting*[1] that have served me well. It is based on personal observations from a career spanning more than 40 years and incorporates many stories from specific client experiences. Although these stories are authentic, some of the details have been modified to protect the identity of the client. It is not my intent that this be perceived as a "tell-all" book in the Washington tradition of political hacks. Rather, the stories are intended to make the concepts real and to reveal the real-life joys and tribulations of consulting to healthcare organizations.

DISRUPTION IS REQUIRED TO OVERCOME RESISTANCE

Healthcare has been at the top of political debates for virtually all of the recent national elections. Consensus exists among most stakeholders that the healthcare industry must transform itself more toward a "value-based model" to be more affordable and sustainable. Hopes that healthcare could change itself in an evolutionary way have simply not been realized on a timely basis; it is taking too long.

Transformation is a more dramatic form of change that benefits from people outside an industry, and is often referred to as *disruptive change*. For organizations, people from the outside are often required to effectively penetrate the organizational cultures that need to change. Those within these organizations tend to be invested in the status quo; to these folks, embracing change is simply too risky. In the healthcare industry, hospitals are the main target of this disruption. The industry is being challenged to bend the cost curve by moving upstream to keep people healthier and less in need of hospital care. Consultants serve as a catalyst for change to help reform organizations by validating necessary changes and assisting to overcome the bureaucracy that often protects the status quo. It is a natural defense mechanism that organizations in every industry exhibit some resistance to change and reform. Healthcare organizations are no exception.

That independent consultants are an essential part of implementing transformational change is not universally understood or acknowledged, despite the fact that some of the most prominent voices in healthcare reform have been professional consultants. Our contributions are evident by our writing and research,

---

1. The term *consulting* is used throughout the book as shorthand for *management consulting*. Jim Allen of Booz Allen is credited with first using this term in a 1929 brochure about the firm.

our speaking, and our functioning as trusted advisors to our clients. Yet, when it comes time to recognize leaders in the industry, the voice of management consultants is often missing. Like many industries, I suspect, recognition tends to go to the traditional players: people who lead hospitals and health systems, medical groups, insurance companies, and regional health networks. For reasons that are not entirely clear, even some of these prominent executives, some of whom might have previously spent significant time in the role of a consultant, have tended to overlook valuable lessons learned as consultants that could be shared when they reflect back on their accomplishments.

CONSULTING IS NOT WELL UNDERSTOOD

Perhaps some of this lack of recognition reflects the reality that consulting remains one of the more misunderstood occupations one can pursue. Many people who use the label "consultant" are doing so "on the side." Thus, consulting is sometimes more an avocation than a vocation. Indeed, some people who have "day jobs" cite consulting as something they do to supplement their income. Selling their time and talents at an attractive hourly rate may appeal to their entrepreneurial spirit. Since there are virtually no legal barriers to carrying the title "consultant," it becomes a convenient label. Yet, it can be argued that such casual treatment of the label only adds to the confusion of what it truly means to be a practicing consultant. It also detracts from its being recognized as a legitimate profession.

CONSULTING, WHILE SEDUCTIVE, IS ALSO RISKY

If consulting is thus easily misunderstood, what are some of the consequences? Among the most onerous consequences is the seduction that can lead many toward attempting to launch such a career, only to find that it can be quite treacherous. Whether it is the result of the cyclical nature of a difficult economic climate, where fewer consultants are being hired, or the simple realization that one's talents are not suited to such pursuits, or perhaps the sudden recognition that marketing one's talents to prospective clients requires a comfort with sales, the warning is real. "Buyer beware," as the lawyers say. Pursuing consulting as a profession is not as easy as most people think. There is much that can go wrong, and much is required to be a trusted advisor on a sustainable basis. In the end, consultants need clients in order to thrive. After acquiring marketable skills (knowledge and expertise), it is through the market—getting and retaining successful clients—that a rewarding consulting career is defined.

Despite these risks, consulting remains one of the most popular careers being considered by new professionals who recently completed undergraduate and graduate degrees with a focus on healthcare. The Association of University Programs in Health Administration is the organization that works with graduate and undergraduate programs in health administration. As of this writing, there are a few hundred undergraduate and graduate programs in health administration. Generally, these programs are housed within a school of public health, business school, or school of public administration or public policy. People who manage healthcare organizations tend to have a graduate degree.

CONSULTING HAS BROAD APPEAL TO NEW PROFESSIONALS AND THOSE SEEKING A CAREER CHANGE

According to a number of surveys, consulting is the most attractive job for graduates of MBA programs (Bloomberg Businessweek 2020). Among recent classes at my alma mater, George Washington University, it is estimated that at least 10–15 percent of those who graduated with a master's degree from the Milken Institute School of Public Health have pursued consulting as a first job (Friedman 2019). However, consulting skills are not typically taught as course content. Often, the most exposure that a student might have to consulting is through a guest speaker or through conversations with a consultant they know. Compared to other, more traditional career choices, universities do not help students understand consulting as a career option. Alas, to be truly understood, consulting is ultimately something that must be experienced. This book aims to close this gap and prepare the reader for that experience should they decide to pursue a consulting career.

It is not only new professionals who are expressing an interest in consulting. More midlevel executives seem increasingly eager for a career change. In addition, experienced senior healthcare executives are migrating toward consulting as they are nearing retirement. Starting some years ago, a few prominent healthcare executives, who later in their careers were CEOs and senior executives of hospitals and health systems, became full-time consultants. What began as a few isolated examples has now become more common—seasoned executives turning to consulting as a potential "soft landing." This trend is worthy of more study and understanding.

That professional consultants play a major role in the transformation of healthcare is not subject to debate. Given that both new professionals and seasoned executives seem increasingly drawn toward consulting, more exposure to the rigors of consulting is warranted. For those who are interested in consulting, there are relatively few resources—other than anecdotes and guest visits by full-time consultants and recent alumni—to provide some enlightenment regarding the experience of consulting to the healthcare industry. Yet, the ability of healthcare to shift more toward value depends, at least in part, on the continued advice of experienced consultants who excel at their craft.

MY CONSULTING EXPERIENCE

Consulting is personal, and every consultant's journey is different. Hence, it is important that I reveal some of my experiences before we get started. As I look back, I had two distinct advantages. First, I was fortunate to work for the oldest management consulting firm, Booz Allen,[2] where I was surrounded by very talented people and where I was introduced to the basics of the profession. My second advantage relates to understanding the intricacies of the healthcare industry. In this regard, I got to work with a cadre of brilliant pioneers in healthcare, including both health system leaders and pioneers in healthcare consulting. Not everyone gets to work with "Hall of Fame" industry leaders. Being exposed to such immense talent just as the US healthcare "system" began its transformation was pivotal to my career. It gave me the opportunity to connect some dots, which after all is what strategists do.

Also, before I get too far into this discussion, I feel obligated to point out a critical observation. One of the great challenges of consulting is to be "in the moment." By that I mean having a presence of mind that allows you to experience important insights at the time of the client interaction. I believe, for most people, this happens only after gaining hands-on experiences through many client engagements. That was certainly the case for me.

The reason to point this out is that, in sharing my experiences, some (if not most) of the enlightenment I gained from these experiences might have occurred with the benefit of hindsight. To claim otherwise is to suggest an omniscience that I don't possess. Sure, I got better at being in the moment as I gained experience and emotional intelligence. But, in some cases, it might have taken years for me to process some insights that I ultimately derived from a particular situation (no doubt there is still some processing going on). There were more than a few times when, following a key client interaction, I said to myself, "What just happened?"

---

2. Founded in 1914, the firm reflected heavily on its founders, Ed Booz and Jim Allen, and their educational roots at Northwestern University. Their values and client orientation have endured the test of time and survive to this day.

That said, I do seem to have a knack for thinking on my feet. As you will see from some of the experiences I share, a few confrontations required quick thinking to be effectively managed.

With more than 40 years of strategy consulting experience as a trusted industry advisor, I am that rare person in healthcare commonly referred to as a *career consultant*. I do not think this happened by chance. In support of this career, I have traveled over 5 million miles to serve clients in 40 states from coast to coast, encompassing literally thousands of engagements, some of which have lasted about a month, but most of which have lasted four to six months. I have served almost 500 specific clients—mostly hospitals and health systems—each having unique programs, cultures, issues, and challenges. Yes, I detect some common patterns, but the people are always different. After all, healthcare is ultimately about people.

CONSULTING IS INTENSE

The workload of a management consultant can be extreme at times. I have always felt either too busy or not busy enough. While the vast majority of engagements have been challenging and rewarding, not every assignment is. Moreover, there are clearly some things that, with the wisdom of hindsight, I would have done differently.

Overall, though, I would not change a thing. The highs are remarkable when a client successfully embarks on a new path or solves a chronic problem as a result of your input. At the same time, one must acknowledge that the lows, when they occur, can be debilitating. To be sure, I have relied on faith and family to take me through a few rough patches over the years.

In the long run, I have spent much more time with my clients in the rarified air of opportunity and have truly been rewarded in many different ways as a servant leader and advisor. I have always defined my success by that of my clients. Both at the corporate level, through superior positioning in a highly competitive market, and on an individual level, through advancement to bigger and better jobs. Although much of what consultants do remains anonymous, there are often opportunities for innovation, and some are occasionally recognized (one CEO, Brian Grissler at Stamford Health, was the Ernst & Young Regional Entrepreneur of the Year for Social Enterprise in the Metropolitan New York Area). Many lessons were learned along the way. While most of these lessons have been positive, others have been difficult to accept. Either way, I am the better for it, as are my clients.

It is my hope that sharing some experiences and observations, warts and all, will help the reader recognize some of the nuances that are so much a part of management consulting. To the new professional, some of the examples might not yet resonate because of the complexities involved. Managing expectations is critical to having a good consulting career experience. To those who read this book, may it help you to develop a set of expectations grounded in reality that ultimately translates into an exceptional and rewarding consulting career, if that is the path you choose.

REFERENCES

Bloomberg Businessweek. 2020. "Best B-Schools, 2019–2020: Where Recent MBA Grads Work." Accessed January 20. www.bloomberg.com/business-schools/.

Friedman, L. H. 2019. Interview with the author, September 11.

Valet, V. 2019. "America's Best Management Consulting Firms 2019." *Forbes*. Published March 19. www.forbes.com/sites/vickyvalet/2019/03/19/americas-best-management-consulting-firms-2019/.

PART I

The Individual Experience

CONSULTING IS ABOUT EXPERIENCES. Experiences with problems that need to be solved, with techniques that need to be developed or applied, with balancing short-term and long-term considerations, with managing expectations (both your own and those of your team and clients). I approach consulting as a set of experiences in the context of the broader *Experience Economy* (Pine and Gilmore 2020), especially for healthcare organizations that should be doing much more to effectively manage the consumer experience.

My intent is to use stories drawn from my own experience to help explain some of the more opaque elements of professional consulting. It has been suggested that one key skill of consultants is to make the complex simple. I use storytelling to try to accomplish this.

Furthermore, I intend to make consulting less an idea and more a reality. Too many people have been seduced by the allure of consulting only to be dashed upon the rocks of an unexpectedly demanding profession. As Jim Collins notes in *Good to Great*, "You absolutely cannot make a series of good decisions without first confronting the brutal facts" (Collins 2001). Anyone contemplating a career in consulting is well advised to confront head-on the realities of life as a consultant, some of which can be quite disruptive.

CHAPTER 1

Why Consulting?

THERE ARE ANY NUMBER of reasons one might choose to pursue a career in consulting. The idea of spending your career sharing your knowledge to help others can be undeniably appealing, especially for those of us who are driven to serve others.

Other things that make the idea of consulting attractive include

- freedom and independence to pursue things that interest you,
- ability to influence change and make a difference,
- ability to gain experience from a wide variety of situations in a relatively short period of time,
- financial security, and
- escape from more hierarchical structures dominated by personal politics.

As one author puts it in describing the motivation of some of the pioneers of consulting, "the wild intellectual adventure was often as intriguing as the prospect of grabbing the brass ring of finance or career success" (Kiechel 2010).

THE PROBLEM WITH CONSULTING

In gaining recognition as a profession, consulting faces a number of obstacles. Obviously, not all images of consulting or consultants are positive. For example, in technology circles, becoming a consultant is openly referred to as going to the "dark side." Patrick Gray, in his insightful *TechRepublic* article titled "Going to the Dark Side: Should You Consider Becoming a Consultant?," advises "Get ready for routine uncertainty" and "Determine your willingness to take on several jobs" (Gray 2019).

What it means to be a consultant is easily confused with a broad array of functions, many of which are inconsistent with what it means to be a *management* consultant. For example, consulting can easily get mixed up in the so-called *gig economy*, about which there is some excitement, especially among the younger generations. As the name implies, the gig economy is "a free market system where organizations and independent workers engage in short-term work arrangements" (Duszynski 2020). Despite some controversy surrounding the gig economy, indications are that it is here to stay. The following excerpt from Duszynski (2020) lists some of the early findings:

- 57.3 million people freelance in the United States. It's estimated that by 2027 there will be 86.5 million freelancers. (Upwork)
- 36 percent of US workers participate in the gig economy through either their primary or secondary jobs. (Gallup)
- One in six workers in traditional jobs would like to become a primary independent earner. (McKinsey)
- For 44 percent of gig workers, their work in the gig economy is their primary source of income. (Edison Research)
- 55 percent of gig workers also maintain full-time or regular jobs. (PYMNTS)
- 75.7 percent of workers would not quit their gigs for a full-time job. (PYMNTS)

The potential problem for consulting posed by the gig economy is that it opens the door even wider for *contractors or hobbyists* with little or no qualifications to try their hand at management consulting. This only adds to the confusion of what consulting is and detracts from any attempts to solidify its perception as a respectable profession. While consulting certainly can be included as part of the gig economy, this book focuses instead on the trained full-time consultant, not the hobbyist who picks up a gig or two on the side, which is often nothing more than temporary staffing.

Another, more general problem facing consulting is the gap that exists between the popular *idea* of consulting and the actual *experience* of consulting. Too many people come to the profession unprepared for what consulting really is. I have heard the profession described as "mentioning the unmentionable in a mentionable way." This is hardly attractive for the weak at heart. Combine a lack of preparation regarding the realities of independent consulting with the inherent complexity of the healthcare industry, and the result can be dramatic and involve precipitous failure.

I completed my master's program in 1975 at a time when jobs were hard to come by. I ended up securing a two-year contract to launch a B-agency planning initiative[1] aimed at facilitating greater collaboration among eight hospitals in central Pennsylvania.[2] When I was still in school, I had sent my resume to several consulting firms, including Booz Allen. A year into my two-year contract, a recruiter from Booz Allen contacted me and asked if I was still interested in a position. I replied that I was under contract and therefore could not entertain the opportunity at that time. After I hung up, I was immediately scolded by my colleagues on the project. I called the recruiter back, and the rest, as they say, is history. In truth, at the time I had virtually no idea what I was getting myself into.

APPEARANCES CAN BE DECEIVING

As an undergraduate, I earned a premedical degree, but ended up going in a different direction. I was struck by the experiences of several friends who were studying to become nurses with a bachelor of science degree. They had put so much time and effort into the didactic work the first two years, yet many grew disillusioned, sometimes instantly, with the practical experience of nursing on a hospital floor beginning in year three.

The enormous administrative apparatus that gets in the way of caring for patients can be quite disheartening to both nurses and new physicians. A common refrain among physicians is "This is not what I signed up for." The soaring idealism that drives many to pursue medicine becomes tarnished by the realities on the ground. More than a few physicians have been forced to conclude that the system makes it virtually impossible for them to provide patients with good experiences, which leaves the physicians themselves dissatisfied and, in many cases, burned out.

The problem of clinician burnout is exacerbated by the dramatic changes taking place in the overall healthcare industry today. For example, the now-ubiquitous electronic health record has yet to prove itself as an efficient tool in day-to-day clinical practice. Physicians and nurses have to be trained on "the latest and greatest" even if these new techniques and technologies do not fit their style

---

1. This refers to the network of community agencies formed as a result of federal legislation put in place to help guide the investment of funds flowing into healthcare after the passage of Medicare and Medicaid legislation. They are better known as "certificate of need" agencies, a few of which still exist today.

2. It is interesting to note that now, over 40 years later, the eight hospitals are now down to seven and part of three separate and competing health networks.

of practice. While there are clear benefits to digital records (alerts and reminders, for example), the transition has not been an easy one.

MYTHS VERSUS REALITIES OF CONSULTING

There are a number of myths associated with consulting (see exhibit 1.1). Of these, the myths relating to work–life balance are probably the most daunting. As we'll see when we look at different consulting firms, work–life balance appears to be a constant struggle as part of the consulting experience.

It is rare in the life of a consultant to think that our work life and personal life are in balance. Though rewarding, serving even the best client effectively is unlikely to occur without some personal sacrifice. It could be a family event that conflicts with an important client meeting. It could be a phone call in the middle of a family vacation (like the one I got from a long-time client as we were en route to a family dinner in Nice, France). To be sure, every career calls for some form of sacrifice from time to time. In consulting, however, it is perhaps more an expectation than an exception. The problem is that those who go into consulting tend to think that not having a boss in the usual sense means that their time is their own. Consultants quickly learn that their clients control their time more than one might expect. As always, managing expectations is crucial.

Consulting can compete with any profession when it comes to fulfillment and reward. Even so, it presents challenges at both ends of the career spectrum. To aspiring students who might be attracted to consulting, it is important that they understand what awaits them in terms of recognition (or lack thereof). Gaining recognition for one's consulting work is a challenge, and it might take considerable time to gain such recognition and establish a personal brand (see chapter 3 for more on personal brand). Not everyone has the patience for this. But then this must be weighed against the career progression of other healthcare occupations. Toward the end of one's career, consulting can be a great way to monetize the experience that has been gained in the trenches over the previous years. Healthcare is complicated. Knowing how to navigate in the culture of these complex organizations is a big part of a successful consulting engagement and is something that only comes with experience.

There is nothing wrong with approaching consulting as a first step in an executive career. Done right, consulting is a great way to begin a career and gain exposure. However, for one interested in becoming a career consultant, it is important to reflect on one's personal needs and the degree to which they intersect with what consulting can realistically offer. Needs, expectations, and reality must converge if one is to pursue consulting successfully over time.

Exhibit 1.1: Some Consulting Myths

Dimension	Myth	Reality
Accessibility	Anyone can be a consultant.	It takes a certain personality to be a successful consultant over time.
Living the dream	Consulting is easy.	There are few professions that are more demanding.
Sales	If you can do the work, you can sell the work.	Consulting requires mastering skill sets that do not necessarily overlap.
Good clients	All clients are good, and clients are always right.	There are bad clients, and clients might be more wrong than right most of the time—which is why consultants are hired in the first place.
Wealth-building	Consulting is lucrative.	Consulting remains an attractive entry-level position due, in part, to high starting salaries. But the correlation of compensation to business-generation can be quite daunting.
Failure	Failure is rare.	Failure is alarmingly common.
Rewards	Consulting is always fulfilling.	Consulting can be and often is fulfilling, but there are inevitably times of great stress and dissatisfaction.
Flexibility	Consulting is far more flexible than the typical position in a healthcare organization.	This can be true at times and during certain stages of a career; but clients tend to limit flexibility, even when you own your own firm.
Learning	Consulting mostly involves applying what you already know.	Successful consulting requires continuous questioning, learning, and unlearning.
Risk	There is risk only at the beginning of a consulting career.	Though success or failure might be quickly determined, the risks get bigger over time.
Transfer of skills	Most operational skills are transferable to consulting.	Relatively few operational skills are transferable.
Occupational hazards	Consultants are better able to maintain objectivity and stay above the fray.	One must work hard not to become cynical about the work and clients over time.

THE STABILITY OF CONSULTING COMPARED TO TRADITIONAL EXECUTIVE MANAGEMENT

Though it is perhaps counterintuitive, consulting can offer more stability than many executive jobs. Most executives have three to five employers during their careers. Of course, this varies considerably by industry. One of the most-watched statistics in healthcare is the administrator turnover rate in US hospitals. This rate has been tracked for many years by the American College of Healthcare Executives (ACHE), the professional association of healthcare executives (see exhibit 1.2). Note that while the number of hospitals has declined in the past six years overall, the turnover rate has held stable at close to 20 percent. Generally speaking, this is a relatively high rate of turnover. It means that, on average, a hospital CEO will change jobs every five years. So much for job security! By way of example, during the more than 40 years I have been a consultant, I have lived in the same general area the whole time; in contrast, one of my hospital administrator friends has moved eight times, including from coast to coast.

Executives and consultants have different *dissatisfiers*. (See chapter 4 for a more detailed discussion on consultant dissatisfiers.) Executives tend to worry about their bosses. They also worry about the people who report to them. Much of their work involves hierarchical relationships. Personnel issues seem to be less worrisome for consultants. Consulting is, by its very nature, a team sport, where a consultant is part of a consulting team for a client engagement. Sometimes, they are part of several teams at one time, related to different client engagements. The number of teams depends in part on the size of the firm and the nature of the

Exhibit 1.2: Hospital CEO Turnover Rate[*]

Year	Turnover rate (%)[**]	Number of hospitals
2019	17	4,438
2018	18	4,465
2017	18	4,435
2016	18	4,401
2015	18	4,448
2014	18	4,501
2013	20	4,546

[*] Nonfederal, general medical, and surgical hospitals.
[**] Rates before 2016 are statistically adjusted to correct for errors in reporting. Based on a telephone survey in 2017 using a sample of 300 hospitals, we determined that adjustment of the rates for 2016 and subsequent years was not necessary.
Source: ACHE (2020).

practice. Some seasoned consultants would argue that involvement with multiple teams dealing with different challenges is part of the fun of the consulting experience because it exposes one to different people and the way they do things.

TIP FROM THE TRENCHES

It is probably the steep learning curve that sets consulting apart from other potential career paths for the new careerist. It is common to hear from recent grads that what excites them the most about the prospect of consulting is the ability to have an accelerated set of experiences with many different organizations, rather than being tied to one organization for an extended period of time. To find success as a consultant, one must try to consolidate lessons drawn from a broad range of experiences. Especially as a new careerist, take some time at the conclusion of each consulting engagement to document what you've learned from the experience. This will accumulate over time.

This complex team experience is not for everyone. It tends to be quite intense, making for an exciting adventure, where your skills are mixed with those of others to solve problems or promote change. Though there is no lack of excitement in the life of a health system or hospital CEO, the issues they face are more often in the realm of so-called "career-limiting acts." These represent difficult decisions, often involving members of the medical staff, where it is easy to get drawn into personality issues that often don't go well for the executive. It is a slippery slope as they say. The volatility of healthcare management today cannot be overstated. In comparison, consulting, while still involving risk, is perhaps less volatile.

REFERENCES

American College of Healthcare Executives (ACHE). 2020. "Hospital CEO Turnover Rate Shows Small Decrease." Published September 15. www.ache.org/about-ache/news-and-awards/news-releases/hospital-ceo-turnover-2020.

Collins, J. 2001. *Good to Great: Why Some Companies Make the Leap and Others Don't.* New York: Harper Collins.

Duszynski, M. 2020. "Gig Economy: Definition, Statistics & Trends." *Zety.* Updated May 19. https://zety.com/blog/gig-economy-statistics.

Gray, P. 2019. "Going to the Dark Side: Should You Consider Becoming a Consultant?" *TechRepublic.* Published December 13. www.techrepublic.com/article/going-to-the-dark-side-should-you-consider-becoming-a-consultant.

Kiechel, W. 2010. *The Lords of Strategy: The Secret Intellectual History of the New Corporate World.* Boston: Harvard Business Review Press.

Pine, B. J., II, and J. H. Gilmore. 2020. *The Experience Economy: Competing for Customer Time, Attention, and Money.* Boston: Harvard Business Review Press.

CHAPTER 2

What Is Consulting?

FEW CAREERS ARE AS POORLY understood as consulting. The term is used to cover myriad things, yet the underlying concept is relatively straightforward. Consultants can be defined as outside experts hired by clients to help solve problems or identify and exploit opportunities objectively and dispassionately. They are paid (often significant) fees for their time and expertise. In return, they bring their knowledge and experience to bear on whatever challenges they face, helping organizations achieve important goals faster or better than they could have without such help. Consultants help transfer knowledge to clients or to develop new knowledge.

Some people will have you believe that anyone can be a consultant. While that might be true from a regulatory perspective (i.e., lack of barriers to entry), few people have the personality, skill set, resources, and energy required to be an effective consultant. Ultimately, the marketplace is the arbiter of success. Later we will discuss the basic skills of consulting and some of what is required to sustain a client relationship. But first, let's start with why consulting exists and what it can realistically accomplish.

Simply stated, consulting exists because the client has a need for it. Usually the client initiates the relationship because an area of its business requires intense focus and expertise, and it hires a person or team to provide advisory services. Implicit in this exchange is that external resources (i.e., outsourcing) are, by comparison, preferable to using internal resources. Sometimes consultants initiate the exchange because they can convince a client that they have a product or service that will be helpful. All leaders rely on advice to succeed. Often, this advice comes from sources within an organization. But many factors can affect such advice that have nothing to do with the issue at hand (e.g., politics). Advice from people outside the organization (i.e., independent consultants) is often required for the purpose of ensuring objectivity. Some leaders succeed without the assistance of independent consultants, but the majority, in my experience, lean heavily on consultants over the course of their careers, often establishing long-term relationships with individuals and firms.

This raises an interesting question. For those who have forgone consulting services, how have they kept up with the latest changes in their industries and successfully integrated those changes into the cultures of their organizations? Some try to manage this by attending national conferences and doing a lot of reading, others by hiring someone internally who has the right experience. But who is presenting at these conferences and writing these books and articles? Who is being hired internally because they have the right experience? The answer: consultants. So whether or not leaders actually take advantage of the services of outside consultants, they nonetheless benefit from consultants' work and expertise.

The influence of consultants has become pervasive, in part because the United States spent 18 percent of its gross domestic product on healthcare in 2020 (Statista 2020). Consultants are an integral part of the tapestry of change in most industries, and healthcare is no exception. Anecdotally, a significant and growing number of graduating students are attracted to consulting, and a growing number of firms are serving different industries in new and different ways. Firms come and go, but in healthcare consultants support many parts of the complex industry. And those who list "consultant" as their primary occupation are no longer restricted to career consultants who enter the profession as soon as they receive their master's degree. More midlevel and senior executives are moving into the profession, to the point where consultants are now commonplace.

Exhibit 2.1 illustrates the Consultant Value Chain and the value components of a professional consultant. At the core of this is the value proposition Knowledge + Experience. Young careerists just starting out begin their first jobs with knowledge, but lack experience. Knowledge without experience, though valuable, has limitations. Inexperienced consultants find ways to project expertise even while learning (Bourgoin and Harvey 2018). Likewise, experience alone is insufficient. It is only by integrating knowledge with experience that professional consultants can support this value proposition, which is essential for professional consultants, although it is not sufficient to sustain a career. These core elements must be supported by others from the consultant value chain. Let's take a closer look:

- *Authentic.* It is no coincidence that authentic is located on top of the value chain. Without it, there is no credibility, and credibility is the key to any consultant–client relationship. Consulting is about persuasion, and those who are influenced must trust the consultant if the advice is to take hold. Authenticity involves passion and empathy. As noted in one article, "Empathy allows you to build trust with your clients—and this is the most

Exhibit 2.1: Consultant Value Chain

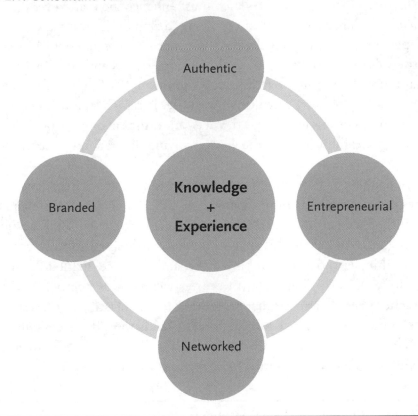

challenging and underappreciated part of any job in the professional services industry" (Runde 2016). It involves emotional intelligence (EQ), which includes self-knowledge of potential biases that a consultant exhibits and how their views might inadvertently influence a discussion. Actions must be beyond reproach and never include surprises. Services must be delivered in a consistent and reliable manner in order to instill confidence in the client that the advice is well formulated and the advisor can be trusted. Ethics permeates everything. Being authentic is being trustworthy and being true to oneself. (See chapter 12 for more on authenticity.)

- *Entrepreneurial.* Consulting is a business. As such, it requires risk tolerance and a certain amount of entrepreneurial flare. Though it might appear straightforward on the surface, successfully managing a consulting business presents a host of logistical challenges. This is why many consultants choose to delegate certain business functions by joining a firm rather than supporting a solo practice.
- *Branded.* Consultants must shape a personal brand. Branding is tied to marketability. To be marketable, a personal brand must resonate with potential

clients or consumers. To be sustainable, the brand must remain vibrant, and consultants' experiences and research must enhance the brand over time.

- *Networked.* Consulting is a team sport, requiring both group and interpersonal skills. It begins with cultivating *social capital,* which is defined as "the value created by leveraging knowledge that is embedded within social networks and interrelationships" (Johnson 2017). Consultants forge a network that requires nurturing over time. It can scale, but it needs to be stoked. To promote growth, the network must encompass prospective clients. (See exhibit 5.2 and the accompanying discussion in chapter 5.)

Every client engagement is a step in a career-long learning experience that distinguishes great consultants from mediocre ones. Consultants can be characterized as part philosopher, part therapist, and part artist (Block 2011). While acknowledging the insights contained in this analysis, I take a more simplistic approach, one in which consulting is understood as both an art and a science. Exhibit 2.2 represents the consulting skills continuum, with process facilitator as one pole and content expert as the other. The more that consulting tends toward the process side, the more it can be creative and artful; the more it tends toward the content side, the more it is like a science. Most client engagements fall somewhere between the two poles. Exhibit 2.3 lays out the art/science contrast in greater detail.

Exhibit 2.2: The Consulting Skills Continuum

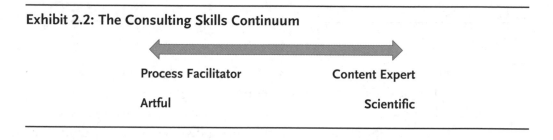

Process Facilitator	**Content Expert**
Artful	**Scientific**

Exhibit 2.3: Comparison of Consulting as Art Versus Science

Dimension	Art	Science
Application	More strategic	More operational
Approach	More customized	More standardized
Frequency	More one-offs	More repetition
Emphasis	Successful execution	Replication of comparative results
Focus of creativity	Application to/by people and culture	Measurement, productivity, and effectiveness
Measurement	Perception and process, feelings	Outcome

THE ART OF CONSULTING

From an artistic perspective, consulting can be understood as a form of expression. What is expressed is a point of view, and the point of view can be tied to a *brand*. Brand is important both to individual consultants and to firms, and the best consultants develop a brand that resonates with clients. Two examples from healthcare stand out to me: the Hunter Group[1] and the Studer Group.[2]

Under the leadership of David Hunter, the Hunter Group developed a reputation for rapid cost reduction, sometimes referred to as "slash and burn." While other firms certainly offered this sort of operational turnaround, Hunter's approach seemed to get bigger and more quantifiable results faster. His brand of consulting was loud; it made a statement. His teams were especially adept at coming into complex and dysfunctional situations and successfully turning them around. Though his techniques stoked controversy in some cases—notably with regard to employees being summarily fired—they succeeded at reducing costs and improving financial performance in a relatively short period of time. Though many leaders lost their jobs after bringing in the Hunter Group, hospital boards and bond trustees continued to hire them when things grew desperate. The Hunter Group's heyday in the 1990s and early 2000s coincided with a period of great upheaval in the healthcare industry.

The Studer Group was built on the personal success of Quint Studer. Studer (2003) tells his story with passion and eloquence in a moving narrative about overcoming developmental challenges as a child. His unique perspectives gave me an entirely new appreciation for the importance of many little things that make quality real to the consumer of healthcare services. The Studer Group's ability to codify quality metrics, coupled with its attention to details, such as follow-up calls and thank-you notes, resulted in the long-term retention of satisfied clients. These clients, who hired the Studer Group at considerable cost over relatively long periods of time (a year or two), marketed the business for them through positive word of mouth. Simply stated, Studer succeeded in helping clients change their cultures in order to produce better experiences for clients who receive services through their programs.

As with the Hunter and Studer Groups, many of the early healthcare consulting firms were built around the personalities of their founders, many of whom tended more toward art than science. They gave compelling speeches and wrote widely circulated articles that resonated with potential clients. Some of these

---

1. Now part of Navigant Consulting, though the brand is no longer used.
2. Now part of Huron Consulting, which continues to use the brand.

firms, like Hunter and Studer, were sold; others folded or ceased operations when their founders retired.

Thinking of consulting as artistic is meant to emphasize that it has a creative, more spontaneous side. Artful consulting involves grasping and navigating the nuances of particular situations ("one-offs"), whereas the science side is more standardized, repetitive, and process driven.

The art of consulting often involves deciphering the culture or pressure points of particular client organizations with respect to the unique needs of each organization at a particular point in time. In cases in which artful consulting is required, pattern recognition, though still essential, is more about recognizing the deviations from typical patterns that make a given situation unique. Two health-care organizations might suffer similar operational deficiencies, but since different people and cultures are involved, each case could need a different solution. The ability to recognize key differences in otherwise similar situations is a particularly valuable skill, one that tends to separate the best-in-breed consultants from the run-of-the-mill.

THE SCIENCE OF CONSULTING

While the creative, context-sensitive side of consulting is a kind of art, the systematic tools and processes used in consulting belong to its more scientific side. Some of the most effective books on consulting focus on the research and development carried out by the big three strategy firms, including McKinsey (Rasiel 1999), Boston Consulting Group (BCG; Stern and Deimler 2006), and Bain Consulting. This sort of consulting tends to be evidence-based (to borrow a medical term) and to rely on huge databases built from extensive global experiences and analytics. These titans of global business are not easily copied, which is one reason they have enjoyed such sustained success. Their empirical research is frequently published (often in proprietary newsletters) and rich in detail, so interesting that it continues to attract both clients and the best and the brightest graduate students looking for a challenge. Competition for positions at these firms is fierce, and compared to other firms and industries (e.g., nonprofits), their billing rates are astronomical.

Their consulting rests on quantifiable return on investment (ROI) metrics. If the firm is willing to invest in exploiting the lessons of the experience curve or BCG's growth/share matrix, then it can reasonably expect to generate a significant return on this investment in terms of growth and/or competitive positioning. This results from the rigor of standardized approaches that focus on such things as a 4-C framework: customer, cost, competition, and capabilities, as noted by PrepLounge (2020). Such ROI-type engagements tend to promote rapid results.

Long-term strategy tends to be more variable, though more sophisticated data analytics could standardize strategic engagements more and more in the future. Clearly, retail analytics have delivered significant benefits to Walmart, Target, and other giants of the retail world. There is significant potential for the same to occur in healthcare, which needs to become more retail-like (i.e., shift toward measurable value). Before it is suggested that healthcare is more complicated than retail businesses, the typical American grocery store or department store, which successfully handles thousands of diverse products (some of which are perishable), is hardly a simple business.

Fundamental to continual quality improvement in healthcare is the realization that there is preventable variation in clinical outcomes. The same holds true when it comes to basic operational functions—there is hope for greater standardization of key functions in healthcare organizations in the future. According to many experts, artificial intelligence is expected to play a major role in this over time.

RISK TOLERANCE

Tolerance for risk is an essential trait of successful consultants. Consultants are constantly being tested as they try to demonstrate the value of their insights and knowledge. It can be relentless. Risk is a central reason that consulting is not for everyone.

TIP FROM THE TRENCHES

Risk is inherent to consulting. Clients are demanding and have their own preferences and needs. Sometimes, even when you can address their needs, you cannot accommodate their preferences. Consulting involves constant challenges. Some people welcome the challenge; others are dragged down by it. Managing expectations is crucial. Not every client engagement will be successful or rewarding. Even so, consultants strive to ensure a positive client experience even when client demands are unreasonable.

That consulting comes with its fair share of risk should surprise no one. In my experience, however, many new or prospective consultants fail to fully appreciate the risk they are taking. If you are in consulting long enough, you are sure to experience disappointment or even outright failure sooner or later. Is that something you can bounce back from, or will it haunt you going forward? Dealing with disappointment and loss is never easy, but it comes with the territory.

THERE IS NO CONSULTING WITHOUT CLIENTS

For professional consultants to exist, someone has to be willing to pay for the services they offer. Anyone can give advice, but that does not mean it is necessarily sound advice, nor does it mean one can find people to pay for it. Consulting involves entering into a *service exchange*. To succeed, a consultant must abide by the usual rules of retail. They must clearly articulate the expertise they offer. They must provide evidence that their expertise is relevant to potential clients. They must provide references willing to attest to the reliability of their services. Those services must be within a price point that is acceptable to a client (taking conspicuous consumption into consideration).[3] Regardless of the level of detail provided or the references offered, in the end, there is a leap of faith by the client that the consultant can deliver on their promises. It is imperative that the consultant not lose sight of this act of faith by the client when they retain their services. It is a sacred trust that is to be honored.

Consultants generally compete for clients. The only exception is the so-called "sole-source" situation. In government work, this is generally referred to as "no-bid contracts." Some visible scandals have emerged from this approach, notably for large defense projects. The concern, especially for big projects, is that a bidding process brings competition into play so that fees are reduced to remain competitive. In the absence of an open bid process, "sweetheart deals" can occur that smack of political corruption. Generally, for smaller, and/or more specialized projects, even in government, some no-bid contracts continue to exist.

As the name implies, sole-source situations are exclusive; there is no competition. In a sole-source situation, the client buys from the firm without other considerations. This might occur for a number of reasons. Sole-source opportunities were far more prevalent in healthcare back in the mom-and-pop days of independent hospitals than they are today. Now, there are far more firms and thus more options from which to choose. Where a sole-source situation exists, it might be that the consultant's expertise is so rare that there are really no other options. It could be that there exists a high level of trust and familiarity (i.e., trusted advisor) between the client and the consultant such that there is no need to test the market or consider alternatives. It could also occur where an existing employee at the

---

3. Conspicuous consumption, in this context, is an interesting and undeniable part of consulting. Clients expect to pay a lot for consulting—to the point that prospective consultants who seem to be priced too low run the risk of their services not being taken seriously. Often, a client buys a service that is priced higher because the client believes it has more value than that offered by a competing firm.

client site decides to go independent in the middle of a project that is dependent upon their continued involvement for successful completion. Make no mistake, consultants prefer sole-source opportunities.

THE SERVICE EXCHANGE

All business transactions involve an exchange of goods or services. Where there is competition, an exchange is also involved. Exchanges function differently depending on the nature of what is being sold.

Goods differ from services. Consulting relies on the service exchange to secure transactions with clients. Similar to other services (e.g., housekeeping, auto repair, medical services), word of mouth can play an important role. Though consulting is relatively unregulated from a licensing perspective, the market imposes its own requirements. This is where the service exchange comes into play.

Participation in the service exchange is all about credibility. To have credibility, one must have favorable references. Credibility and a sound reputation are the currency of consulting. Unfortunately, not all references are positive. Therefore, successful consultants cultivate favorable references who are willing to share their experiences with others. Ideally, the experiences of references will relate to the new, prospective engagement.

REFERENCES

Block, P. 2011. *Flawless Consulting: A Guide to Getting Your Expertise*, 3rd ed. San Francisco: Pfeiffer.

Bourgoin, A., and J.-F. Harvey. 2018. "How Consultants Project Expertise and Learn at the Same Time." *Harvard Business Review*. Published July 27. https://hbr.org/2018/07/how-consultants-project-expertise-and-learn-at-the-same-time.

Johnson, W. 2017. "The Critical Role of Emotional Intelligence in Consulting." Management Consultancies Association. Published January 26. www.mca.org.uk/blog/the-critical-role-of-emotional-intelligence-in-consulting.

PrepLounge. 2020. "The 4C Framework Is a Good Framework to Structure a Firm's Positioning." Accessed September 9. www.preplounge.com/en/bootcamp.php/case-cracking-toolbox/structure-your-thoughts/4c-framework.

Rasiel, E. M. 1999. *The McKinsey Way*. New York: McGraw-Hill Education.

Runde, J. 2016. "Why Young Bankers, Lawyers, and Consultants Need Emotional Intelligence." *Harvard Business Review*. Published September 26. https://hbr.org/2016/09/why-young-bankers-lawyers-and-consultants-need-emotional-intelligence.

Statista. 2020. "U.S. Health Care Expenditure as a Percentage of GDP 1960–2020." Published June 8. www.statista.com/statistics/184968/us-health-expenditure-as-percent-of-gdp-since-1960/.

Stern, C. W., and M. S. Deimler (eds.). 2006. *The Boston Consulting Group on Strategy.* Hoboken, NJ: John Wiley & Sons, Inc.

Studer, Q. 2003. *Hardwiring Excellence.* Gulf Breeze, FL: Firestarter Publishing.

CHAPTER 3

Types of Consultants

IN A SENSE, THERE ARE AS many kinds of consultants as there are problems to be solved. That said, it is helpful to distinguish in broad, general terms among a number of different consultant types or roles. That is our task in this chapter. For prospective consultants, it might prove helpful as you read to think about what type of consultant you aspire to become or what role is more in your comfort zone.

SCOPE AND APPROACH

Let's start by characterizing consultants in terms of the actual tasks of consulting. This can be reduced to *scope* and *approach*. With respect to scope, we can distinguish between generalists and specialists. Scope refers to the nature of the subject that is being explored. (It is commonly used in consulting to refer to the dimensions of a specific consulting engagement.) A subject that is broad in scope, for example, that might cut across the enterprise would be best served by a more generalist role. In contrast, one that is more focused on a small operating unit would tend to be in an expert's or specialist's sweet spot.

In terms of the consulting skills required to address these different issues, the approach ranges between process (facilitator), which is employed more by generalists, and the content (expert), which is less dependent on process and more focused on the answer (see exhibit 2.2 in chapter 2), where specialist experts tend to reside.

When I first entered the industry, generalist approaches were the primary form of consulting, and continue to be a focus of the global firms that train general consultants able to address myriad interests across industries. In healthcare, however, increasing specialization has made it more and more difficult to be considered a generalist, let alone to establish a successful career as one. There is little demand for generalists in healthcare, except perhaps when it comes to strategy (more on this later) or where "breakthrough" concepts are sought for an intransigent problem. The contrast between generalists and specialists is outlined in the scope diagram that appears in exhibit 3.1.

Differences in approach refer to the methods that tend to be employed toward resolving the issues under consideration. Approach can be understood in terms of the contrasts shown in exhibit 3.2 and should be viewed as a continuum, since many engagements reflect elements of both extremes.

Exhibit 3.1: Types of Consulting: Scope

Generalist	Specialist
Knows a little about lots of things	Knows everything about limited things
Able to deal with complex, intransigent issues	Focuses on specific "fixes"
Works at highest levels	Works in the trenches
Strategic/connects the dots	Operational/improves things
Every client is unique	Does similar studies many times for many clients
Highest billing rates	Varies billing rates

Exhibit 3.2: Types of Consulting: Approach

Process Facilitator	Content Expert
Deals well with uncertainty/lots of gray	World is black and white
Willing to ask tough questions and trusts process to find answers	Never asks a question they can't answer
Data limitations acknowledged	Data becomes information
Is decisive/does something	Embraces informed decisions only/strives for certainty

PROCESS FACILITATOR

All consulting involves some form of expertise. What can be overlooked is that some people are not *subject* experts, but rather are *process* experts. They might know little to nothing about an industry or the subject at hand, but they know how to manage groups and how to leverage their expertise to help solve problems. They know what questions to ask. These people are process consultants or "facilitators." Since the vast majority of consulting engagements involve some degree of facilitation, it is important for all consultants to have some facilitation skills whether they are process consultants or subject experts.

Pure facilitation involves spurring and steering a dialogue among a small group of people (preferably no more than 12 in a group) who possess the necessary expertise among them to address an issue. Harnessing the collective knowledge of the group, the facilitator assists in defining the challenge faced by the group in such a way that, ideally, consensus is reached regarding the nature of the challenge, clear options are isolated, and a targeted solution is developed.

Though consensus is sometimes unachievable, the participation of stakeholders in this sort of dialogue usually results in a higher level of commitment to the proposed solution, as opposed to a decision that is made solely by an executive in isolation (i.e., more top-down). Sometimes such processes are used to provide input to the decision-maker who retains the right to decide but still seeks advice from the group.

The facilitator brings to the table expertise on conducting constructive dialogues (including "critical conversations"). Skilled facilitators are like catalysts in a chemical equation; the best facilitators are often barely noticed as the dialogue unfolds. They quickly get each participant to explore their own thinking and to engage with the rest of the group. Skilled facilitators keep the conversation moving in a positive direction to avoid taking contentious positions on issues, thus allowing for consideration of alternative perspectives and ultimately arrive at a solution that might incorporate a number of elements from the different perspectives.

One challenge facilitators often face is to avoid the process becoming an end unto itself. The concern of clients is that some of the more complex processes, such as quality improvement and value-based transitions, run the risk of taking too long and having no clear endpoint. Thus, the facilitator must mark progress made and keep the scope of the discussion within clear boundaries. Setting time limits is particularly important to most processes (e.g., negotiations). In merger discussions, interest can quickly be lost if the group is unable to resolve certain conflicts in a timely manner. A skilled negotiator knows to start with some easy issues, thus allowing the group to gain confidence in their collective ability to move beyond key differences. Regardless of this initial success, if the process takes too long or begins to backtrack where certain issues that were thought to be resolved are raised anew, then the whole process can collapse. The analogy commonly brought up about process is that it can be like fish: If it takes too long to cook up, it starts to smell.

CONTENT EXPERT

Unlike process facilitators, content experts tend to be faced with focused problems that require a specific sort of solution that relies, at least in part, on the expertise of the consultant. Often the content expert is in a teaching mode with the client, sharing their experience and knowledge. Part of what content experts add to the mix is their ability to precisely define the problem at hand and to zero in on what is needed to solve it. They often rely on the experience that they bring, having dealt with this same issue in other situations. The more specialized the problem, the more predictable the outcome. Many such specialized problems seem to have more binary solutions—right or wrong. These are more problems that cry out for "fixes" with immediate feedback, versus more complicated, long-term problems less amenable to easy fixes.

Content specialists understandably have less tolerance for ambiguity than process consultants. For them, problems tend to be somewhat black and white, whereas there is far more gray area involved in the work of process facilitators.

COMPARISON OF CONSULTANT TYPES

Taken together, scope and approach make for an interesting matrix of consultant roles, as shown in exhibit 3.3. While one is hesitant to use labels, it does help to distinguish one type of consultant from the other. It is somewhat common that consultants find themselves in more than one role over time, but their brand would tend to reside mostly in just one.

Some firms offer parts of each of these types of consulting, while others tend to specialize by industry, function, or both. Let's look at each of these different roles that a consultant might play:

- *Guru/strategist.* These people tend to be widely recognized within the industry. They focus on future trends and strategy development. They conduct large projects that call for significant resource allocation. Their currency is managing risk in a competitive world. In healthcare, these consultants work in the realm of change and transformations. They help

Exhibit 3.3: Comparison of Consulting Roles Based on Scope and Approach

position the client to achieve advantage in a competitive market. Their focus is often more on the long run than the short run.

- *Industry specialist.* Experience is the key driver here. Few people are experts in more than one area or discipline. Some consultants specialize in third-party contracting, others in clinical practice. Whereas the guru/strategist can cut across industries, specialists tend to focus on a particular industry.

- *Facilitator/dealmaker.* The work of facilitators/dealmakers tends to be rather generic, as they apply similar processes to multiple situations. The process by which two hospitals merge, for example, is not that different from how a medical practice is acquired or two practices merge. It should be noted, however, that mergers between nonprofit organizations and commercial enterprises can often be quite different.

- *Niche player.* Whereas industry specialists focus on industry segments (e.g., medical practice versus hospitals), niche players are more functionally oriented (e.g., nursing versus finance versus IT) within industries. These consultants tend toward areas where operational experience is highly valued. This is the preferred type of consulting for highly skilled senior executives looking to make a career change.

INTERNAL VERSUS EXTERNAL

One of the attractions of becoming a consultant is that people from outside an organization are often listened to differently than those from within. External consultants are usually referred to as independent consultants. They are hired external to an organization and are considered to be experts. This is part of the reason that clients are willing to pay them more than they would an inhouse employee (i.e., higher hourly rate). Thus, they are routinely given the benefit of the doubt, and they tend to stay above the fray, immune to internal politics. That, however, does not diminish the role of internal consultants.

Unlike independent external consultants, internal consultants tend to play more or less fixed roles within organizations—for example, training or line responsibility for major transitions such as integration. Under Jack Welch, General Electric was famous for approaching strategy within the firm, using internal consultants to disrupt existing business models in anticipation of future change. Though this sort of consulting can be effective, it is often hampered in ways that external consulting is not. In most cases, internal consultants cannot remain forever immune to internal political pressures. External consultants, by definition, tend to have more varied experiences from more firms than internal consultants, who in contrast might go more in depth into a firm that employs them. Internal consultants, being more familiar with the inner workings of their employer than most independent consultants, tend to be more involved in operational issues.

One of the key differences between external and internal consultants is the kind of compensation they receive. Internal consultants tend to be paid a salary, whereas independent consultants bill for their time or on a per-project basis. (For more on internal consultants, see chapter 8.)

TIP FROM THE TRENCHES

Internal consultants are often seduced into operating on commission or some other risky compensation model. This can lead to significant conflict. For example, it can be difficult to wrestle a percentage of a shared commission from someone for whom this is their sole form of compensation. Moreover, unorthodox compensation models can compromise the objectivity that is crucial for delivering unbiased service. A time-and-expenses compensation model is standard for consulting services. Any alternative to this might involve judgment that can quickly get beyond your control, and few things are more demoralizing than being accountable for things over which you have no control.

INDEPENDENT VERSUS FIRM

A key decision facing prospective consultants is whether to start out as an independent or solo consultant, or to join a firm. For those coming in as a senior executive, the big global firms are hard to crack, but smaller regional and specialized firms are often more receptive. Going the independent route seems to be the trend, as healthcare executive Georgia Casciato points out in a recent Healthcare Consultants Forum[1] newsletter: "The 'gig economy' has become increasingly ubiquitous in most industries, including healthcare consulting. A newer player on the spectrum of consultancies, the executive leader-turned-consultant is one of the fastest-growing categories of talent" (Casciato 2019).

Global firms tend to have strong cultures and intractable ways of doing things. Promotions come almost exclusively from within the organizations because these firms invest considerable time and effort in developing their people. For the executive attempting to come in from outside the firm, it is challenging to be considered for anything other than a beginning consultant. The exception to this might be an individual who can bring in a relatively large, well-defined book of business.

The decision to join a smaller regional or specialized firm should rest largely on the firm's infrastructure support and the consultant's fit with the other partners. Many a senior executive has overestimated a firm's resources and ability to help them transition to consulting. A firm's client list, brand recognition, and ability to launch a new practice are all items to consider in such a move. This is discussed in far more detail later in this book.

---

1. The Healthcare Consultants Forum is a platform of the American College of Healthcare Executives that focuses on the interests of consultant members.

For those who go the independent route, the most important issue is securing clients. Most successful launches require one or two clients to get started. The client engagements might be small, but they put the new firm on the map. From there, success depends on effective networking.

TIP FROM THE TRENCHES

Friends don't buy from friends. Starting out, I assumed that many of my colleagues and peers would be eager to engage my services. I could not have been more wrong. It is one thing to work and become friends with a client over time; it is quite another to start out as a friend and then get hired as a consultant. Perhaps this relates to that well-known biblical story that you cannot be a prophet in your own land. Or, as Will Rogers offered, "An expert is a man 50 miles from home with a briefcase."

GOVERNMENT VERSUS PRIVATE SECTOR

Healthcare is dominated by private nonprofit organizations, which extends from smaller institutes focused on a single cause (e.g., Autism Speaks) to multibillion-dollar health systems operating across multiple markets (e.g., Trinity Health). Until recently, the number of hospitals in equity-based, for-profit health systems was growing, but then Community Health Systems and a number of other investor-owned chains began to experience financial difficulties (Ellison 2019). This was due, it seems to me, to their assumption of significant debt from acquisitions as margins were being squeezed by more aggressive policies from both government (i.e., Medicare and Medicaid) and private payers.

My experience with government consulting contracts goes back to my early days with Booz Allen. Unless you are part of a large firm, it probably doesn't make sense to do both public and private sector work, as the infrastructure required to support each is quite different. Medium to smaller firms tend to focus on one or the other. The other interesting observation, in my experience at least, is that the public-private networks tend to be quite distinct, with relatively little exchange between the two, at least from a consulting perspective. It should be acknowledged that increased public-private partnerships are starting to better integrate some of these distinct networks.

CONSULTING VERSUS INTERIM MANAGEMENT

Interim management is increasingly common in organizations attempting to enact fundamental changes. Thus, it is worth discussing the similarities and differences between consulting and interim management.

In 2019, I attended a roundtable discussion that was described as "among consultants." It was a lively and constructive event. Interestingly, however, nearly every one of the participants was functioning more in the role of an interim manager than as an independent consultant.

Interim managers are independent contractors who are brought in by an organization to accomplish a specific task for a set period of time.[2] This does not sound that different from consulting, but it is. The people in the roundtable were essentially doing the same work that they had done as full-time executives. However, it was for a shorter time period.

Interim managers are given the authority necessary to complete their work, and this can include line authority with people reporting directly to them. Unlike interim managers, independent consultants have no such authority; they are advisors, and their advice can be accepted or rejected by the client. If a client wants a solution to a problem, they should hire a consultant; if they want someone to run things better, then they should hire an interim manager. Confusing these roles can be disastrous. When the role is as advisor, things can go genuinely sideways when the consultant attempts to assume operational authority. One cannot both advise and compete with the operators to whom they are offering such advice.

There are many temporary staffing firms. Some focus exclusively on interim management, while others might characterize themselves as professional search firms that also offer contingency or retained search services.[3] Not all search firms offer temporary staffing, and most consulting firms do not normally offer interim management.

Some basic tenets should guide the use of interim managers. Done right, the value of interim managers is that they should not be eligible to compete for the open position that they have temporarily assumed. Instead, they are there to enact needed changes that are difficult, if not impossible, to make by someone concerned about keeping the position. As noted earlier, such difficult actions are commonly referred to in healthcare as "career-limiting acts" or CLAs. It should be noted that interim management is a tangible competency that highly skilled people can develop. Their brand involves the unique ability to manage dramatic change in a relatively short period of time.

---

2. Note: In this context, we are not using the term "interim" to describe someone in a temporary role awaiting final vetting and potentially moving into a position full-time.

3. Contingency searches are nonexclusive. The client, who may have contracted a number of firms for the search, is under no obligation to pay unless the consultant finds the candidate who ultimately takes the position. In contrast, retained searches are exclusive: A single firm contracts with the client for a specified period of time, depending on the difficulty of the search.

The use of interim leaders can be very effective, especially in the context of succession planning. The interim leader is charged with gauging the current state of the organization and making changes that might have been neglected by prior management. They do so with no illusions of continuing in their role, but rather with the clear understanding that they are paving the way for the next appointee to effectively fulfill their duties. Some churches have helped pave the path for interim managers by requiring that an interim pastor be hired before the search is started for the permanent replacement, especially where a pastor has been in their position for an extended period of time (e.g., 15 years or more). It is rare that a person in a position for so long is able to leave without some skeletons in the closet that, if not addressed, can be perceived as a significant burden to the next person in line, thus adversely affecting the recruiting process. Often these interim management engagements are for a minimum of 6 months up to 18 months, depending on the level of challenge involved.

The danger in confusing consulting and interim management falls mostly on consultants.

Consultants must create space between the advisor (themselves) and the person acting on the advice (the client) because they have no authority to act on their own advice. Shifting from advisor to actor can be quite risky. It can result in a loss of objectivity, and at the same time places a consultant in a very different light that might represent competition to members of the client team. Let me share a story to help illustrate this point.

I allowed myself to get drawn into this sort of situation with a high-value client I had worked with for years. I was hired by the board and not the existing CEO, with whom I had worked for well over a decade. When it contacted me, the board expressed concern that the actions of the CEO were no longer aligned with those of the board. I was willing to be hired under these difficult circumstances, but only if I was given an opportunity to convince the CEO of the need to change if he wanted to remain in this position. Unfortunately, the CEO and the board remained on different paths, and the CEO was terminated. Since there was no clear successor within the organization, the board needed to hire someone from outside the health system. But the firm or person hired would likely have little to no knowledge of the crisis situation they were walking into and it would be very expensive to take the time to bring them up to speed. Ultimately, since I was intimately familiar with the situation and had been for many years, I let myself be considered for the position, but only on an interim basis—something I came to regret.

What I failed to recognize at the time, but became very clear to me soon after, was that taking on this role adversely affected my ability to return to the role of trusted advisor. People I had worked with in a consulting role looked at me very differently. In this new role, I had authority to hire and fire; it was not the same advisory role. The moment I assumed operational responsibility, even on an interim basis, it seriously undercut the enduring client relationship that I had cultivated for more than 15 years.

An alternative that was not available to me at the time might have been to fill the interim manager position with someone else from the firm. In this way, some consulting firms are able to successfully offer both consulting and interim management services. In my experience, though, grouping consulting and interim management under the same roof introduces unwanted difficulties, except perhaps in the case of junior interim positions, which often come down to simply keeping a chair warm until a permanent occupant can be found.

ACADEMICS

Many academics supplement their incomes and enhance their reputations by consulting on the side. Doing so both enriches the learning experience of their students and gives them practical experience as they attempt to bring their research to life in real client situations.

Not all academics are comfortable in the commercial world. Those who do consult have to manage it alongside their teaching, research, and publication duties. Such people tend to be very talented. Two examples stand out in my mind:

- *Bill Cleverley, PhD, Cleverley + Associates.* A truly gifted professor, Bill Cleverley staked out for himself an unusual position, with a PhD in finance from the University of California, Berkeley, with a focus on healthcare. He taught at Ohio State University in the graduate program for health administration from 1973 to 2001. Steve Loebs, the chairman of the program from 1980 to 2002, encouraged members of his faculty to spread their wings in an effort to open up markets to hire their graduates. Bill was quick to take advantage of this encouragement. Eventually, he ended up reducing his teaching to half time and worked out an arrangement with the Healthcare Financial Management Association (HFMA) to collect hospital financial statements and undertake some basic analyses and benchmarking for hospitals. In 1992, he acquired the program he had started from HFMA. He then established the Center for Healthcare Industry Performance Studies (CHIPS). After a few other mergers, CHIPS was sold to United HealthCare in 1998 (Loebs and Cleverley 2020).

  Bill did more than data research. He was one of the first academics to teach seminars at the annual Congress on Healthcare Leadership of the American College of Healthcare Executives (ACHE), and for many years he was a regular speaker at their two-day seminars, both at ACHE and HFMA. Through these seminars he helped establish a platform: "Profit is not a dirty word." In time, he became widely published and was a well-known speaker to HFMA chapters and at board retreats. Bill's book is a classic that is now in its eighth edition (Cleverley and Cleverley 2018). Cleverley + Associates was formed in 2000 to provide pricing and payments studies for hospitals and healthcare organizations.

- *Daniel K. Zismer, PhD, Castling Partners.*[4] Dan Zismer is the inaugural Wegmiller Professor Emeritus and Chair in the MHA Program of the School of Public Health at the University of Minnesota. He is cofounder and managing director of Castling Partners, a healthcare advisory and development firm. His resume includes healthcare leadership and governance positions, as well as roles in developing healthcare services–related entrepreneurial ventures. Zismer served as chair and director of the MHA and executive studies programs in health administration at the University of Minnesota from 2013 to 2016. Prior to that, he focused his 20-year career in healthcare on provider-side mergers, acquisitions, and related integrated strategies. He served as the head of two national healthcare consulting firms (one of which he cofounded and sold) and headed operations for a large, multistate integrated health system. Zismer has been on the faculty of ACHE, the Governance Institute, and the American Association of Physician Leaders.

Exceptional, to be sure, both examples serve as an inspiration to others who might be looking to leverage their research and knowledge into lucrative offerings. Most academics who do consulting have far more modest practices or are hired by firms to participate in various projects where their expertise can be applied.

DEVELOPING A PERSONAL BRAND

Since virtually anyone can claim to be a consultant, it is important to distinguish between those who merely list "consultant" on their business card versus those who are genuinely qualified to do so. This is why it is so important for consultants to cultivate a personal brand (see exhibit 2.1, "Consultant Value Chain," in chapter 2). How can you distinguish yourself in a crowded market?

Unlike CEOs, who change jobs frequently as operators of healthcare organizations, consultants have the opportunity to develop a reputation, to become

---

4. Printed with the permission of Dan Zismer, October 25, 2019.

known for something specific (e.g., a subject area or specialized performance such as an operational turnaround) based on their knowledge and experience. Successful consultants tend to specialize based on certain capabilities or experiences, and to have a brand upon which they can build. Firms also attempt to brand themselves. A consultant's personal brand tends to be somewhat separate from the firm that employs them, unless the firm carries their name. The brand should reflect the specific expertise of the individual. What do you want to be known for as a consultant?

As an example of the branding phenomenon, some consultants have become popular speakers to leverage their expertise and generate consulting business. A few examples stand out to me in this regard, and some of the best are from the past:

- Russell Coile had an uncanny ability to look to the future and provide meaningful insights. He published no fewer than ten books in his career and had a popular newsletter, *Health Trends*.
- Lee Kaiser, one of the first popular futurists, was able to look into the future regarding what healthcare could become, and offered a fresh perspective on common issues that have long occupied people in the industry. His currency was stories. The listener tended to walk away with a totally new way of seeing things.
- Nathan Kaufman, at one point a colleague of Coile's, has created a practice that routinely takes the contrarian point of view. His wicked sense of humor has made him one of the most popular speakers at ACHE's annual Congress on Healthcare Leadership and in other forums. He has developed a consulting practice focused mostly on physician practice mergers and acquisitions.

Consulting is never easy. However, a consulting career can have many advantages over other career paths. Most notable, perhaps, is the consultant's steep experience curve and the sense of adventure that comes with it. To explain what I mean, let me share a story from some years ago.

Alex McMahon,[5] in his twilight years, joined the faculty of the Fuqua School of Business at Duke University (my alma mater). One year, he invited me to participate in a discussion panel on hospital mergers and acquisitions during one of the annual alumni health forums held by the university. I spoke last, and when my time came it occurred to me that although all of the other panelists had first-hand experience of their own mergers, as a consultant I had participated in the

---

5. Alex was the president of the American Hospital Association (AHA) before he went back to Duke to teach. He had previously been the chairman of the board at Duke University at the same time that he served at AHA.

successful completion of more mergers in my relatively short career than all the other panelists combined (and they were considerably older than me).

To be sure, my fellow panelists offered some useful insights, but none of them had the experience that I had accumulated. By that time, I had been involved in more than 35 mergers valued at well over $20 billion. I had become a recognized expert in this specialized area. Clearly, facilitating a merger is different from experiencing your own (something I did later in my career). My broad experience was different from that of the other panelists, and this was clearly part of my brand. I have benefited from that recognition, which reinforced that experience is a great asset that is valued by the marketplace.

Success is certainly part of an effective brand. There are those who are drawn to the relatively high salaries and exciting lifestyles of successful consultants. It should be acknowledged, however, that not all consultants achieve a high level of financial independence. Consulting is a risky profession. It is true that successful consultants make a good living and enjoy a relatively high level of compensation. But it should also be understood that compensation is correlated with revenues generated by sales and billed hours. Consulting is not for the timid or the insecure. Done right, having a successful brand as a professional consultant can surely be part of a rewarding career with many benefits, both experiential and financial.

REFERENCES

Casciato, G. 2019. "Considerations for the Healthcare Executive-Turned-Consultant." Healthcare Consultants Forum newsletter. American College of Healthcare Executives. Published Spring. www.ache.org/learning-center/publications/newsletters/healthcare-consultants-forum-newsletter/spring-2019.

Cleverley, W. O., and J. O. Cleverley. 2018. *Essentials of Health Care Finance*, 8th ed. Burlington, MA: Jones & Bartlett Learning.

Ellison, A. 2019. "CHS Sees Net Loss Quadruple, Revenue Sink in Q1." *Becker's Hospital Review*. Published May 1. www.beckershospitalreview.com/finance/chs-sees-net-loss-quadruple-revenue-sink-in-q1.html.

Loebs, S., and W. Cleverley. 2020. Interviews with author, February 28 and March 3.

CHAPTER 4

So You Want to Be a Consultant?

WHATEVER YOUR REASONS for wanting to be a consultant, you should try to understand what you'll be getting into. Consulting, especially full-time consulting, is not for everyone, but bear in mind that, for both new and seasoned professionals, consulting can be a valuable stage of your career, even in cases where full-time consulting is not a good fit. There is a difference between the concept of consulting and the experience of consulting. This chapter shares some issues that should help you evaluate more specifically where, or if, consulting might be appropriate for you.

ATTRIBUTES COMMON TO CONSULTANTS

Though consultants come from a wide array of educational and professional backgrounds, we can identify attributes common to those who seem to have the best experiences. Ultimately, what successful consultants share is not so much a personality type as it is an attitude, and a common skill set that includes a command of the roles a consultant plays.

In this chapter, we'll look at issues commonly faced by consultants, with a focus on fit. While there is no single "consultant personality," the checklist in exhibit 4.1 can serve as a helpful screening tool. The intent of this list is to help set expectations of what the consulting experience is like and what attributes are brought out in pursuit of this demanding profession. Let's look at each of these attributes in turn:

- *Self-direction.* Except at large global firms that have a structured hierarchy, or upon entry when they are lacking experience, consultants tend to answer on

Exhibit 4.1: Consultant Personality Screen

> **ATTRIBUTES OF SUCCESSFUL CONSULTANTS**
>
> *How many can you check off?*
>
> - Self-directed
> - Excellent at time management
> - Tolerant of ambiguity
> - High energy
> - Passionate
> - Skilled at multitasking
> - Focused
> - Flexible and able to think on your feet
> - Creative/innovative
> - A lifelong learner

a day-to-day basis mostly to themselves. Thus, they must be self-motivated, driven by an "inner flame" that keeps them productive and on track with client assignments. Self-direction includes discipline with strong work habits. Those who are self-directed learn to gain confidence in approaching issues, both familiar ones and others that are entirely new. Approaching the consulting experience as an adventure can pay dividends.

- *Time management skills.* Time management skills are critical to any successful consulting career, particularly during orientation for new professionals. Effective time management helps complete tasks on schedule and provides time for new consultants to learn on the job and to volunteer for various assignments (e.g., proposal writing) that will help advance their careers. This is a skill that managers will evaluate quickly among entry-level consultants.

- *Tolerance for ambiguity.* Many client engagements lack clarity at the start. Clients might not always know what they want or need. This lack of clarity can be frustrating and consume valuable time. Sometimes, clients are hesitant to share what the real problem is that they're facing. "The key to winning business is getting the client to trust or like you enough that they will tell you what issues are worrying them. . . . The real problem is getting the client to tell you the problem" (Runde 2016). Uncertainty prevails, even with regard to how the client is reacting to your work or to you personally. It is relatively common for ambiguity to usher in a rich opportunity for new learning and to assist the client in adding clarity and understanding to the problem(s) they are trying to solve.

- *High energy.* Self-motivation is essential, but not sufficient. Entry-level consultants not only have to deliver value on client engagements, but they have to learn how to do so in real time. Consulting engagements require consultants to maintain a high level of energy throughout the process. Sometimes this can be difficult to sustain, especially when confronted by a disinterested individual or institutional apathy, but it comes with the territory. Consultants quickly develop an "on-stage" persona that they must bring to life, especially when physically present in the client setting. There is little doubt that most clients look to the consultants to supply essential energy to enable the team experience to be successful.

    While teams take their cue from consultant leaders and facilitators, this can become overwhelming at times. The requirement for high energy can also be risky, so you should learn to pace yourself to avoid potential burnout—a very real occupational hazard of the consulting experience.

- *Passion.* Having passion for the work you do makes it easier to maintain a high level of energy throughout a client engagement. This is particularly true when it comes to aspects of consulting that you might not enjoy. For instance, interviewing can become tedious after the first few. Others may find producing reports to be a pain. Debriefing the CEO is not in every consultant's sweet spot. Being able to lift one's vision above the tedium of an individual task allows clients to witness your buoyancy, which can be contagious. Without passion for the work, it is difficult to find success in consulting. Being constantly on stage and feeling like you are in a fishbowl consumes significant energy. It is perhaps urban legend that it is not work if you enjoy what you do. Consulting is hard work, but it sure goes much easier if you have passion for your chosen career.

- *Skill at multitasking.* The demands of the consulting experience are summarized well in the term "multitasking." Over the duration of most consulting assignments, the consultant is required to balance a number of issues simultaneously. This is not always easy to do, so keeping lists can be helpful. It is hard to imagine a consultant surviving without lists. One learns quickly that, at the end of each day, the day's list must be fully checked off.

Also, developing reliable routines can be helpful (e.g., finish expense reports within a day of completing trips).[1]

Most client engagements center around one or two key issues, but also involve managing many smaller sub-issues. Each client engagement is but one part of the daily tasks of a consultant. There are marketing calls to be made, timesheets to be filled out, internal teams to be staffed, team meetings to be attended, and the list goes on. Not to mention the time required during your "spare time" to tackle activities of daily living. Without excellent multitasking skills, it is all but impossible to find success as a consultant.

- *Focus.* What allows multitasking to succeed is the ability to block out other tasks, thus allowing for intense concentration on issues one at a time during critical periods. While balancing multiple things in a given day, what often happens with an engagement is that it requires an intense focus on a particular issue for brief periods of time. Once all available input is received, the consultant will need to produce a crisp set of observations with clear conclusions and recommendations. Timing and setting priorities help with this. It is often important to put off dealing with a particular issue until all available input has been received. This is not always easy, and many issues suffer from limited information. Part of focus can involve identifying key questions that frame an issue and require further exploration.

- *Flexibility and ability to think on one's feet.* Great flexibility and adaptability are required of consultants because the workday will rarely take form as anticipated. Consultants learn to expect the unexpected. I offer a story as an example of where this became important.

One time, after careful preparation with the client, I showed up for a final client presentation only to be waved away on arrival and told we had to change our approach. Somehow the process had failed to deal previously with some issues that the client considered important, and we needed to quickly pivot our presentation to address them. Although several of the issues exceeded the initial scope of work that had been carefully negotiated, we needed to find a way to satisfy the client. No matter who in the client organization requested the change, we were ultimately responsible for the process failing to identify the issues earlier. As this example demonstrates, you need to develop the ability to change direction rapidly even in situations that do not seem fair. Losing connection with the client can happen from

---

1. This may seem a bit mundane, but it is surprising how disrupting basic things like filling out a timesheet or an expense report can be in the life of a consultant.

time to time, despite your best efforts. Part of the consulting experience is learning to observe subtle cues that the client provides along the way. Consultants who are truly client-centric find a way to read the signals accurately and shift their approach as needed.

- *Creativity and innovation.* Consulting tends to attract smart, clever people. Thus, a key challenge of consulting is how to manage such people. Doing so effectively begins with observing that they don't want to be managed at all. "The cleverness of these people is central to their identity so the manager has to work with that. The close association between what they do and who they are also means that clever people often see themselves as not being dependent on others. The leader must, therefore, start by acknowledging their independence and difference. Their skills are not easily replicated and they know what they're worth" (Goffee and Jones 2009).

  Another key attribute of smart people is their drive to look at issues in novel ways and persuade people to take on new perspectives—in other words, creativity. Virtually every consulting engagement provides opportunities to innovate, to introduce new ways of thinking or approaching issues or problems. Consulting is a good fit for those who love to challenge the status quo. The key, of course, is to convince your clients and colleagues to adopt your innovations. Stark differences exist among firms regarding their receptivity to such innovation.

- *Lifelong learning.* With technological advances, it is becoming increasingly rare for any profession today not to require lifelong learning. Consulting is no exception. The interesting thing about management theory is that it is constantly developing new ways to look at old issues. The pandemic in 2020 is perhaps a dramatic example of this. While healthcare has dealt with infectious diseases for centuries, the scope and severity of this latest virus have challenged conventional wisdom at every level. Creating new knowledge is one thing, putting it into action in effective ways is another. Consultants must be receptive to new ways of thinking and maintain a healthy skepticism about the status quo with an abiding commitment to improve it.

CONSULTING AS A CAREER

Obviously, the foregoing list of attributes is intended only as a rough guide and should not be considered determinative of future success. From a broad perspective, the path of most career consultants follows the progression illustrated in exhibit 4.2.

Exhibit 4.2: The Consulting Career Path

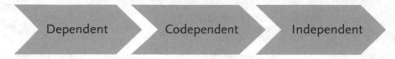

The *dependent stage* for early careerists is to team up with either a solo consultant (mentor) or a firm and start out dependent on managers and others to train them and bring them work. Early client engagements usually include a team of consultants and the initial focus is on data gathering and analytics. This may or may not initially involve direct client contact, depending on the firm and the nature of the engagement. Most people starting out want client contact as soon as possible. This is not lost on the more progressive firms.

Rookie consultants must complete their work successfully and in a timely manner. They must exhibit energy and initiative. Long hours are common at this stage, as significant learning is part of the process, which includes a fair amount of "re-work" designed to help the consultant learn what standards exist and how to edit their own work. Often, reviewing prior work and case studies from similar client engagements can be instructive. Partnering with a key manager is often part of this initial experience, one that is enhanced when the manager is patient and willing to spend the extra time working with the consultant on the issues and how the firm likes to approach them (each firm tends to have its own style).

While many promotions provide some recognition along the way, this initial stage lasts from one to four years, depending on the nature of the consulting and the culture of the firm. If one spends more than four years at this stage, it could indicate that consulting is not a good career choice or you are with the wrong firm. "Up or out" is a common phrase used at consulting firms, referring to the potential that must exist for consultants to be promoted to new levels on a timely basis.

Over time, as successful consultants develop confidence and the ability to operate with greater independence, they experience more responsibility and become more involved in client interactions. Those with ambition, energy, and initiative can progress rapidly through this stage. As noted before, it is during this stage that consultants often find mentors or "sponsors" to help them. Consultants should not be bashful but rather very eager to ask for help. Most managers are willing to act as mentors. In many firms, mentoring is a requirement for a manager to be promoted. Often, new consultants will know when they're succeeding in this stage because colleagues will begin competing for their involvement in proposal writing and client engagements. "The best litmus test of your ability to work with others is whether others are eager to work with you" (Runde 2016).

As one evolves to the *codependent stage,* a relationship develops where consultants and managers begin to work together as peers. This relationship involves mutual respect, each contributing to the success of the other. There is also shared accountability, where the work of each reflects on the other. This stage is where "minders" begin to manage "grinders," who are in the dependent stage. (See chapter 9 for a more detailed discussion of *finders, minders,* and *grinders.*) At larger firms, the manager phase can have multiple tiers, with some consultants advancing no further. It is more difficult to cover the cost of a full-time minder at smaller firms. Usually, this phase lasts two to five years, after which you are either out (failing to be able to sell work) or move up to the finder or partner phase. As the name implies, the firm becomes codependent on the consultant during this stage. The value represented by each consultant has increased as they have accumulated more skills through training and gained experience by completing a variety of engagements. They also begin to attract some additional work, mostly with existing clients with whom they have worked.

Not everyone who excels at basic analytics is attracted to sales. Small- to medium-sized firms tend not to support permanent codependence of this sort. In some rare situations, some small firms are able to apply a model where one partner is "the outside person," responsible for sales, and another partner is "the inside person," responsible for the work itself. This is unusual in my experience. It is only in the larger firms that consultants can make a career in which they don't progress beyond the codependent stage. The future of most firms rests with partners who are responsible for generating revenues by selling work to existing and new clients.

One achieves *independence* at the partner phase (*finder*). At this stage, the firm becomes dependent on you to generate the clients and the work (i.e., future revenues). You might lead a "division" or "practice area." You might form teams tailored to each client engagement. Sometimes teams are organized around a client, other times around a function or type of study (e.g., revenue cycle). You will work with a number of managers, all of whom form teams and oversee various consultants.

Being a finder is not for the timid. Finders are often in competition, possibly even internally, to secure engagements and opportunities. There can be considerable pressure to meet revenue targets, with significant parts of one's overall compensation linked to these numbers. The good news is that the practice can be quite lucrative and rewarding if you meet these targets. The bad news is that failure at this stage can occur rapidly and has significant financial implications. For most finders, some years are better than others, with a significant part of compensation usually tied to sales.

CONSULTING AS A STEPPING-STONE

For many people, consulting is more of a stepping-stone rather than a permanent career choice. Some of the better-known healthcare executives started out as consultants, though this is not always openly acknowledged. The global consulting firms tend to recruit right out of school and train for success internally. Gaining employment with a global consulting firm tends to be highly competitive because these positions are very attractive and come with high starting salaries.

As a place to start a career in healthcare, consulting has a number of advantages over other options, such as line-management positions in a hospital or healthcare organization. There are a number of additional factors you should consider when deciding whether to pursue consulting as a career.

IS CONSULTING RIGHT FOR YOU?

There is no simple way to determine if consulting is right for someone. One key observation is to focus on the *experience* of consulting and not just the *concept*. Force field analyses, of which exhibit 4.3 is an example, are often used to assist in decision-making. Using force field analysis can help in deciding if and when consulting is right for you. When enablers can overcome resisters, you have a green light to proceed.

One thing to remember while going over this force field analysis is that people change. What is important to you now might differ from what is important to you at another stage of your career. It also matters whether consulting is a career calling rather than just a starting point, or perhaps it is more a detour, or end stage of your career.

Now let's take a look at each of the enablers and resisters listed in exhibit 4.3.

Exhibit 4.3: Force Field Analysis

Enablers	Resisters
Exposure/experience	Lifestyle and health
Fits my personality	Don't like sales
Stepping-stone	Intensity/being on the clock
Accelerated learning curve/training	Travel and aging
Competitive/recognition	Isolation
Make a difference	Burnout and stress
Wealth creation	Repetition/boredom
Soft landing toward retirement	Competition/politics
	Risk

ENABLERS

We discussed the allure of consulting earlier. The following is a more detailed discussion of some of the more important enablers, by which I mean reasons for making consulting part of your career path.

Exposure/Experience

Early careerists recognize that, though their resumes may be strong, they lack experience. In many cases, one of the best ways (if not *the* best way) to remedy this is to work for a while as a consultant; a consultant will be exposed to several clients with different issues and will gain valuable experiences. This rapid exposure provides them with a sense of the various options that exist in the industry, as well as invaluable insight into best practices and many of the ways things can go wrong. With this exposure will come confidence and familiarity. Even if it is merely a first step in a career choice, consulting has a lot to offer.

Fits My Personality

Earlier in this chapter, we discussed attributes common to consultants. Possessing any particular attribute isn't required in order to find success as a consultant. For example, an aversion to sales is often cited as prohibitive, but even if sales isn't your thing, you can still find success as an entry-level consultant, particularly if it is positioned as a stepping-stone to a non-consulting career in healthcare. That said, I would nonetheless be wary of consulting where the requirements of the profession do not match up well with your personality. Some people are attracted to the challenge of consulting precisely *because* it's not a natural fit for them. But the work of consulting is rigorous and made more difficult where one's personality does not fit the requirements of the job.

Stepping-Stone

Even if you envision consulting as a stepping-stone to another career path, it is not necessary to admit as much in the interview process. For one thing, you never know for sure what path your career will take. What you thought was a stepping-stone might in fact become your destination. Either way, consulting can be a useful first step because of the training it makes available to you.

Accelerated Learning Curve/Training

Consulting has been sustained, especially at the global firms, by investing considerable resources in the accelerated learning curve. Clearly, the level of investment correlates with the size of the firm, with the more elaborate infrastructure available in the larger, more traditional consulting firms. But even some of the medium and smaller firms have elaborate training programs that are a genuine source of pride. The value proposition for the firms seems clear: Accelerated learning enables the consultants to be productive and generate revenues for the firm. It is for this reason that the bigger firms have full-time employees devoted to this process. The differences between firms can be quite dramatic with regard to the resources and talent devoted to training, as discussed in more detail in part II—The Firm Experience. Training routinely involves case studies, role playing, and simulations, and it is increasingly shifting to more of an immersion *experience*. Orientation, in particular, tends to be focused on covering the basic skills required of consultants.

When I went through orientation, we affectionately referred to it as "charm school." Clearly, firms view these programs as an investment in their future. Not only does it allow for accelerated learning of the basics, but it also allows them to standardize their values and bring their proprietary techniques to life. The global firms tend to have a strong culture and to promote from within. The more training a consultant receives, the more value they have to the firm. It is truly difficult for someone to enter into the more traditional firms at anything higher than entry level, since so much information is communicated through the training programs. The longer you stay with the firm, the more exposure you get as you go through the natural progressions and training provided at each level.

Competitive/Recognition

Consulting appeals to people who enjoy competition. You first compete to get hired. Over time, clients and the market will tell you if this is your calling or if you are better suited for another career. *If you do not like to compete, consulting is probably not for you.* Darwin's law of natural selection arguably applies to consulting. Not only is there individual competition among consultants, but your success in the market will ultimately be determined by how well you compete to develop clients and future engagements.

The college selection process exposes smart people early on to the rigors of competition. Rhymer Rigby at the *Financial Times* says that "a good start is to recognise what these people want. Generally, they want to be recognised and get on their work. They like complexity, challenges, and problem-solving, and tend to gravitate to like-minded people. The trick is to appeal to what drives them but at the same time, it's important to recognise that a lot of really smart people are not necessarily that well-equipped with social skills or emotional intelligence. So feedback is important" (Gettler 2015). People who compete successfully do so, in part, for the recognition that follows. Consulting provides recognition, not only among peers and clients, but also to a wider audience, by way of opportunities to share your expertise through writing and speaking. The best firms acknowledge achievement. As Quint Studer (2020) has noted, "The more we recognize the more the behaviors are repeated, and our recognition chips are always replenished."

Make a Difference

Many people are drawn to the professions because they offer opportunities to make a difference in the world. Consultants are often called in to address problems that clients have been unable to solve using their own resources. Clearly, part of the fundamental value proposition of consulting is being able to leapfrog a client into a position to solve problems faster or more effectively than the client could have done on their own. Not all engagements provide immediate feedback, but some do and it can be very gratifying. Of course, there is a corresponding risk of failure, which can be both motivating when successful and discouraging when not. Fear of failure, which is a constant, can also be a motivator when experiences learned from failures help to reduce future risk.

Wealth Creation

Consultants are generally well compensated. The highest earners are invariably owners or partners rather than staff consultants. Ownership comes in different forms, however. For example, participation in profit-sharing plans, where the firm matches and contributes to a fund in which you are vested, is a form of ownership. These plans are subject to significant regulations, so pay attention to the fine print.

Restricted and unrestricted stock also provide opportunities for wealth creation. This can take the form either of "warrants," if the company is not publicly traded, or stock/stock options if it is publicly traded. The importance of stock is related largely to taxes. Stock options, for example, allow you to accumulate wealth without triggering a taxable event until they are sold. If the option increases in value, then you pay for the option out of profits (profit = current value − initial strike price of option). If it does not increase in value, then you don't sell it, and there is still no taxable event. Some firms have used this approach to tie up members of their team, who then find it too expensive to leave the firm since options could be granted or vested over time.

Soft Landing Toward Retirement

More and more executives seem drawn to consulting later in their careers. It is not clear why this is, although burnout on operations is no doubt a contributor. The constraints of managing within a system that is increasingly standardized can feel oppressive over time. There is a lot of bureaucracy and external regulation in healthcare that tends to limit innovation. This subject deserves more than casual treatment and will be the subject of a follow-up book.

RESISTERS

Consulting is not for everyone, especially as a full-time career path. *Resisters* refers to some of the barriers that might stand in the way of a successful consulting career. Resisters should be carefully weighed against enablers before pursuing such a career.

Lifestyle and Health

I've heard consulting described as "a young man's sport." Though consulting is reserved neither for the young nor for men, there is more than a little truth to the cliché. Consulting is hard, grinding work. As such, it can take a toll on one's health and can set fairly strict limits on the sort of lifestyle consultants can lead.

Before we married, my fiancée and I spent a year together to see if we could make the consulting lifestyle work for us. Over time, as some colleagues advised me early in my career, I was able to prove to myself that my consulting career almost never got in the way of major family events. I was always there for key athletic events, graduations, and the like.

I must say that having some skill in communications is required. I will also suggest that being a road warrior does limit one's ability to participate in community events, something I have truly missed at times. Volunteering to serve in various community leadership opportunities may be limited more to the weekends.

Yet, some consultants end up in a trap where their professional and personal lives become indistinguishable. They do not know what else to do with their time except work, and they feel they must always be productive.

In my own case, the need to separate my professional and my personal lives became particularly acute when I spent about ten years operating out of a home office. I designated space in the house as office space. I was careful not to work in other parts of the house, and my family knew not to bother me when I was in "the office." I found this physical separation extremely helpful.

Lifestyle challenges can be particularly difficult for women. During my time as a professional consultant, a number of progressive practices have worked hard to moderate these disparities, but they are still real and worth noting.

When I first began as a consultant, women generally left the profession when they decided to have children. As in so many other industries, firms were ill equipped to address the impact of their absence and to face the challenges of reintegrating them into the workforce. Some women were able to overcome these barriers to reentry, though it was anything but easy. Fortunately, this has changed rather dramatically.

Most global consulting firms have since done a good job of addressing these problems. Technological advances have helped. Video conferencing, in particular, allows professionals to remain engaged while working remotely. One of the lasting effects of the COVID-19 pandemic is the accelerated acceptance of digital technologies (e.g., virtual health) and internet conferences (e.g., Sling, Zoom, and Google). One concern that is often expressed by younger people who are considering consulting is the ability to have a family, especially when travel is involved. Granted, family can be affected when both parents are consultants. For example, it is far more challenging to manage family life when both partners travel than when only one spouse might be on the road three to four days a week. Often, clients take over your schedule when you are involved in a significant engagement. In doing so, clients are not being rude or inconsiderate. It simply comes with the territory.

Don't Like Sales

I teach a seminar for the American College of Healthcare Executives that focuses in part on digital strategies for attracting customers. We go through an exercise where I ask people to share what first comes to mind when they hear the word "sales." I tend to get back things such as "slick," "snake oil," "used cars," and "deceitful advertising." At least in healthcare, it seems that there is little regard for the proverbial salesman.

Clearly, many people have an aversion to sales and want nothing to do with it. But there is no denying that sales is part of consulting as a whole, even if some individual consultants can succeed with little involvement in sales. This is perhaps an area where the career stage you are in matters. For early professionals, an aversion to sales shouldn't be prohibitive. Later on, however, an aversion to sales can be catastrophic. I have known many people who, though successful as leaders and line managers, were unable to monetize their experiences as a consultant. The reason for this failure invariably includes an aversion to or lack of competence in sales.

Intensity/Being on the Clock

Consulting can swallow you up. The focus on billable hours can create significant pressure. Finishing one engagement only to immediately shift to the next one can be challenging. Consultants often find it difficult to focus on selling their next engagement while still working on the current one. Achieving work/life balance is challenging at best, impossible at worst. The long hours and sheer mental effort required to solve intransigent problems can be all-consuming.

Constantly being on the clock is stressful in itself. Many people who enter consulting (or the law) find this surprising. While some business models are built around a more value-based retainer approach, one that is less dependent on tracking hours, most still require keeping a timesheet. This is important not only for billing purposes, but also for budgeting and planning. It teaches you how much time various tasks take, and since most engagements are priced by time and expenses, such familiarity can make the difference between being competitive versus being overpriced, or between making versus losing money on a particular engagement.

Travel and Aging

Some people travel better than others. One consultant friend of mine dislikes not only traveling but also the stress of making travel arrangements and filling out expense sheets. Regional practices tend to be more operational and might involve less travel—more often by car or train versus by plane.

Aging is another important consideration when it comes to travel. Simply put, it becomes more and more difficult to travel as you get older. Travel affects the body in many ways and can be quite taxing psychologically. The good news is that experience usually makes one a better traveler. The rigors of travel and stress notwithstanding, it has been my experience that people can find success in consulting well into their retirement years, if they wish. Since consulting is truly an experience-based business, those with the most experience can find themselves in demand beyond normal retirement age.

Older consultants tend to be more selective in taking engagements and might work with fewer clients over time. I think this is one of the reasons why many senior executives are drawn to consulting during their later years, for it allows them to focus on what interests them most. But there is a danger lurking here.

Consulting is seductive, and this can pose problems for those who do not or no longer have the stamina or mental capacity to keep up. A dear colleague of mine with whom I collaborated on many engagements, Larry Pixley, was one of the founders of Stroudwater Associates. As we were working together, Larry learned at age 64 that he had developed Parkinson's disease. Otherwise, he seemed like he had plenty of gas left in his tank, and it was my impression that he hadn't slowed down one bit. Even so, he made the difficult decision to retire early.

As he explained, one symptom of this progressive disease is diminished mental capacity (something I hadn't realized about Parkinson's). He had found himself in a client situation where he accidentally divulged a sensitive piece of information to the wrong party in the midst of a highly sensitive negotiation. He was a perfectionist, and this slip-up rattled him to the point that he retired, unwilling to jeopardize any future client work.

Isolation

Not only travel itself, but also time away from home and family takes a toll. Technology has made it easier to stay in touch with loved ones, but nothing can replace being there with them.

Travel can be very isolating, and I have seen it wear on those not used to extensive travel. It is important to learn how to stay healthy on the road. Exercising, socializing, and eating a healthy diet are crucial, though often hard to keep up away from home, so you should take advantage of gym facilities, seek out a yoga class, and avoid the constant temptation to eat fast food.

Burnout and Stress

Burnout is a clear and present danger of consulting. To avoid burnout, some people find ways to take occasional breaks. Many academics who do consulting on the side have found a good formula for balancing time among teaching, research, and consulting. Burnout largely results from poorly managing stress.

You ignore stress at your peril. Learning to manage stress comes with experience, and people approach it in different ways. We each learn what works for us. I find working out regularly is very helpful. Walking has been essential for me and is, of course, something you can do on the road. Because consulting requires you to be constantly onstage, it is imperative that you find some downtime. This is where you get lost in a book, a movie, or some activity that requires concentration. As mundane as it might sound, I actually had an advisory board for my own firm that, at one point, counselled me to play more golf, both to learn to be more patient and to get away from the stress of the office. (Not sure I ever developed much patience from this, but it was fun regardless.)

Repetition/Boredom

There is no getting around the fact that certain forms of consulting lose their luster through repetition. Though experience with similar kinds of engagements has value, especially when it comes to things such as standardization and process efficiencies, too much repetition can lead to boredom. Your tolerance for repetitive tasks should inform the type of consulting you pursue.

Competition/Politics

It should be noticed from this force field analysis that competition appears as both an enabler and a resister. A great deal of consulting is done by teams formed to carry out individual client assignments, and this exposes a consultant to potential internal competition. How can that happen?

Things can begin to go sideways when, for example, people take credit for the work of others. Over time, it generally works out because most people are able to find their niche on a team. But there are often setbacks, and sometimes intervention is necessary.

At larger firms, competition to advance to the next level can be fierce. There are only so many positions available, and limits to how many people can be promoted.

Where things go bad, it is not rare to hear complaints that people were not given credit for a major sale or were excluded from an opportunity to work with a client that they had secured. While this sort of thing is fortunately rare in my experience, it can and does happen.

Politics in consulting firms can turn negative. It is in the nature of a consultant to view things critically, and there is a constant drive to improve things. This can morph to internal firm practices as well. In my experience, the internal grapevine of consulting firms can be quite caustic. It only takes one manager to sour the consulting experience at a given firm. The choice is then to work with other managers or to leave the firm. There is no getting around the reality of the consulting experience that there is some cultural negativity to internal politics. The larger the firm, the more you might be able to move away from negative interactions and find managers to work with who are positive and reinforcing—you have more choices.

Risk

An accurate understanding of the consulting experience recognizes that consulting carries high risk. Key contacts that one develops might change jobs, clients retire, and firms merge. I have been involved in several major engagements where the CEO was terminated halfway into the engagement, at which point the engagement was summarily cancelled. Moreover, one must worry about health concerns, particularly as they might impact one's ability to travel, as noted before.[2]

The risk in consulting does not wane. Most consultants I have known take great pride in their work. A major letdown with a client engagement can take the fun out of things and can indeed be a bellwether for change. I urge my consulting friends to avoid the pursuit beyond the point where the work no longer provides the pleasure that it once did.

DISSATISFIERS

Dissatisfiers are more unavoidable than resisters because they are built into the nature of the profession, and every profession has them. Among the major dissatisfiers of consulting are the following:

- *Long workdays.* Too often, there is insufficient time to do a project as well and as thoroughly as you would like. This can be very frustrating. It gets tiresome to keep trying to stuff 18 hours of work into 12-hour bags.
- *Bad clients.* Fortunately, having a bad client is rare, for the selection process tends to ensure client–consultant chemistry. Over the years, I have walked away from a number of client opportunities because I was not a good fit for the client or vice versa.
- *Bad engagements.* Even if you have a good relationship with the client, you still might find yourself stuck in a bad engagement. What makes an engagement bad? It could be poorly planned or executed. It could require working with incompatible personalities. It could end up involving issues outside your area of interest or expertise.
- *Inadequate budgets.* Most budgets are reasonable. Rarely are they excessive. The rub comes when budgets are simply inadequate to complete the designated engagement. Frustration over budgeting issues can surface and sour an otherwise solid client relationship. In such cases, the options are clear: Either finish the work and take the hit on budget (i.e., get paid less than the time that was required), attempt to adjust the scope of the project, or increase the budget.

We have sought in this chapter to present a realistic platform of what is required to have a good consulting experience and to sensitize you to some of the

---

2. I recommend maintaining a disability insurance policy as a practicing consultant. I have seen many people in the profession get run down over time and benefit from such policies. Most firms offer this as part of benefits packages. (Be sure it includes long- and short-term disability.)

realities of consulting that should not be overlooked. Ultimately, only you can judge if consulting is right for you. While preparing for such a move is critical, the final judgment might not occur in the preparation but will have to await your immersion into consulting. But that is OK, since it is not necessary to enter into consulting with the requirement that it become your career. You can view it as a station worth stopping at on your journey, at least for some period of time, especially at this early point in your career.

Given this orientation, what consulting can expose you to, and the attributes you possess that allow you to consider such a move, it can be argued that the upside potential outweighs any downside. Regardless, if consulting is ultimately not the right career for you, the skills and experience that you gain from consulting cannot help but raise your profile and contribute to your next successful career move.

REFERENCES

Gettler, L. 2015. "Managing Smart People." CEO Institute. Published March 11. www.ceoinstitute.com/member-experience/ceo-insight/blog-article/managing-smart-people/.

Goffee, R., and G. Jones. 2009, updated 2013. "9 Ways to Harness the Special Talents of Clever People." *Management Today*. Published September 1, updated October 9. www.managementtoday.co.uk/9-ways-harness-special-talents-clever-people/article/929304.

Runde, J. 2016. "Why Young Bankers, Lawyers, and Consultants Need Emotional Intelligence." *Harvard Business Review Blog*. Published September 26. https://hbr.org/2016/09/why-young-bankers-lawyers-and-consultants-need-emotional-intelligence.

Studer, Q. 2020. "Don't Underestimate the Impact of Positive Recognition." *The Busy Leader's Handbook*. Published October 26. https://thebusyleadershandbook.com/dont-underestimate-the-impact-of-positive-recognition/.

Consulting Skills: The Basics

HERE'S WHERE I BEGIN to address consulting skills. This topic has been divided into two chapters because there is so much to discuss. Chapter 5 focuses on some of the more obvious basics, and chapter 6 looks at what we will call the intangibles. The concepts presented are reinforced through case studies and tips. A review of these chapters reveals not only what it really means to be a professional consultant to healthcare organizations, but also why consultants tend to be perceived as varying widely in their skills. Mastering the basics is a critical way to get started.

I was first exposed to the essential consulting skill set early in my career, when I was with Booz Allen. Realistically, there is no substitute for the sophisticated orientation and skills training courses offered by the older, more traditional management consulting firms. As a graduate of such a program, I tend to refer to myself as a "professionally trained" consultant. Though words alone cannot hope to replicate the full immersion experience, I share with you some of the insights that I have learned along the way.

Not all consultant training is vested in formal didactic programs. While formal training is essential for new careerists, observing seasoned consultants in action is also of immense value. Often consultants are thrown into the proverbial pool, left to sink or swim. It is far more preferable to learn from an experienced swimmer first—or at least to find one in the pool who is willing to help you as you flail around. Ideally, part of rookie training should come from working closely with veterans employing an apprenticeship model. In fact, this may be one of the real differentiators among firms. Which firms have people who model basic consulting skills best? To what extent do they emphasize teaching as part of a manager's skill set? Do they recognize the value of an apprenticeship model in their training activities?

Many sources are available to study consulting skills in more depth, including numerous online resources. The intent here is to place these generic skills in the context of what is required to serve healthcare clients.

THE POWER OF OBSERVATION

Consulting is about gathering data, manipulating it to become information, and then, through wisdom and experience, using this information to form conclusions and recommendations. In considering the variety of sources available, nothing compares to what is provided through client interviews. It is for this reason that we go into great detail about the nuances of the interview process at the outset of this discussion. Impressions that consultants make on the client are largely based on the interview process and how they interact in interviews and in group meetings.

In conducting a client engagement, consultants rarely start with a blank slate; they take time to understand how the client views the data and get their interpretations of the issues at hand. Clients seek advice from the consultants for which they are paying good money. They are usually eager to share their thoughts on what the problem is and some ideas of how to attack it. Consultants partner with clients throughout the consulting process, sharing observations and interpretations to gain consensus. Interviews and data interpretation are dependent upon keen observation skills. Because this can be subtle, it is something that cannot be overemphasized.

At the core of consulting is observation—what we see, hear, feel, and understand, which is made powerful by what we absorb. The simple reality is that two people sharing the same event can have very different experiences based on what they observe and what they retain. It must also be recognized that we all have "filters," and the lens through which we see the world is guided by these filters. As a result, some of us see things others miss. Still others notice the same thing but do not retain it or put it in the proper context. The ability to quickly assess a new situation, to sort one's initial impressions and determine what is important and what is not, sets experienced consultants apart from rookies. Honing the power of observation is perhaps the most essential consulting skill.

Observation involves the senses. But observation skills tend not to be something we are born with; rather, they are developed over time. Sherlock Holmes helps to illustrate this point. In one story, Holmes instructs Watson on the difference between seeing and observing (Konnikova 2011):

> "When I hear you give your reasons, the thing always appears to me to be so ridiculously simple that I could easily do it myself, though at each successive instance of your reasoning, I am baffled until you explain your process. And yet I believe that my eyes are as good as yours."

"Quite so," [Holmes] answered. "You see, but you do not observe. The distinction is clear. For example, you have frequently seen the steps which lead up from the hall to this room."

"Frequently."

"How often?"

"Well, some hundreds of times."

"Then how many are there?"

"How many? I don't know."

"Quite so! You have not observed. And yet you have seen. That is just my point. Now, I know that there are 17 steps, because I have both seen and observed."

Along with sight, listening is also a very important sense of observation. "While knowledge and experience can get individuals 'through the door,' an ability to listen, adapt, collaborate, empathize, and build trust is what will set a firm apart from competitors and individuals from their peers" (Johnson 2015). Consultants can easily fall into the trap of talking when they should be listening (more on this later). As with interviews, consultants can initiate a discussion with a good question, but the real value comes in listening to the response and putting it in the proper context.

Observing body language is every bit as important as what is being said, and what is not being said. In addition to the senses, a consultant must possess the mental discipline to connect the dots. As Peter Drucker pointed out, "The most important thing in communication is hearing what isn't said." Just how forthcoming is the client with regard to the issues and possible solutions? This involves trust and candor, commonly combined in the term "authenticity," and it can apply to the client just as much as it applies to consultants. Being authentic is one of the core elements of the consultant value chain reviewed in chapter 2. Listening well can go a long way toward establishing an authentic relationship with a client.

Using a few key interview techniques can help make a consultant more authentic and a better listener. Three specific tools are engagement, pace, and interaction.

- *Engagement.* Usually, people can tell whether or not you're interested in what they have to say. My experience is that people like it if you take notes. Nurses refer to their "paper brains," meaning what they have written down while speaking with a patient. Exceptional listeners not only listen in real time, but are able to recall key things that were said by studying their notes afterward.

  Asking a question and then drifting off does not engage the client. Do you acknowledge comments, ask follow-up questions, nod your head in agreement? Ultimately, it does not take much to express interest; it can be as simple as making eye contact and acknowledging, "Got it."

- *Pace.* I do not like to do more than six interviews a day, and I prefer to separate them by at least 15 minutes. This time allows you to study up on who is next and to reflect on what you just heard. It also allows you to go over time a bit if an interview demands this. Sometimes it is necessary to schedule a follow-up interview. The truth is that, after a while on any given day, it gets hard to keep listening and easy to tune out, which is why pace is so important. Have some refreshments handy. Walk around. Be willing to accept a drink of water when it's offered to you if you conduct the interview in someone's office.
- *Interaction.* While it is not always possible, best practice dictates that interviews should involve two consultants—one takes the lead while the other takes notes. For group meetings, things might be a bit different, depending on the size of the group.

Most consulting engagements involve a "task force" of executives who, with the consultants, form the *engagement team.* (Sometimes the task force is called a "steering committee," though I prefer the former because it tends to disband upon completion of an engagement.) Ideally, the task force will involve 12 or fewer people from the client side. That's large enough to cover the critical components of the organization, but not so large that anyone gets left out of the discussion. It is common practice for larger engagements to create focused subgroups that feed into a central group or task force.

It is important to begin most projects with individual interviews of the engagement team. For physicians, I have found group interviews to be most helpful, because getting physicians in a group allows them to speak openly about their feelings. For example, interviewing three physicians from the internal medicine department generates more participation and can help to get reactions to a number of questions to gauge consenting views versus differences of opinion.

There is a difference between a group interview and group meetings. A group interview can make use of the same interview guide as individual interviews (see Interviewing Techniques later in this chapter). Group meetings represent another kind of listening challenge. A group meeting should have an agenda that is prepared ahead of time. If you are not responsible for the agenda, get a copy of it before the meeting. This will allow you to prepare. It is important to remember that you can't listen while you're talking. It's essential, then, to have another team member involved if you expect to do some of the talking.

Listening better enhances your powers of observation. Experience teaches consultants to see and hear things that clients often miss. Now that you understand the power of observation, we are prepared to begin our orientation to consulting.

ORIENTATION TO CONSULTING

Onboarding the new consultant usually begins with in-depth orientation training—what we affectionately called "charm school" back in the day. This process varies considerably by firm, but my experience suggests that three things should be reviewed to get started:

1. Key questions and the 80/20 rule
2. Data gathering
3. Interview techniques

Although some of this might seem like common sense, it is worth looking at each of these components in depth.

Key Questions and the 80/20 Rule

Booz Allen is generally given credit for coming up with the concept of key questions. Peter Drucker, one of the original business gurus, is known to have said, "My greatest strength as a consultant is to be ignorant and ask a few questions."

It is rather amazing to me how few consultants learn to interview well. Yet interviews are among the most intimate interactions that a consultant will have with a client. There is no better place to establish your *authenticity*. Imagine if a retailer had the ability to interview every customer the way consultants do in the interview process. Instead, retailers pay significant dollars to survey customers and conduct focus groups. When you think about it, it is rather ironic that consultants get paid to interview the client and to then produce what the client wants. Interviewing is an incredibly powerful exchange as part of the consulting process.

For any consulting engagement of consequence, preparation for the interview process is critical. Such preparation involves reflection with both empathy for the client and anticipation of the specific situation being examined. There is mental discipline involved in the preparation; what my Catholic clients refer to as a period of "discernment." It requires looking at an issue from every angle.

As an example, interviews for operational issues tend to be very different from interviews involving strategic issues. Knowing who to interview, while important, follows from determining *the right questions* to ask. Anyone can ask a question; what is important is to find the right questions, and to determine which questions are most important. Identifying key questions is a critical technique for injecting efficiency into the inquiry. The seasoned consultant not only asks the right questions, but asks them in the right sequence (i.e., structure). Focusing on just the few key questions allows you to get to the finish line faster, and better. Clients appreciate this because busy executives cannot afford to waste time.

In practice, formulating key questions is best approached on a team basis, allowing for insights from a variety of perspectives, especially in the case of projects that involve complex issues. Mastering the skill of identifying key questions also allows us to avoid "rabbit holes" that waste time and resources. Important engagements call for the consulting team to meet preceding an initial client visit, making a conscious effort to identify the key questions related to the issue(s) at hand.

Similar to key questions, McKinsey focuses on a number of tools in attempting to solve business problems, including the 80/20 rule, summarized by Rasiel (1999) as follows:

> The 80/20 rule is one of the great truths of management consulting and, by extension, of business. You will see wherever you look: 80 percent of your sales will come from 20 percent of your sales force. . . . 20 percent of the population controls 80 percent of the wealth. It doesn't always work (sometimes the bread falls butter-side up), but if you keep your eyes peeled for examples of the 80/20 rule in your business, you will come up with ways to improve it.

Invoking this rule allows you to quickly focus on data that is relevant versus data that is of little consequence. It makes you answer questions like "What are the three most important things I need to know to answer this question?" The 80/20 rule is about the experience curve: The more one becomes familiar with a particular issue, the easier it is to focus attention on key components of a problem, adding efficiency to the process.

Data Gathering and the Rule of Thirds

There is a saying that you don't get a second chance to make a first impression. For some people at the client organization, their first impression of the consultant is formed when the consultant asks them for data. Unfortunately, many client engagements get off on the wrong foot because the data request is a burden and involves many extraneous items. It is important to understand that gathering data is an imposition on the client. The more consultants and firms can draw on in-house databases, the less they will burden their clients. An ability to efficiently gather data without bothering the client is what sets some firms apart from others.

At the outset, efficient data gathering requires an organized "data requirements list." This list can sometimes be appended to the proposal. Depending on the client and the issue involved, preparing the data requirements list alone can be time-consuming. A note of caution here: Healthcare is unique when it comes to gathering data because of the issues of privacy and regulatory compliance.[1]

Once the data has been received, it requires analysis. More often than not, firms have requested certain data (e.g., utilization statistics) in standardized formats that allow for relatively efficient populating of analytical tables, charts, and graphs. Firms tend to have developed templates for this purpose. Data analytics are becoming increasingly sophisticated. In fact, some firms now outsource key elements of this (e.g., clinical service line analytics), because it requires manipulation of large amounts of data (e.g., 18 months of medical records for all inpatients and outpatients) using sophisticated analytical tools.

Once the analysis has been completed, the results must be summarized and packaged in an easy-to-understand way. Do not underestimate the time required to finalize this deliverable. A helpful presentation technique is to organize the summary material into three distinct categories: findings, conclusions, and recommendations (discussed in more detail later in this section).

In completing an assignment, it is useful to divide the time among three key components: data gathering, analysis, and producing reports. Separating a consulting engagement into these three segments is referred to as *the rule of thirds*. Correctly estimating the time required to complete each segment is truly an art form and can often make the difference between a successful project and one that goes over budget. The advantage of splitting this process into thirds not only reminds you that data gathering is critical, but that it is important to not underestimate the thinking and processing that comes after gathering the data. While a crude measure perhaps, the value of the rule of thirds is that you can reasonably determine the time it will take to complete the engagement if you can first determine what it will take to gather the necessary data, then just multiply by three. It is a simplistic estimate, to be sure.

---

1. The Health Information and Portability and Accountability Act of 1996 (HIPAA) governs the acquisition and manipulation of personal health information (PHI). This one piece of legislation has helped pay the salaries of countless lawyers and consultants focused on regulatory compliance. To greatly oversimplify the issue, contracting with a provider in possession of PHI (medical records) will require significant contract language for any consultant. If there is no reason to capture patient-specific information, then the consultant will be able to indicate to the client that they are not interested in PHI and any related information should be *de-identified*. However, many lawyers counsel clients to list themselves as a *business associate* from a liability perspective, because it is always possible that the client will inadvertently send PHI. The liability is that this information may somehow become public (e.g., through hacking). This liability carries hefty financial penalties, which is the reason for such caution.

Interviewing Techniques

Healthcare is first and foremost about people. Healthcare organizations exist to serve people, and there is no more important asset for these organizations than their employees and their patients. Accordingly, obtaining input from these people is critical to a consulting engagement. We take a deep dive into interviewing because it is such a valuable tool for consultants. Interviews provide context for the engagement and insight into the people and culture of the organization. Many consulting engagements begin with an initial round of interviews involving key people at the client site. There may also be follow-up interviews or a new set of interviews with other people depending on the nature of the engagement. Clearly, interviewing is an integral part of data gathering. It represents some of the most intimate interactions that a consultant has with a client. If a key goal of any client engagement is to meet or exceed client expectations, there is no better place to learn about those expectations than through the interview process.

Interviews can have any of a number of objectives. At a minimum, the interviews should introduce you to key players in the organization with whom you will be working. Ideally, this should include the people who will be responsible for implementing your recommendations. Interviews should also shed light on the dynamics of the particular issue that you are studying. This can involve helping to define a problem or identify opportunities for improvement. It can also bring to the surface certain sensitivities of this client. It is common to identify a few "sacred cows" during this process. Identifying sensitivities does not necessarily mean that they are to be avoided but rather shows how they are best approached. For example, issues that are political in nature could involve more interviews than ones that are not. Sometimes, rather than restricting the number of interviews, it might be important to have an "open" interview process. As an example, one medical center that was challenged with the need for greater physician engagement opened up the interview schedule, and anyone interested could participate. (We completed 96 interviews!)

Clearly, one of the central aims of the interview process is for key people in an organization to provide input. To understand this in more depth I'd like to share an exchange that took place between an independent physician and the board chairman of a health system during a board retreat. Board retreats are one of my favorite formats for group discussions because they represent the rare occasions when leaders can get out of the shop, gather as a group, and discuss key issues without being interrupted. During a variety of breakout sessions and general discussions, one physician was rather disruptive and kept carping about the lack of input on key decisions and the need for more physician involvement. Toward the end of the retreat, after several comments from him about the lack of input on a particular issue, the chairman had had enough. "Bob, what are you talking about in terms of lack of input? You were on the task force that studied that issue."

"That's right Joe, and I told them what we should do. But they did not agree with me. You see? I had no input."

Rest assured, Bob was serious. The group had a good laugh, but Bob was not laughing.

Interviews come in a variety of forms, but I want to focus on so-called *structured* interviews. A structured interview follows from an *interview guide*. It is always best to share a draft interview guide with a client in advance. Each client will designate a *liaison* or key contact for a client engagement. The guide should be shared with this person with the understanding that they will share it internally as they deem necessary. Through this process, trust is established as clients know what is being asked of their colleagues. Done well, an interview is a discussion, but these discussions will invariably reach the client grapevine.

It is essential to understand that interviews have consequences—they should be confidential, but that does not mean that they take place in a vacuum. Discussing a topic with one executive in an interview can lead that executive to continue the conversation later with another executive, and so on. Therefore, it is important that the organization be prepared for the interview process and provide some introduction internally to the client team that the consultants will be visiting and outlining the purpose of their visit.

Each interview should begin with a brief description of the engagement and the purpose of the interview. A basic rule of consulting is *no surprises*. Picture a CEO talking with a subordinate about a recent interview by the consultant: "What did they ask you about?" You do not want the answer to surprise the CEO.

Structured interviews tend to be confidential. At the outset, the interviewer should inform the person being interviewed that the comments are confidential and "not for attribution," but that the results of all the interviews will be summarized to provide feedback to the group.

The content of interviews is invaluable to the consultant attempting to understand the issues and arrive at recommendations that are compatible with the culture of an organization. This is important from a background perspective, but how are the results of interviews to be shared with the client? Some engagements might involve dozens of interviews in order to gain clarity on a complex issue. The client needs to understand what came out of the interviews—what did the consultants hear and what did this mean to them? In summarizing the interviews, some segmentation is required. It is common to share a list of people who were interviewed and segment them by major function, or position, as there tend to be palpable differences in the views held by various groups. For example, hospital groups tend to be segmented by management (corporate, unit, middle), the board, and members of the medical staff (primary care, specialty, independent, employed).

Interviews can also be summarized by topic (e.g., governance, financial performance). For a strategic planning process, it can be helpful to segment issues by internal versus external. It is also common to segment issues according to a planning technique that attempts to identify strengths, weaknesses, opportunities, and threats (SWOT analysis). Interview summaries will vary by the nature of each engagement.

Interviews are time-consuming, so it is common to set expectations by providing a target number of interviews by segment in the proposal (e.g., ten interviews with members of the senior management team, ten with board members). To assist in such segmentation, it is therefore important to know which segment applies to which interview; interviews generally begin with a clarification of what position interviewees hold, how long they have been in their positions, and some general information about their backgrounds. How many interviews are enough?

In developing the interview list, set a target number to provide a representative sample of viewpoints that might exist in the organization. Depending on how "open" the organization is to interviews, it is somewhat common to ask a person at the end of an interview if there is anyone else who might be important to interview on the same topic (and then privately check if that person is already on the list). The interview list should be determined in collaboration with the client, not solely by the consultant. You know you have conducted enough interviews when they start to sound the same and you no longer hear any new thoughts.

Interviews can be conducted individually or in groups. There are advantages and drawbacks to either approach. A central consideration concerns what is being sought through the interview process. Better understanding of a client culture is always an underlying purpose of the interview process. Few things say more about the culture of an organization than how openly people behave in a group setting. Where cultures involve fear, or are more restrictive in certain ways, group discussions tend to be stilted and lack candor.

Please note that interviewing involves ethical considerations. For example, it is important when preparing a summary of interviews that you not include any content that might be traced back to a particular individual or group. Sometimes, CEOs request feedback from interviews along the way, and this presents problems from both sides. Information provided can potentially identify views expressed by a particular individual, and the interviewees need to know that they can rely on your promise of confidentiality. Therefore, only general responses should be provided, and I never quote anyone specifically from an interview. General impressions are another story. For example, how do you handle if a CEO asks if someone seems resistant to the consulting process? This does not involve sharing a specific comment but rather impressions that I own. Given that the answer can be material to the engagement, this question strikes me as in bounds, but you can see where this can require a delicate balancing act.

Hearing different points of view is essential to the overall interview process, but the trick is to contextualize the comments so as to distinguish genuine, systemic issues from personal or interpersonal axe-grinding. Often, after a series of interviews, consensus emerges around key issues. Other times, unique comments are of interest because they might stimulate some useful dialogue. Still other times, patterns can be difficult to discern.

Interviews do not always go well. It may be important to point out when an interview seems to hit the skids.[2] Ideally, you should acknowledge this with the person being interviewed at the time, with a question such as "I sense that this is not going well for you; is there something I should know?" This allows you either to get things on a better path or to share later with the key contact that a particular interview seemed to have gone sideways and ask for a follow-up to see what might be learned. Perhaps there is some sensitivity for which you or the person being interviewed were not prepared. Either way, some follow-up is in order and can prove to be important. While this is a rare thing, it can and will happen. Again, done right, interviews are one of the most valuable tools available to consultants.

DELIVERABLES THAT ARE ACTIONABLE

Effective consulting requires clear communication with the client at all times. For clients, consulting engagements are an investment. Naturally, they expect a return on this investment. Boston Consulting Group (BCG) is one of the big three global strategy firms (along with McKinscy and Bain). At one time BCG used to boast of a measurable return on its work from increased profitability tied to applying a specific technique to a particular engagement. Part of the return takes the form of the final report and related deliverables (e.g., presentation slides, management letters, progress reports, worksheets). But such reports benefit clients only if they are actionable.

It can be argued that the real value consultants bring comes from the plans they recommend, help develop, and ultimately implement—in other words, the results. Different firms emphasize different approaches. Bain, for example, attempts to differentiate itself from BCG by taking more of a results approach (versus report), which also involves a unique monthly retainer billing process (versus a fixed fee).

---

2. A note of caution here: It is not always possible to know what might have set someone off during an interview. You will tend to know when a line has been crossed, but you may never find out what was *really* involved. This is where things can get off the rails and it is best to steer clear.

"The product of Bain's efforts was to be not a report or a study—the firm's consultants still drip with distain at the mention of such things—but rather a strategy and, even more important, *results*—results that you could see first on the bottom line, then in the stock price" (Kiechel 2010). Creating competitive advantage for their clients has long been the goal of the big three global strategy firms.

However, having the right solution to a problem is not enough in itself; the client must understand and be in a position to act on that solution. This can be subtle but needs to be made clear as it represents a trap for consultants. Nothing is worse than making a recommendation to clients that they are incapable of implementing. While it could be the right solution to the problem, it serves no useful purpose if the client lacks the capability to make it a reality. When this is the case, the consultant tries to find a solution that can be implemented or makes clear what capabilities the client might be lacking (and must acquire) if it is to successfully implement the recommendations.

Regardless of form or format, it helps to present the final deliverable of an engagement under three distinct categories: findings, conclusions, and recommendations.

Findings, Conclusions, and Recommendations

A key objective of final reports and related deliverables is to make it easy for clients to read and absorb their contents. Clients seek clarity, especially in an area as nuanced as healthcare. This is why it's so important to have clear organization to your work. I have long thought that a key benefit of consultants is to take something that is complex and make it simple. While this might not always be possible, the result should be a clearer understanding—if not consensus—on the nature of a problem and its recommended solution(s).

Findings
What is *found* are facts, specifically demonstrable and therefore incontrovertible facts. Grounded in data analytics, findings tend to be restricted to observations and to what can be quantified (e.g., trends, outcomes) without regard to implications. For example, "Volume of cardiac visits increased by 1,500 patients year over year (+3.5 percent)." Note that this statement says nothing about whether the increase in volume is good or bad, or about possible implications of the increase. Findings are judgment free.

Conclusions and Recommendations
Conclusions and recommendations, on the other hand, are all about judgments. Conclusions are the "so what?" of consulting. Why is this or that fact important?

What are its implications? What new questions does it raise? How can it help inform recommendations? Back to the previous example, a 3.5 percent increase in cardiac visits might be well below the peer average increase for that same time period, which could suggest that it is important to drill down to each type of cardiac visit (e.g. medical versus surgical) to better understand some of the reasons for this observation. Reviewing the comparative observation about cardiac visits, we can see that there is an improvement in performance (volume) year over year, but that it represents below-average growth. The context added by the comparison might suggest the following: "It is recommended that additional lines of business (capabilities) be entertained to get closer to meeting the peer group growth average."

Recommendations need to be succinct and actionable. Ideally, they should result in an action plan that is assigned to an executive and includes accountability (e.g., timing) and incentives, to help ensure that the recommendations are carried out. It can also be sequential over an extended period of time (short-term and long-term). Often an action plan has some dependencies—for example, action A must be completed before one can address action D.

DATA ANALYTICS

Data analysis used to be relatively simple. Over time, analytics has taken on significantly more importance as consultants have attempted to know infinitely more about a particular client business. The phrase *manage what you measure* comes to mind; we now measure everything. The goal of data analytics is to transform raw data into clear and actionable *information*. I like to say, "Analytics is to data as storytelling is to words." Analytics has become so important to the profession that graduate schools are now offering degrees in analytics alone.

TIP FROM THE TRENCHES

In the past few decades, data analysis has shifted from manual manipulation of numbers to the collection of vast amounts of data that are manipulated using increasingly sophisticated software. Years ago, Lotus and Microsoft Office enabled this data manipulation through automated programs that greatly sped up worksheets that had previously been done manually. This has since been followed by increasingly sophisticated business intelligence (BI) software suites that have greatly expanded the ability of day-to-day users to manipulate data and to complete tasks in hours that once took days. Master these software applications; they are invaluable tools.

Financial feasibility studies were all the rage when I first began my consulting career. We used to carry our Hewlett Packard "scientific" calculators everywhere we went, so that we could "punch the numbers" on a moment's notice. We've come a long way since then thanks to computers and advanced analytical software.

Today, data analytics is less about manipulating columns of numbers and more about slicing and dicing vast fields of data (big data). With modern tools and approaches, we are more able than ever before to make information out of data.

PROJECT MANAGEMENT

Project management is an essential skill for a consultant. Even for the solo consultant working individually on a single project, you are likely to be coordinating the activities of a small group, including the client. But for larger projects, involving a larger consulting team and/or a more complex issue, project management can get quite involved. This discussion provides only a high-level view of the importance of project management, which has become a bona fide specialty unto itself with many graduate programs now sponsoring a major or certificate in project management.

Perhaps the central skill of project management is excellent time management. That project management is essential to consulting is evident by the simple observation that most projects are completed on a *time and expenses* basis, often with a *not to exceed* budget target. Therefore, it is necessary to track and manage time carefully. Projects that exceed the time limit result in cost overruns that cost the firm money and count against the managing consultant. Projects not priced on a time-and-expenses basis might be done by retainer (e.g., fixed monthly charges) or a fixed-fee basis (completed for a specified amount in professional fees). Usually, the consulting firm assumes some risk for managing under a specific budget. In certain specialized cases, the consultant might actually assume full risk for the results and charge on a *percentage of savings* basis or some similar format. Such risk-based contracting is not for the faint of heart but can be quite lucrative, while creating true value for the client. (See chapter 9 related to billing practices.)

Project management also involves staffing appropriately. The proper staffing mix can make or break most decent-sized consulting engagements. Staff projects carefully so that people working on specific parts of a project have the appropriate skill set. Where a junior consultant lacks a required skill set it usually falls upon the lead consultant to either find someone else to do this work or to pitch in personally. The lead then must decide whether to charge the client for the additional time and thus incur an overrun or to "eat" the costs by not charging them. A cost overrun often results from time spent by a consultant with a higher billing rate who was required to perform a task that was originally assigned to someone with a lower rate.

Every project needs to be managed. From the small engagement to the large turnaround, there are phases and deliverables along the way, and there is always a beginning and an end. The client is often concerned that there be a clear end and that work is completed within a specified time frame. The argument against some process consulting is that it becomes self-perpetuating. This is especially true in the bigger turnaround and more complex projects that can last years. The global firms tend to specialize in these projects that can involve dozens of consultants. Keeping them on task and managing to a budget in these big projects is indeed a highly valued skill set.

Disassembled, these larger projects are really a series of smaller engagements designed to bring about the desired outcome—for example, to meet an overall cost reduction of 10 percent. Each engagement or subproject might be led by a different expert responsible for obtaining the results in that area, such as revenue cycle or materials management. Ideally, these many engagements are aligned with the client to achieve change. The intent is to hand the project back to the client so that the change can be operationalized. This does not happen by chance. It requires careful planning and execution, which can be challenging. Project *planning* is a key component of the discipline of project *management*. Certain tasks are dependent upon and sequenced with other ones. That is to say that certain things need to happen first before other things can be developed to follow. This interdependence among tasks is carefully planned through a diligent project management process.

Some tasks are more important than others. Usually there is a set of tasks involved in a given project that will ultimately determine the success or failure of the project. *Critical paths* are identified that isolate a few key tasks for a given project. These usually help simplify the project from an oversight and monitoring perspective. Since most projects tend to involve many tasks, critical paths allow projects to be closely monitored without having to review each individual task.

In the more complicated projects, an Office of Project Management is very helpful in planning and executing the project. Regular monitoring and reporting are required to track progress and make adjustments along the way. Deliverables need to be organized. Regular client meetings and progress reports are required. The COVID-19 pandemic has taught all of us that many of these meetings can be done by phone and video. Some meetings, however, always will be done face-to-face. In my experience, the more sensitive client engagements always involve content that the consultant prefers to convey in person rather than in writing. I am not comfortable conveying certain sensitive information via Zoom or phone.

The experienced firms use detailed templates from similar projects to provide for efficiency and help limit wasted pursuits. They have many tools at their disposal, including Gannt charts and dashboards designed to monitor progress. Group video calls have become far more common, especially in the aftermath of COVID-19 lockdowns, and are expected to become far more popular in future consulting engagements as a result, which represents significant savings in time and resources over the more traditional travel for face-to-face meetings. An example from healthcare that allows for a drill-down of what is involved in project management comes from strategic planning, as shown in exhibit 5.1.

Sometimes project management is outsourced to a third party as a matter of routine. A building project, for example, might involve a construction manager who is independent from the builder, and in fact is contracted as an owner's representative, overseeing all elements of the project on behalf of the owner. Most consulting engagements tend to include project management as part of the skill set that the consultant brings to the project. The science of project management is now quite advanced due to the upgraded engineering that has been developed from endeavors such as airplane assembly and implementation of electronic medical records.

I have been involved in many strategic planning engagements in which I functioned as lead facilitator and my firm effectively acted in the capacity of a *virtual firm* (see chapter 8 on virtual practices), contracting with other firms to provide expert input in key strategic areas that appeared seamless to the client. Such engagements involve a high level of coordination and standardization, where key elements of the process were started and concluded on a synchronized basis,

Exhibit 5.1: Strategic Planning Gantt Chart

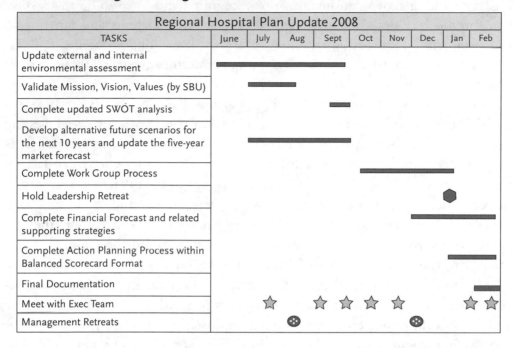

Regional Hospital Plan Update 2008									
TASKS	June	July	Aug	Sept	Oct	Nov	Dec	Jan	Feb
Update external and internal environmental assessment	▬▬▬▬▬▬▬▬▬								
Validate Mission, Vision, Values (by SBU)	▬▬								
Complete updated SWOT analysis			▬						
Develop alternative future scenarios for the next 10 years and update the five-year market forecast	▬▬▬▬								
Complete Work Group Process				▬▬▬▬▬					
Hold Leadership Retreat						⬢			
Complete Financial Forecast and related supporting strategies						▬▬▬▬			
Complete Action Planning Process within Balanced Scorecard Format							▬▬		
Final Documentation								▬	
Meet with Exec Team	☆		☆	☆	☆	☆		☆	☆
Management Retreats		⊛			⊛				

thus allowing for assimilation of the output and consolidation into a final deliverable (a strategic plan). It is similar to preparing a meal for a large group. You want the different dishes to be ready at the same time so that the whole group can be served and eat together. Anyone familiar with high-volume kitchens marvels at the intricate methods used to provide such synchronization.

NETWORKING

As noted in chapter 2, in the Consultant Value Chain section, a consultant must maintain a strong professional network to achieve success. Most of the discussion up to now has focused on the work of consulting; not yet discussed is having the work to do. It takes a client to provide a consulting opportunity, and getting clients is rarely easy. Conventional wisdom suggests that you cannot label a startup business as viable until it has been operating for at least three years. This might have changed in light of the new e-commerce unicorns, but I consider three years a good rule of thumb in consulting. This allows you to accumulate some clients and test the theory that there will be add-on work. Said differently, your completed work was valued by your client so much that they rehire you for additional work. For sustainability, this is vitally important as a key performance indicator.

Networking is a term that applies to a broad spectrum of areas. In consulting, networking allows consultants to be recognized and hired to do their work. Networking includes not only potential clients, but also peers and others who might be part of a broad referral network. Most consulting engagements result from referrals, and word of mouth is the most powerful advertising that a consultant can ever achieve.

Network is both a noun and a verb. For a consultant, networking is an essential skill that must be constantly honed to remain relevant. It involves investing time and resources to gain name recognition and to reveal opportunities. It is about encounters that can lead to future business. Opportunities rarely surface by chance. *Out of sight, out of mind* applies in this regard. It is therefore necessary to be seen interacting on a proactive basis with peers, clients, and prospects. "So if expertise is important but not enough on its own, what truly determines the success of your firm? It is the ability of your experts to start, nurture, influence, and manage relationships with clients" (Johnson 2015).

It should be recognized that networking comes naturally to some personalities, less so to others. Certain personality tests (e.g., Myers-Briggs) suggest how people with different personalities should approach networking. It is not a one-size-fits-all pursuit. Some people like to interact over a drink, others like to take in a ballgame, while still others focus on email or phone conversations. Regardless of the approach or approaches taken, networking should be a formal consideration for anyone thinking of consulting as a career.

One approach that can be helpful in this regard is a continuum of care value chain developed by Jim Morell,[3] shown in exhibit 5.2. Using this approach, a clinical continuum model is applied to the services/programs that are involved in a practice. Answering several key questions can help determine where and how to position efforts to achieve recognition and be visible to potential firms, with a focus on services and programs that are of interest to clients.

Referral sources are an outgrowth of networking. While this might not matter as much to the new careerist who joins a firm where clients are generated by others, it is worth noting early in one's career the dependency on referral sources for future clients. The natural sources that come quickly to mind include fellow alumni from your college or graduate school, people with whom you work along the way, and especially previous clients. Exceptional consultants can usually point to significant work that was generated by former clients where they had completed successful projects.

Less obvious referral sources might be those generated from other activities. Not everyone I have worked with agrees with me on this, but I believe attending

---

3. James C. Morell of JCM Advisors is adjunct faculty at DePaul University in Chicago.

Exhibit 5.2: Continuum of Care Value Chain

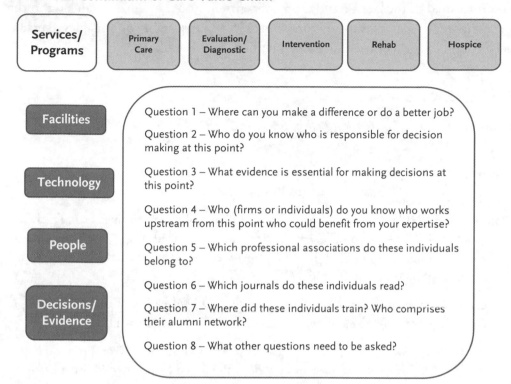

Source: James C. Morrel. Used with permission.

meetings where you interact with other attendees can also lead to potentially significant business. It is through meetings like this that one is able to build a network. As mundane as it might sound, interactions involving simple card exchanges can truly result in the occasional business opportunity.

Networking applies not only to clients and prospects, but also to peer consultants. I have been gratified to have received numerous peer referrals. This can occur when another consultant has a conflict with a client or feels that their skill set is not applicable. This might happen more in specialized work such as turnarounds and merger and acquisition studies. Peer referrals might come from people in your firm who are part of teams formed to complete specific engagements. It also encompasses relationships with other consultants who might represent collaborative opportunities. "Though networking can be beneficial at any point in one's career, it can especially help young professionals find sponsors who can change their career trajectories. . . . It is like holding multiple lottery tickets—it can help transform you from being relatively unknown in your firm to being a well-known contributor with a diversified career portfolio, multiple advocates, and a range of opportunities" (Runde 2016).

Networking can also encompass educational programs where people help keep you informed of the latest trends and concepts, as noted in more detail later in the next chapter. It can refer to advisors who help you maintain your business, such as accountants, legal counsel, financial planners, and the like.

REFERENCES

Johnson, W. 2015. *The Critical Role of Emotional Intelligence in Consulting.* Oxford, UK: Oxford University Press.

Kiechel, W. 2010. *The Lords of Strategy: The Secret Intellectual History of the New Corporate World.* Boston: Harvard Business Review Press.

Konnikova, M. 2011. "Don't Just See, Observe: What Sherlock Holmes Can Teach Us About Mindful Decisions." *Scientific American.* Published August 19. https://blogs. scientificamerican.com/guest-blog/dont-just-see-observe-what-sherlock-holmes-can-teach-us-about-mindful-decisions/.

Rasiel, E. M. 1999. *The McKinsey Way: Using the Techniques of the World's Top Strategic Consultants to Help You and Your Business.* New York: McGraw-Hill.

Runde, J. 2016. "Why Young Bankers, Lawyers, and Consultants Need Emotional Intelligence." *Harvard Business Review Blog.* Published September 26. https:// hbr.org/2016/09/why-young-bankers-lawyers-and-consultants-need-emotional-intelligence.

CHAPTER 6

Consulting Skills: The Intangibles

IN THIS CHAPTER, we continue to focus on consulting skills, but with an eye toward some of the more subtle tools in the tool chest. There are four key *leadership intangibles* of high performing healthcare professionals: humility, compassion, kindness, and generosity (Kaissi 2019). Given the demands placed on leaders of healthcare organizations, it is easy to see the appeal of these qualities.

In the case of consultants who achieve success, there are intangibles that many people might miss. The hope here is to make some of these intangibles better understood with some things that might seem like common sense, but, as the French philosopher Voltaire put it, "The thing about common sense is that it is not so common." Mastering the intangibles, like the basics, is critical to the authenticity required of a professional consultant.

Intangibles are not the same as exceptionalism, which is covered in part III of this book. For purposes of this chapter, intangibles refer to those attributes that, while not obvious, are nevertheless essential—not optional—for any successful consultant to possess. This includes at least the following, which are explained in more detail in the subsequent discussion:

- Know when to speak and when to listen
- Maintain objectivity and an absence of bias
- Focus on situational awareness
- Always observe ethics
- Manage expectations
- Understand collaborative work and team dynamics
- Gain assistance from lawyers and others
- Be flexible with your work environment
- Manage billable time

KNOW WHEN TO SPEAK AND WHEN TO LISTEN

As noted earlier in the last chapter, a common mistake by new consultants is to talk when they should listen. Interviews involve listening. In one of my graduate school courses, the instructor shared the "Rules of Good Listening," which began with "stop talking." Knowing when to speak and when to listen is definitely a skill that gets refined over time.

The reason new consultants might be inclined to talk can be related to insecurity. It is natural for new recruits to feel challenged to demonstrate their expertise by talking. While this is understandable at one level, credibility can better be established in more formal interactions, such as a presentation, instead of during an interview. In an apprenticeship, the value is in first observing the professional in action, and then adopting a style that works for you. The experienced consultant should take the lead initially on interviews, allowing the consultant-in-training to observe and begin to experiment with different approaches to see what is most comfortable.

Interview techniques vary. Some interview techniques require some introduction. In the typical open interview, questions tend to be structured around "How do you feel about . . . ?" or "Tell me about . . ." Follow-up questions are a normal part of this process. In the best structured interviews, you will likely get into a conversation that covers the outline from the interview guide but also goes into some sidebar issues. That is OK. It can be quite revealing to let people being interviewed have some flexibility to take the conversation where they want to. It reveals how they are looking at things and helps them get something off their chest. This is tantamount to "unaided feedback" in a focus group. However, try to avoid getting trapped in rabbit holes that do not lead to anything.

It can be tempting to enter into conversations and end up talking more than listening. This can still generate valuable information provided that the overall objective is not lost—namely, to generate feedback from the client in the context of this specific engagement. If "perfect is the enemy of good," in interviews, "interesting is the enemy of focused."

MAINTAIN OBJECTIVITY AND AN ABSENCE OF BIAS

As noted earlier, consultants get hired for different reasons and are often asked to develop an opinion. However, they need to know when they are being asked to express an opinion versus when they are being asked to provide objective input to a process. The most valuable consultant engagements occur when different internal views exist, and the consultant is asked to sort out the options and make a recommendation. This can be especially dicey if things have progressed to the point where separate camps have been formed (i.e., people have taken positions) and a "win–lose" scenario now exists. In these situations, the role of the consultant includes avoiding taking a position by recognizing common interests (Fisher and Ury 1981). This is not the time to express a point of view, at least not at the outset. Even more than that, it is essential that the consultant be aware of any personal biases that could color how they are perceived during the process. This is the essence of emotional intelligence. Similar to the psychiatrist who undergoes analysis, consultants should be aware of their biases, and careful not to somehow allow these to enter into the evaluation. They are only able to do so to the extent they are aware of those personal biases, which is not always easy, but it is an essential tool for the trusted advisor.

Some subscribe to the theory that there is no such thing as objectivity. Everyone has a lens through which they view the world. As such, trying to approach something objectively is to disclose a point of view—for example, "Usually I tend to favor . ... for these reasons. However, in this situation . . ." It often becomes obvious when the client is seeking objectivity versus a point of view. When in doubt, ask the client lots of questions.

It is common to structure a set of interviews with members of a team and to then summarize these around a few central themes. Often, the sponsor or CEO might like some preliminary indication of the results of these interviews. While this is an important part of the process, it is also a time for caution. All attempts should be made to shield those who were interviewed from being identified with a specific comment. Remember, these are confidential interviews. It might take some reflection to put comments in context. In my experience, it is helpful to resist the temptation to summarize recent interviews because it is relatively easy to let slip a phrase or word that could identify the person who made the comment. Overall, such a preliminary review should focus more on generalities and promise more detail in the future. There is trust involved between those who have been interviewed and the leadership with whom results are being shared.

When the interviews are complete, summarizing is important but tricky. Clearly, the interviews provide context for any meaningful engagement. At the same time, sharing the results in a meaningful way with the client takes skill. A technique that I like is to highlight "interesting" comments in addition to consensus comments. In healthcare, for better or worse, most decisions seem to be made on a consensus basis. Using this technique, consensus comments are listed in **bold**. I then try to segment the comments by major topical area. Such divisions might include clinical care, branding and marketing, culture, governance, and the like. From an innovation perspective, "interesting comments" most often stimulate some good discussion.

FOCUS ON SITUATIONAL AWARENESS

All new engagements involve an orientation process, during which the consultant becomes acclimated to the client's situation—a situation assessment (discussed in more detail later). With new clients, this process can take up as much as 30 percent of the total project time. Obviously, then, orientation accounts for a substantial part of the cost. This is one reason why, rather than bringing in a new firm, companies tend to use the same consultants time and again—their familiarity with the organization decreases time spent on orientation, which can represent significant savings. Doing an orientation process well gives the client confidence that you are genuinely interested in the project and working hard to become well informed.

Generally speaking, most clients hire consultants for their personal expertise. What can be less obvious is that they also expect consultants who are paid significant fees to be well informed. What does that mean?

Clearly, clients expect that the experience that consultants bring to an engagement will allow them to frame the issue quickly and effectively in order to determine how best to address it. *Quickly* means that they have seen something similar before (pattern recognition), they know what to look for (80/20), and what questions to ask (focus), thus saving valuable time. *Effectively* means that they are looking at the right things and are thorough in their evaluation, determining whether the issues tend to fall into three general categories: people, process, or system. Surely, there are often combinations of all these issues. Experience is therefore not a random consideration, and it could be the primary reason a consultant is hired. To be sure, it takes a certain level of smarts to go into consulting, but I have found that clients make selection decisions based more on experience rather than smarts. Or, to put it another way:

> Early in your career . . . you will discover that all of your colleagues are as smart and hard working as you. You'll learn that the key to being successful must be something else. . . . I've learned that the critical distinguishing factor for advancing in the professional services is emotional intelligence (EQ). . . . Developing EQ is just as pertinent for the recent graduate who is starting out, as it is for the seasoned veteran (Runde 2016).

Part of awareness is understanding not only your surroundings, but also how you affect your surroundings—that is, how people respond to you.

So far, we have discussed situational awareness in the context of the issue at hand. But being well informed goes beyond that, since healthcare is experiencing dramatic change as a result of being highly regulated (policy) and subjected to considerable reform.

While related to some extent, policy and reform are not the same. For our purposes, policy is developed by government for the most part. Federal, state, and local governments all pass laws that require compliance and myriad actions in order to function—for example, requiring providers of care to be licensed. To these legislated activities, one must add the regulations of the agencies that are responsible for executing these laws. These regulations are constantly changing, often with significant implications. Hospitals, for example, have the unique attribute of having one very large customer on which they are dependent for a majority of their revenues—the government (notably the federal government through the Centers for Medicare & Medicaid Services). While government has always been a large customer (at least since 1965 when Medicare and Medicaid became part of the Social Security Act), in my experience, it is only in the last five to ten years or so that government has become recognized as the largest single hospital payor and, as a result, the *market maker*. So, staying informed means understanding both the intent and the effect of new laws and regulations at the policy level.

But it gets more complicated. There are also private or voluntary regulations through such organizations as The Joint Commission. Accreditation and licensing can involve public–private partnerships among a variety of organizations to provide a "seal of approval" or other recognized designations, which can be important to decision-makers in determining where to receive a service.

In contrast to policy, there is reform. Reform happens, sometimes in spite of policy. Much of what has changed in healthcare in the past decade or two has started out as reform. Whereas policy often takes a variety of paths, many of which can be quite tedious before the policy is finally implemented, reform evolves. Reform is particularly interesting because it is largely sustained by market forces. It is Darwinian—survival of the fittest. Reforms reflect innovation as well as trial and error. Certain reforms come and go. Those that are sustained seem to provide a distinct advantage over the status quo, hence their widespread adoption. *I have found over the years that policy can change market forces, whereas reform generally responds to market forces.*

Missing in the past but increasingly an important and growing market force in healthcare is *consumerism*. Much of reform today is focused on providers' need to attract those who have choices as to where and how they receive care. Reform brought about such changes as ambulatory surgery, urgent care, convenient care centers, and virtual health. Notice that some of these reforms are very much driven by technology and the flow of capital into the industry toward innovative and less costly approaches to deliver care. (See chapter 15 for a more complete discussion of the healthcare industry.)

Given that change and innovation are constantly occurring in the healthcare industry, how does one stay well informed? There are many methods that can help, but some of the most useful in healthcare are summarized in exhibit 6.1. The key thing is to maintain a level of industry knowledge on a routine and regular basis. Being knowledgeable is the rule, not the exception.

Exhibit 6.1: Specific Methods of Staying Informed

Method of staying informed	Frequency	Expense	Primary benefits
Books and periodicals	Regular periodicals come out weekly, monthly, and quarterly and range from academic to operational. *Modern Healthcare* is a popular information source.	Can be expensive, especially textbooks. Some books on strategy cost more than $100 each.	Best place to seek in-depth understanding of key issues. It is where true experts tout their expertise. Much of what is written is from consultants in the field.
Newsletters and digital content	Daily, weekly, and monthly. *Becker's Hospital Review* is a popular source.	Some are free and supplement larger meetings.	Put out by associations (e.g., American Hospital Association) and private groups (e.g., Becker's). One of the best sources of current information.
Proprietary documents	As needed.	Subscription models tend to apply, such as the Advisory Board. Tend to be expensive. Often allow for customized research.	Driven by member demands. Tend to rely on case studies that can be quite useful. Focus on hot topics.
Association meetings	Hospital associations and the like offer meetings at least annually. The Healthcare Information and Management Systems Society is the largest association/affinity group for information technology professionals.	Membership is often covered by employer. Firms tend to buy memberships or sponsorships that can be expensive. Meetings are a separate expense. Often held in attractive sites.	Some are better than others. Great for networking. Presentations at some are exceptional because they result from competing proposals (e.g., the annual Congress of the American College of Healthcare Executives).

(continued)

Method of staying informed	Frequency	Expense	Primary benefits
Affinity groups	A primary networking vehicle. Some are private (e.g., CEO Roundtable) while others are tied to associations (e.g., Society for Health Care Strategy & Market Development). May include bulletin boards and other asynchronous forms of communication.	Annual dues required. Meetings often held at attractive sites for 2–3 days.	Excellent for networking. Some of these groups attract members for many years who share information in addition to what is prepared for each meeting.
Networking and individual contacts	Every professional should develop a "top 10" list of peers whom they stay in touch with on a regular basis. These interactions include discussing what key issues are emerging and the like.	Takes time to do well. Some set goals tied to customer relations management systems (e.g., at least one call per day to a key contact). Often, people with specific expertise (e.g., legal) are part of your network.	Done well, this can be a primary source of current information. Some result in local groups that get together on a regular basis for breakfast, lunch, and so forth.

At the strategic level, this might involve learning the key talking points of a particular strategy or policy. The more specialized the practice focus or engagement, the more detail you might need to know. For a health strategy consultant, at least an hour every day devoted to digital content and reading is required. Regular attendance at national meetings (e.g., Health Forum) is also a must to keep up with the latest innovations and to interact with industry leaders. A fundamental attribute of the best consultants is that they are knowledgeable about a wide array of subjects, and therefore always prepared to enter into a substantive discussion on a policy issue such as site-neutral payments, or a reform issue like total joint procedures in ambulatory surgery centers. They also are eager to ask questions and find out new information from everyone with whom they come into contact. It is a two-way interaction in which trusted advisors must be able to hold their own to be credible.

Most of these resources are obvious and self-explanatory, but affinity groups are worth discussing in a little more detail. Many of these resources reflect the adage "You reap what you sow." Nobody is going to spoon-feed you. You have to be proactive. Some of these local affinity groups have become quite sophisticated with large memberships, both corporate and individual. My experience with a local affinity group, Healthcare Technology Network of Greater Washington (2012) is a good example worth sharing.

In the 1990s, a small group was gathered by David Main[1] to discuss the impact of the growing technology industry on the healthcare field. According to Healthcare Technology Network's website, "The membership uses the group as a forum to advance the use of technology in healthcare, to identify and facilitate financing and capital sources, and as a resource for exchanging information in this sophisticated and ever-evolving marketplace." The group continues to meet monthly with a rotating membership around a core group of technology specialists. Mind you, this is an entirely volunteer group. The topics are never determined more than a few months in advance to allow a short-term pivot depending on current events (e.g., changes in regulations). Speakers are wide-ranging, taking advantage of policymakers in Washington as well as the little-known entrepreneurial community that exists in the Capitol Region, including from the pharmaceutical industry. Members have changed jobs, started companies together, and published award-winning articles and books. As you can imagine, the discussions can get quite lively at times. Main has an uncanny ability to offer occasional opinions without getting political to the point that anyone gets uncomfortable. Such interactions are invaluable. Not only does a group like this help to stay informed on emerging issues, but it also pushes people into areas that might become important in the future. Similar groups exist in Nashville, Chicago, and Boston, to name a few. The Health Council of Nashville that just celebrated its twentieth anniversary has a substantial budget and sponsors fellowships. I believe these groups make a major contribution in helping their members stay informed.

ALWAYS OBSERVE ETHICS

In the absence of licensing requirements or other means of regulating the profession, consulting can be at risk for ethical lapses. Lapses can take many forms and demand a certain consciousness. The primary exposure to ethical transgressions relates to three key areas: confidentiality, conflicts of interest, and documents and sources. This last area might be somewhat surprising, which requires some additional explanation.

---

1. David Main is an attorney with Nelson Mullins. He was originally part of Senator Richard Schweiker's staff and counsel to the Senate Health Subcommittee. A skilled networker, David has had an active healthcare law practice with several firms, worked on the original HMO Act, and played a pivotal role in the development of the David A. Winston Health Policy Fellowship Program.

Confidentiality

As advisors, consultants require access to key information with which to formulate conclusions and recommendations. This can include proprietary information and private conversations, so building trust is essential. Any violation of trust, whether actual or perceived, can be a disaster. Regarding confidentiality, this can take many forms, some of which involve careful judgments that can go awry.

In one embarrassing situation, I inadvertently replied to an email in which we were in the middle of a merger discussion. My observation in the email was that I did not want the other party to lose interest by having unrealistic demands made on them by our client. I did not intend to be sharing this comment directly with the party with whom we were negotiating, but I did so when I pushed "reply all" instead of "reply." This created some temporary panic and could have been a disaster.

Fortunately, in our next conference call shortly thereafter, I apologized. I knew the other party well enough that we had a good laugh over it. She was a professional who recognized the error and actually appreciated my concern. Thus, I was able to dodge that one.

I am truly strident about not sharing who told me something in confidence. I never divulge the source. Once, I was confronted by a senior executive regarding the performance of a member of the client's team. I indicated some concerns, adding that I had heard similar concerns expressed by a few other team members because I thought this was something they should look into. He was adamant that I share who I had heard this from. I was not willing to divulge the source, as these comments were shared with me in confidence. To say the least, he was not pleased.

I am not sure there is anything ethically more sacred in consulting than maintaining confidentiality. It is not the job of the consultant to spread rumors or become an informant. Yet, it can be uncomfortable when a client demands such information as part of the engagement. Under these circumstances, when asked who said something, my experience suggests that it is best to simply say that I treat the source with the same sensitivity and respect as I am treating the current conversation with the executive. Usually, this is accepted and no more need be said.

Conflicts of Interest

Conflicts of interest arise for most consultants at one time or another. Perhaps the most common form, at least for a strategy consultant, is when you might have worked for a competitor in the same market. As a strategy consultant, this takes on far greater meaning than when an operational service is involved. For example, a revenue cycle engagement for client A in the same town as client B should not represent a conflict. What is critical in this case, in which an operational service is involved, is that there be full disclosure up front and that nothing pertaining to either client be shared with the other (e.g., client A does something better than client B).

Where strategy is involved, such as developing an ambulatory care strategy, it would be inappropriate to work for the other client competing in the same market. Some of the larger firms would approach this conflict by using a different team on the engagement, but I do not believe that this fully eliminates such a conflict. If both engagements are pursued, one way firms try to shield one client from another involves constructing a firewall between the two clients. This means that there are two separate teams working within the same firm, and that both teams are explicitly restricted from exchanging any information. While logical, I have found this difficult to implement, especially when the two teams come from the same office.

When a firm engages in a strategy job, it is investing its time and effort in the competitive success of that client. I do not believe that the same firm—even with a separate team—should simultaneously engage with competitors in the same market when it comes to strategy. There is also an interesting issue evolving in this area; the intense consolidation that is occurring in healthcare, especially among physicians and hospitals, has significant implications for the definition of the relevant market. As regional health systems cover larger and larger markets, positions change. For example, you might have two hospital clients for whom you have worked in the past that are separated by ten miles, and their markets did not overlap at the time. But now there exists a genuine conflict as each has joined different, competing networks. Both new networks involve the larger combined market that now fully encompasses the markets of the two hospitals. Some clients would be nervous knowing that we had done *any* consulting work for a competitor in their market. While this might not be reasonable on their part, disclosing up front any prior work for competing organizations in the same market is the safer way to go, even if the engagements were years apart. I have found that strategic information enjoys a shelf life, usually around three years. When it is clear that a former client is not likely to rehire you, it becomes less of an issue to be hired many years later by a competitor.

In an interesting situation early in my career, I was accused by a client of having a conflict of interest during a merger discussion. I had been involved in many similar discussions prior to this one, so I was keenly aware of the potential for conflict. Unfortunately, one of the two CEOs in a merger discussion between two competing hospitals in the same town felt that I had become biased. My role at the time was that of a *facilitator*.

Under this facilitator arrangement, I was retained by both clients. Unlike in a legal orientation, where competing attorneys embrace an adversarial process, I had an equal obligation to each; the process was designed to be collaborative, not adversarial. It was therefore possible that the best arrangement that could be worked out might tend to favor party A over party B. It was clear at the outset of any such discussions that a key issue to be resolved would be the leadership of the surviving organization. Ideally, such mergers are not viewed as a takeover of one organization by the other, but I have found this to be challenging to achieve. The goal is to find a balance, so that the choice among executives in consolidating the staffs from the two organizations fully considers the skills of all involved (i.e., based on merit and not politically motivated).

Feeling slighted, this CEO took it upon himself to write a formal complaint to my professional society. I was completely blindsided by this letter and felt compelled to defend myself because he chose to go around me and put this in writing. I can only guess that he must have felt that things had shifted to where he was unlikely to be selected as the surviving CEO for the combined entity. Clearly, I had failed to maintain the necessary balance to keep this CEO engaged in the process. Obviously, there very well could have been other factors involved, but we moved on (and the merger did not occur).

The antidote for conflict is disclosure. It is imperative at the outset of every engagement that *any potential conflict* or *appearance of conflict* be disclosed **in writing**.

Documents and Sources

An area of ethics that is less obvious relates to sourcing and documentation. Nothing is more important to the integrity of the consulting product.

A constant challenge to any consultant, whether solo or part of a team, is version control. When working on a document or presentation, it is common to have multiple versions of the same document. This can quickly become confusing, even for a solo consultant. Firms have all developed conventions, especially for shared documents, that can range from daily renumbering to various other labels such as *final*. So, where does ethics come into play with documentation and sourcing? There are several areas.

First is sourcing. It is important to identify sources for key materials when the materials are not yours or attributed to others. Without proper sourcing, it will be assumed that the material came from you. It's better to be clear on this and not allow for any confusion. This is especially true where an opinion is being offered. Depending on the nature of the opinion, there could also be legal liabilities. For better or worse, the consultant owns their work.

A second ethical focus of documentation is far more subtle than sourcing. To best introduce this concept, let me share a difficult story. I was involved with a sensitive assignment that was rife with political intrigue. This is not all that rare in working with complex healthcare organizations. It seems the more complex the organization, the more that politics can enter into the equation. Politics also requires flexibility beyond what is necessary in typical consulting engagements. For example, there can be certain "hot button" items for which there is a clear sensitivity. Look for these and avoid them. These sensitivities are not always that obvious until one steps into it.

In this situation, the client organization was confronted by a disruptive form of clinical practice that presented both an opportunity and a threat if not managed correctly. As often occurs, the engagement that was ultimately authorized was significantly reduced from the comprehensive approach to the issue that was originally proposed. (Notably, there was no request for proposal, or RFP, for this engagement but only a detailed scope of work.)

Near the end of the engagement and after significant back and forth with the client while preparing for a task force meeting, we arrived at the client site for our last meeting only to be greeted by our client liaison, who told us, "We need to change the presentation completely." While this is almost unheard of, it is not rare to have to make a few last-minute adjustments. *Consultants are often challenged to think on their feet.*

After informing us of the need to take a different approach, in retrospect, the client was less than candid about what had happened since we last spoke. *Why the need for this dramatic change? Had we done something wrong?* No. But confidentiality prevented the client liaison from disclosing more information regarding the stakeholder's concerns in question. The person simply did not feel at ease in sharing more details on a key conversation or two that had occurred. There was a lot happening at the time.

Obviously, we were working under severe time pressure, so in an effort to facilitate the revisions as best we could, we immediately split our team into two small work groups. One group was focused on adding clarity to how some data had been displayed. This was a relatively straightforward request, albeit unsettling to have to do it at the last minute. The second group attempted to revise other elements of the presentation, and it was in this second group that something quite disturbing happened. At the time, we were not quite sure *when* it occurred, but it ultimately became apparent *how* it occurred.

Remember that we started this discussion around version control. Due to the urgency of making these changes the day of the presentation, and lacking further details on what was required, we allowed the client to actively edit our presentation on our computer. This on its face has some serious risk to it, and it was terribly uncomfortable. While I was looking over their shoulder trying to keep up and discuss the changes as we went along, at some point it got away from me. In retrospect, I should never have given up my computer, but instead should have made all the changes myself based on real-time suggestions from the client.

I was careful to review the final version that was used for the presentation because it was our work, and we were making the presentation. But the client had clearly made a number of important changes. Mind you, this was *our* presentation to the client. Sometime during or after the presentation (we were never sure), a slide had been added that involved a recommendation related to a highly sensitive decision. We only discovered this at a later point while preparing what was then labeled as the final presentation. No one from our team remembered this slide being presented during our session with the client, but there it was in the file in front of us.

Had we been asked to offer an opinion on this sensitive item, we would have gladly identified and reviewed the options, analyzed each, and come up with a clear recommendation. Such was not the case, and this report was supposed to represent our best thinking for which we were being paid good money. Recall that the scope of this engagement had been reduced from its original proposal.

We were then left with how to handle this unauthorized addition to our report. Confronting the client was going to be very complicated. We had to choose either to go directly to the individual involved or inform someone higher up in the client organization of the breach. But how best to do so? If this were to be treated as the ethical breach that it was (though without malice), it would have started with a conversation with the individual involved. That would have been followed immediately with going over that person's head and indicating that this was not a recommendation that we were in a position to make. We could have done so with or without pointing out the ethical violation (essentially, forgery).

Rather than initiate a process that could quickly have escalated, it was my determination to casually bring attention to this slide during a regular conversation with the person involved, and simply state that we were not sure where this came from. We chose not be confrontational, but made it clear that we were not in a position to make such a recommendation. Being transparent and direct in this manner helped resolve the issue.

This example illustrates how important it is that consultants control access to their product (e.g., final report, letter) up to the point of delivering it to the client. This is why we create a PDF of the final version of every document that is provided to the client.

MANAGE EXPECTATIONS

A basic tenet of successful consulting is managing the client's expectations. There should be no surprises. Unfortunately, it is rather common to begin a client engagement with expectations that are out of line with reality. This can happen by reducing the scope of engagement to fit it into a budget reduced from what was originally suggested. If left undocumented or undiscussed, this set of unrealistic expectations will lead to a poor outcome. Beginning with the RFP, there could be major miscommunications with regard to scope, duration, and cost. It is important to address these questions up front, and doing so requires a certain amount of skill.

On the positive side, it is good that clients expect a lot from an engagement. This shows they are motivated and have a real need. However, when what is expected differs considerably from what can be provided under the given budget, there is a problem. Each of the following core areas involves different dynamics: scope, duration, and cost.

Scope

What consultant hasn't experienced an engagement in which the client asked for the sun and the moon, and then choked upon seeing the price tag? After spending weeks trying to whittle the scope down to something the client can live with, the consultant learns that things haven't changed all that much. Make no mistake; the client still expects substantial completion of the original scope, despite these cutbacks. For this reason, it is essential for one to develop a clear scope of work (SOW) statement coming out of such negotiations upon which both parties can agree. Additionally, the instant the work request begins to exceed the SOW, the consultant must point this out to the client. This is bound to happen, and if the client is not made aware immediately, the engagement is subject to that dastardly disease known as *scope creep*.

Unfortunately, many client situations involve a lack of clarity in scope. Those that are clear have a higher probability of a favorable outcome. The purpose of a proposal is to share with the client what the consultant sees as the scope and how the consultant intends to address it. It is imperative that there be agreement on this at the outset and/or agreement to examine this along the way. (For more discussion on scope of work, see chapter 13.) Also, any variation from the scope should be identified *immediately* by either the client or the consultant at the time the decision is made to do so. This will avoid conflicts later.

Duration

How long a project takes to complete is subject to some variation. Regardless, expectation is created at the outset. *How urgent is this? Are there other initiatives depending upon the completion of this one?* These are among the key elements that should be understood up front. There are expectations that should only be modified by mutual agreement and with a clear understanding of why. Otherwise, what is agreed to upon initiation should be honored. An important sidebar consideration could be physical presence at the client site. Make sure you are clear on what the client expectation is in this regard. The COVID-19 experience might have altered traditional expectations, but don't take this for granted. If they want to see you on site, you need to be there.

Cost

Oddly, it has been my experience that this area of expectations is the one that is best understood. The client is generally clear on what the engagement will cost and budgets accordingly. Sometimes there is a purchase order involved, sometimes not. Managing payments should be routine, with a payment schedule indicated in the proposal. An interesting part of the cost component is what economists typically refer to as *conspicuous consumption*. It has been my experience that, depending on the nature of the engagement (e.g., commodity or highly customized "one-offs"), clients expect to pay a great deal for the best consulting. Every consultant works out a price niche, but clients can be rather knowledgeable about the market rates and understand what is required to secure the services of a consultant. Consultants too often subject themselves to discounts and underprice their services in comparison to what other firms charge.

UNDERSTAND COLLABORATIVE WORK AND TEAM DYNAMICS

Consulting is a team sport. It can't be done alone or in a vacuum. Even pursuing a solo consulting model does not mean you rely on yourself for all elements of a project. We used to refer to consulting as occurring in a closet and then shared with the client. Consulting work today is far more participative. Three key forms of collaboration are worth noting: use of independent contractors, collaborating with the client, and multidisciplinary teams. These are explained in more detail below.

Throughout my consulting career, I have relied upon a cohort of *stringers*, or independent contractors, to do specific parts of an engagement. I worked with a cadre of such people for many years and even invited them to participate in our semiannual company retreats. For many years, one person in particular (perhaps a gig worker in today's nomenclature) provided valuable analyses that were internet-based or involved manipulation of large amounts of data. This person was very computer savvy, comfortable working from home, incredibly productive, and could turn around needed analyses quickly and accurately with little to no oversight required.

Collaboration with clients must also be carefully cultivated. While the client has hired you to complete certain work and analyses, it is important to understand what the client might have attempted before and to keep them engaged in that process. There have been numerous times when I have been very comfortable advising the client on an analysis in which I ended up using the client's original model with some refinements, rather than take the time to develop an entirely new model. Where I have done this, clients have appreciated the recognition of making productive use of their prior work.

A particularly interesting development in team dynamics is the advent of multidisciplinary consultant teams. It can be argued that this is nothing new in healthcare, where administrative and clinical staff are often combined to address certain issues (dyad management).

As healthcare continues its transformation, notably into regional health systems, the challenges are becoming more complex, cutting across more diverse platforms. This calls for an ever-widening array of skills that are less likely to be vested in just one or two people. Larger consulting teams with more diverse skills are required. But unlike focused teams from the past that tended to combine like competencies (e.g., planning, finance), multidisciplinary or cross-functional teams now offer a diverse set of competencies that are increasingly required to meet an ever-expanding set of challenges facing healthcare clients.

Combining the collective competencies of these teams can be both somewhat challenging and exhilarating. Different disciplines look at situations through different lenses. They even speak different languages to describe the same situation. Sharing these different perspectives can lead to novel viewpoints that are more enlightened than when only one discipline is involved (e.g., finance). The way a marketing person looks at an issue is not the same as a clinician or a finance person. Yet their insights can lead to new perspectives, resulting in a richer set of choices in how to address a particular issue.

That said, not everyone is prepared for or built to be part of a multidisciplinary team. It requires experience and patience to sit through discussions that don't necessarily connect for you, but where you still might be called upon at any time to jump in with your perspective. This dynamic approach to problem-solving represents a serious investment of time and effort and has been known to foster novel solutions to chronic problems—often described as *breakthrough thinking*. Global firms tend to specialize in these large and complex projects that borrow expertise from multiple industries.

Healthcare is one of the richest environments begging for more multidisciplinary teams to address complicated issues like social determinants of health (see chapter 15).

GAIN ASSISTANCE FROM LAWYERS AND OTHERS

As mentioned, in its three forms (with independent contractors, with clients, and as part of multidisciplinary teams), collaboration is a skill that is both profound and hard to teach. Collaboration comes more into play with more complex engagements. These can be both exhilarating and scary. The more you get away from your skill set, the more intimidating it can get. You must rely on the skills of other specialists to plug the gaps. I have had the good fortune to work with highly skilled lawyers, architects, accountants, and other specialists on numerous occasions.

The danger with this interdependency with other specialists is the tendency for other team members to migrate into your space. The lines can become blurred rather easily; everyone fancies themselves a strategist. To be sure, there are lawyers who are strategists. But I have also found that there are many who think they are, but in reality are not. I am not a lawyer, so the lines of demarcation should be somewhat self-evident, at least as the law is concerned. But with experience, my knowledge of the law increased over time, and I found myself in many legal discussions related to client work, based largely on "the way we handled the issue in another client situation."

In these more complex engagements, it really helps to work closely together during the proposal stage to forge different work streams that make up the work process. This is the time to determine who does what. This becomes even more necessary when a budget specifies how much of whose time is involved in each task. And even this much preparation still might not anticipate the issues that will come up during the engagement.

I always found that having one team member take the lead on each work stream is helpful. This structure gives that one person the authority to control the conversation related to that part of the process. This way, the other team members are there to support them in this task. Comments or thoughts regarding this segment of the engagement go through the lead. When meeting with the client, the lead manages the conversation and has the right to cut off dialogue with the team if it starts to drift away from the agenda.

Familiarity can help immensely with the challenge of a highly diverse consulting team. At the height of my career, I had the good fortune to work with the same lawyer from a prominent firm on many engagements, and we got to the point that we were routinely finishing each other's sentences.

Over time, I easily worked with more than one hundred attorneys, mostly well-known professionals from larger firms. They tended to be specialists in corporate law, healthcare regulation, mergers and acquisitions, governance, and the like. I also worked with many local attorneys who were counsel for their local hospitals and health systems. While there was much more variation in performance and knowledge at the local level, I must say that this too proved to be a mostly enjoyable experience. When people live and work in their community, there is a certain level of dedication and commitment that is infectious.

Local counsel, almost without exception, provided valuable insights into the history and personalities of the leaders involved in the process. My experience was that local attorneys were eager to embrace special counsel when complexity merited their involvement. For example, it was rare that local counsel would have much experience with mergers and acquisitions, especially when federal antitrust and other compliance matters came into the picture. They welcomed the help navigating these complex mazes of regulation.

BE FLEXIBLE WITH YOUR WORK ENVIRONMENT

Consultants are required to be productive wherever they are, and travel is a big part of the job. Fortunately, the fundamental resources required to be productive in consulting are not much more than a laptop and internet access, both of which enable mobility. With tight deadlines looming, it is common to set up shop while waiting for a plane, in a restaurant, and the like.

The simple point is that anyone who is more comfortable being tied to a desk will find the mobility requirements of consulting to be taxing. One of the things that I routinely ask of a new client is a secure space where the consulting team can work when at the client site.

MANAGE BILLABLE TIME

Depending on what firm you join, as a relatively inexperienced new careerist you will be expected to be between 80 percent and 100 percent billable for at least 40 hours per week. Think about that for a minute. That is eight hours a day, five days a week. When are you supposed to plan? Answer the phone? Go the bathroom? You get it. Were you thinking of eight-hour days? How about 10- to 12-hour days? Moreover, you don't control this, since someone else assigns your engagements, at least initially.

The reality is that by the time you can take a break from billable time, it is probably most welcome. Without periodic time away from client assignments, you will be on the track for burnout. Yet, in doing so, you are officially "on the beach." You are eating sand. You are not billable. This strikes terror in new consultants and can make them uncomfortable. It creates stress.

The idea behind being billable is to make yourself available for other assignments when you have completed your current work. Managers will not know this unless you let them know. The exception to this is your *sponsor*. Most firms assign a new consultant to a manager who is designated as the new hire's sponsor. It is the responsibility of the sponsor to work closely with the new consultant. In this capacity, the sponsor is the "go-to" person for the recruit and has some responsibility for making sure that the consultant stays busy and gets the support needed to succeed. It stands to reason that some people are really good in the role of sponsors and others are not. There is little question that people are somewhat dependent on the luck of the draw here. There is some comfort in knowing that they had to have considerable skills and experience to rise to the level of manager in the first place. However, it is not rare to have a new recruit switch sponsors at some point because it does not always work out.

For the new recruit, when you finish with one engagement from one manager, you should look for a new engagement with other managers. Most firms have ways of tracking this and making sure other managers are aware of your availability, but you can also help to make this known. *Don't be afraid to advocate for yourself in advance of completing an engagement.*

The first few years are often a bit different from later years in consulting firms. As you rise up the ladder, your billing rate goes up and the number of hours you bill tends to go down. The reason for this is the recognition that managing a project tends to involve some unbillable time, such as selling additional work. In order to make time to write proposals and hold sales meetings, your billing targets are reduced. However, know you will now be held to other standards (e.g., favorable reviews of subordinates, hitting sales targets).

In my experience, most consulting firms are meritocracies: The better your downtime is managed, the faster you advance. Doing good work efficiently results in managers fighting to get you on their projects. The more exposure you get to different managers, the more likely you will be picked up by someone when you experience downtime. These things go hand in hand. It is also logical that the amount of time billed (translated into revenues) influences compensation at review time. Not that this is the only thing that counts, but it definitely counts.

REFERENCES

Fisher, W., and M. Ury, 1981. *Getting to Yes*. Boston: Penguin Books.

Healthcare Technology Network of Greater Washington. 2012. "Welcome to the Healthcare Technology Network of Greater Washington." Accessed March 2, 2020. http://healthtechnet.net/.

Kaissi, A. 2019. *Intangibles: The Unexpected Traits of High-Performing Healthcare Leaders*. Chicago: Health Administration Press.

Runde, J. 2016. "Why Young Bankers, Lawyers, and Consultants Need Emotional Intelligence." *Harvard Business Review Blog*. Published September 26. https://hbr.org/2016/09/why-young-bankers-lawyers-and-consultants-need-emotional-intelligence.

CHAPTER 7

Understanding the Client Perspective

THE NUMBER ONE RULE in public speaking is "Know your audience." The same can be said for consulting. Understanding the client's perspective and the client's current situation (situational awareness) is imperative.

Are you connecting with the client? What are its expectations? How are you doing in meeting them? The consulting transaction has a buyer and a seller, and the seller must understand the buyer in order to yield a good outcome. To be perceived as authentic the professional consultant must understand the client. The knowledge and experience that are the core of the consultant value chain (see chapter 2) must include understanding the client. You must have knowledge not only of the industry and best practices, but also about the client, coupled with the ability to put your experience to work on the client's behalf.

David Maister is the guru of professional service firms. "Buying professional services is rarely a comfortable experience" (Maister 1993). Being a good consultant begins with empathy regarding a client's perspective toward consulting, and a critical part of any engagement is being aware of how the client looks at consultants in general, as well as the project at hand. Some people are genuinely uncomfortable hiring consultants and reluctant to pay the fees involved, or to trust outside people with confidential information. To get a look at how clients approach consultants, I refer you to Agwunobi (2019), who does a nice job of outlining for prospective clients how and when to hire a consultant versus completing the work internally, and specifically addresses healthcare turnaround clients.

Clearly, the market supports a grapevine about consultants, and those who have positive reviews tend to do well. The opposite, though not as clearly defined, is also true. It may surprise you to know that there also exists an active grapevine among consultants regarding clients. If a client has a poor attitude toward consultants or is difficult to work with, this does get around. Such a reputation might come from a poor track record of paying for services or disputing fees, and some memories can last a long time. I have been confronted in a number of situations where something went wrong in a previous assignment completed by a firm that I worked with, and it had implications for future work even though. I had a good relationship with the client. It is interesting to note that I was not always aware of this until later, when I was informed that we were not selected in a shoot-out (final competition). It was quite disappointing, after putting in considerable work on a proposal, to learn that the firm had a negative history with this client. Had we known at the outset, it is doubtful that we would have chased this work in the first place. A more accurate grapevine on this client could have helped us avoid this situation.

In considering the client perspective, some education is in order regarding the correct role of the consultant, but only after a clear understanding of who the client is.

WHO IS THE CLIENT?

It might surprise you to find that there are some differences of opinion about who the client ultimately is. To be fair, it is complicated. Is my client the organization as a whole? Or is it the person who hired me within that organization? I believe the client is ultimately the organization for whom I complete a specific client engagement. The more complete answer gets at the essential purpose of a consultant, which is to provide advice that is both dispassionate and objective.

Clearly, people hire people. Unless you please the people who hire you, your billable hours might be limited. But it is more complicated than that. It really comes down to the legal concepts of fidelity and obedience, which are often applied to governance functions and obligations of board members. Some argue that obedience becomes more relevant when discussing nonprofit organizations, and the healthcare industry is dominated by nonprofit organizations. Therefore, it is important to understand these concepts. Rather than asking "Who is my client?" ask "To whom do I owe devotion?"

I have had the privilege of working with several CEOs who have changed jobs and taken me with them to their new organization as a trusted advisor.[1] As a consultant, this of course is very gratifying. It becomes even more so when a board of directors at a client site reaches out to you and continues to hire you after there has

---

1. This represents the pinnacle of professional services, according to David Maister, Charles Green, and Robert Galford (2000).

been a change in leadership at the organization. When this occurs, the trust that the CEO placed in you has transcended to the board (and, ideally, key members of the medical staff).

TIP FROM THE TRENCHES

As a consultant, it is ultimately the success of the client organization to which you have a duty. CEOs and other staff come and go, and they are the customers who deserve your attention at the time of a given engagement. The organization, however, is the ultimate client that remains over time. Regarding boards of directors, members tend to have lengthy terms and can remain on the board longer than many CEOs. Boards have the obligation to provide oversight and ensure that an organization is carrying out its mission and purpose. The board hires the CEO, the CEO hires the staff, and the CEO and/or staff hire the consultant. Rarely do boards hire a consultant, unless it is for governance work, executive search work, or to work in conjunction with the CEO.

Most of the time, viewing the CEO as separate from the organization is not necessary. They can be regarded as one and the same. The reason for this is quite simple—usually CEOs are working in the best interest of the organization, which is why they were hired in the first place. When this ceases to be true, that CEO is no longer the right person for the job.

In my experience, most (but not all) CEOs tend to realize when a change in leadership is required in their organization, and they are prepared to move on. When the skills of the CEO and the needs of the organizations diverge, it gets more challenging for a consultant. It is not unusual for consultants to be placed in a situation in which there is some suspicion that the interests of the CEO and the organization (usually represented by the board of trustees or directors) are not in sync. Of course, this is a high-risk scenario and might be the real reason that the consultant was hired in the first place. Clearly, some CEOs do not want to hear this news, and by sharing these observations, the consultant may be talking themselves out of a client engagement. On the other hand, sharing information with the CEO regarding the lack of alignment allows the CEO to make a determination of what is best for all parties involved. I have been confronted by this scenario on numerous occasions during my career.

What happens when it is not the CEO who hires you but another member of the C-suite? This can get a bit more complicated. In my career I have often been hired by the chief strategy officer (CSO). Most of the time this works fine because the CSO reports to and is aligned with the CEO. However, how do you handle it when they're not? In one situation involving a strategic plan, I had worked previously with the CEO but was new to the senior vice president (SVP) of strategic planning. During the initial contracting process, this individual made it clear that he did not support hiring a consultant to help with this process and felt that the organization could do this themselves. This was awkward to say the least. Ultimately, we were required to make it clear to the CEO that the resistance we were experiencing from this individual did not allow for a constructive process. This was a situation only the CEO could manage. After a short time, it became clear that the SVP needed to move on so that the process could be completed.

Consultants occasionally speak of *sponsors* in a client organization or related to a particular engagement. This is the person who brought you into the engagement, and in situations when it is not the CEO, this can require a bit of a balancing act. We all know that the CEO is ultimately accountable, which is why a consultant has to be careful. It can appear both unseemly and counterproductive to be engaging the CEO when another person is your sponsor. One usually has to be careful and owe allegiance to the sponsor (this is sometimes referred to as "chain of command"). Yet it is more than tempting to seek out the CEO because of the potential future work the CEO represents. *Don't go there.* Focus on your sponsor's needs.

In one situation, I was confronted with a difficult set of circumstances—a non-CEO sponsor who had health problems. This was one of the most challenging situations I have encountered. It was further complicated because I had previously done work for this organization, had known the individual for some time, and was genuinely fond of this person. After a short time on this strategic planning engagement, it became clear that the individual was experiencing dementia. I was immediately confronted with two very difficult issues. First, there was a privacy issue, which I took very seriously. Did his peers recognize this? Second was the competency issue. At what point would I be obligated to address this more directly? The second issue was easier to manage.

Upon further examination, I felt that I could exercise some control as it involved a strategic planning process over which I clearly had some influence. But even here, I was limited because there were certain meetings in which I was not involved and therefore could not impact a certain work product. I could not easily invite myself into these other meetings. Although it felt very uncomfortable at the time because his impairment was becoming more obvious and he was less able to fulfill his role, the larger group process ultimately prevailed, the final work product was excellent, and it enjoyed wide consensus among all the stakeholders.

It was about a year later when I was first able to deal with the more difficult privacy issue. I felt a moral obligation to share with the CEO my experience and how I had chosen to handle it. The ailment of the executive in question had since become known, and the person had taken disability and left the organization. We had a frank discussion about the situation and determined that it had been handled as best it could under the circumstances.

There is no substitute for trust in the consultant–client process. This can sometimes be taken for granted, but it shouldn't be. In one amusing situation, I was involved in scenario development with the executive team of a health system, and we were engaged in an open dialogue to determine alternative partners for a potential merger. Part of the exercise was to play out the different scenarios of such a transaction, both good and bad. While this was somewhat hypothetical, it was openly acknowledged by the executives involved that their jobs could be in jeopardy through such a merger. At one point, I painted a particularly negative outcome under one scenario, to which the CEO blurted out in anger, "You are full of s___!"

There were gasps all around, and you could feel the air leave the room. Mind you, up to this time the discussion had been mostly constructive and dispassionate. I had done a lot of work for this client in the previous few years, so I had their trust, or at least I thought I did. This is where emotional intelligence and knowing your client are key. Without skipping a beat, I responded, "You did not mean that! Clearly, I am not full of s___. You meant that the scenario I described is not plausible." To which the CEO responded immediately, "Yes, that is exactly what I meant." We all subsequently could breathe again and had a good laugh. There is no substitute for trust in a client relationship.

So, who is the client? In short: It's the organization. However, know that during many engagements you will touch different people within that organization, and no two of them will see things exactly the same. Sorting this out is one of the truly exciting and challenging tasks of the professional consultant. More on this later.

BEING CLIENT-CENTRIC

While all firms claim they are client-centric, what does this really mean? Does it mean that we will tell the client only what it wants to hear? (While I wish that this wasn't so, a remarkable number of consultants seem to operate in this realm.) Some consultants wave the flag that they will be easy to work with and reinforce whatever the client tells us. Is the client always right? What happens when this is not the case?

I believe that being truly client-centric is nothing more than being customer-oriented. Clients are customers and want to be treated accordingly. But unlike brick-and-mortar retail, the consultant is in the client's house, not the reverse (the retail store). What most of us want is a positive client interaction. This is no different from customer relations or the consumer experience in the retail world. Considering retail can truly be helpful in understanding this concept. When trying on a dress or a suit, would you rather have your representative tell you everything looks great, or reject those things where there does not seem to be a fit? The good retail experience focuses on outcome as much as process. If someone buys an expensive piece of clothing, it should look good and fit well. This is also true in consulting.

One difference between consulting and retail is that *the consultant is a guest in the client's house*. Retailers (think car sales) like to control the customer setting. They like to be able to drive the process, which lends itself to the customer being served in the retail setting. In the consulting world, the consultant usually spends time in the client world, over which the consultant has virtually no control.

What is consistent between the perfect retail experience and consulting is that the client wants to be treated like a most favored customer. What then makes for a positive retail experience?

This happens to be the subject of a public blog post (Watkin 2017) that identifies five pillars. I have taken these and translated them into what I believe most clients are looking for in a positive consulting relationship, as noted in exhibit 7.1.

Exhibit 7.1: Attributes of a Positive Retail/Consulting Experience

Retail	Consulting
Engagement	I want to know that you care about me and my issues.
Executional excellence	. . . that you do good work.
Brand experience	. . . that you have solid references and experience relevant to what I need.
Expediting	. . . that I will be a priority for you and you won't waste my time.
Problem recovery	. . . that you are able to admit when you have made a mistake and be a real partner to me by making a fair recovery.

Source: Adapted from Watkin (2017).

DIFFERENT NEEDS REQUIRE DIFFERENT SKILLS

As I pursued my consulting career in healthcare, a noticeable change occurred over time. Problems that were relatively common and straightforward tended to become more complex as the industry, already criticized for its complexity, evolved. This is not only challenging for those of us experts who focus on healthcare, but it also makes it even more difficult for healthcare organizations to achieve greater transparency, something that is increasingly being demanded by critics and policymakers. As health systems have become larger and more diverse, a series of complex issues that have significant implications for consulting have emerged.

As noted later, there will always be room in healthcare consulting for the specialist who focuses on a narrow area of expertise. This is one of the reasons that niche or solo consulting will always have a role to play in the spectrum of consultants. However, as the problems become more complicated, it becomes more necessary to bring multidisciplinary teams into the picture.

Problems that have previously been thought of as primarily operational or strategic now are recognized to have elements of both, with highly specialized knowledge increasingly required in more and more situations. Obviously, this tends to favor the larger firms that employ a more diverse stable of experts covering a wider swath of the healthcare industry. However, even the larger firms must, on occasion, contract with independent specialists to access highly specialized and rare skills.

AN ENGAGEMENT IS A RELATIONSHIP

Brand can be a key driver in the case of some engagements and some firms. Where the engagement is standardized and predictable, it might be a bit more commoditized and less dependent upon a well-established relationship. For most other types of engagements, hiring a consultant creates a relationship. As such, the principals of the client and the consultant must interact and work closely together. The interpersonal dynamics can be at least as important as the technical expertise.

Each party is placing *trust* in the other to deliver on expectations. The result, ideally, is that expectations are met (or exceeded) and it was time and money well spent. There should be a return on this investment. If it is a positive experience, it can lead to more work with this client (add-on work) or with other clients (through a reference). Like all experiences, there are different components to consider. Was the client better off as a result of the engagement? Did it accomplish what it set out to do? How did the client feel about the engagement upon completion? How did the consultant feel?

There are certainly cases where consultants are involved in *one-off assignments*, where it is understood that there is no additional work to be done—generally, crisis situations in which there is a need to arbitrate (i.e., there is a winner and a loser) and the likelihood of additional work is slim to none. Some firms specialize in this type of work, but most avoid it since it does not lead to follow-on work. What these different types of consulting engagements have in common is the need for trust. There is no relationship without trust.

Most relationships evolve. Yet not all engagements will enhance a relationship. For those that do, the professional consultant will earn the opportunity to be considered for more work in the future.

WHY CLIENTS HIRE CONSULTANTS

There can be many motivations for bringing in outside consultants. It is rare that this is done casually, because introducing outside people to any internal process brings with it certain risks and expense. Oftentimes, there are multiple considerations. For example, it is common that the consultant role will include some level of education and coaching, and it must be acknowledged that there can be hidden agendas involved.

To generalize, consultants are usually hired for one of three reasons:

1. *Problem-solving expertise.* Consultants tend to be highly educated and experienced. Such expertise often involves skills not available within a client organization or experience that far exceeds internal expertise. Most of the experience the new recruit has gained starting out as a new careerist comes from someone else, through the academic review of case studies and hearing from others who share their experiences. Over time, new careerists add their personal experiences to the mix, and with this added experience comes expertise. Expertise is important to all consulting engagements, of course, but sometimes it is the firm that represents this experience, not necessarily the consultant assigned to the engagement. Experience can come from referencing related case studies where the firm has achieved success in the past. For example, Firm B is known for successful implementation of X. Clients will hire Firm B to provide oversight and hope that personnel assigned to the engagement have familiarity and experience with the issue at hand.

2. *Objectivity and credibility.* Sometimes competing initiatives need to be sorted out by an objective third party. Many healthcare organizations attempt to achieve consensus during decision-making. Usually this is achievable. When it is not, it may be time to call in a consultant. Any decision of consequence involves some level of risk. Consultants play an important role by lending their expertise and experience to the process of defining and understanding the risk, or pros and cons, of each alternative. This can include development

and implementation of a process such as strategic planning, or a key initiative like a women's health service line. The client organization may already have similar skills but is seeking objectivity or credibility. The consultant might be asked to offer an opinion on a topic or arbitrate among competing interests.

3. *Supplemental staffing.* Sometimes the client clearly has the ability to develop or implement a specific initiative but lacks the staff capacity to do so. Perhaps the task is time-limited and not worth hiring additional full-time employees. Consultants can be brought in to perform a specific task for a brief period of time.

When a company is considering hiring consultants, there is generally an identified need. This need could be urgent or something more routine. The difference is important. Some needs are driven by problems such as financial losses, personnel issues, and other challenges. These engagements might tend to be more *urgent*, especially when operating at a financial deficit. Other needs are related more to opportunities and can be either short- or long-term. Longer-term issues tend to be less urgent in nature.

Other situations that involve supplemental staffing can be broken into two categories:

1. *Client-initiated engagements.* A client has tried to resolve an issue internally but was not able to do so, so the client turns to a consultant.

2. *Consultant-initiated engagements.* A consultant could be selling a specific initiative, such as a revenue cycle, that the client had not considered but realizes there is a genuine opportunity.

In either case, the client will benefit from a process it could not otherwise have accomplished as effectively on its own. This is the value proposition of many consulting studies.

HOW CLIENTS SELECT CONSULTANTS

When competition arises among consulting firms, two important components should be part of every engagement: a request for proposal (RFP) and a shoot-out.

Request for Proposal

Not all clients can consolidate a specific issue down to an RFP. In my experience, this process is usually reserved for larger or more complicated assignments. When an RFP is required, the client usually is considering a few different consultants or firms to complete the work. The value of a written RFP is that the client has invested some effort to define what is required. Ideally, such effort involved some internal review and edits based on feedback. That is not to say that all RFPs represent consensus, but chances are that some consensus exists around an issue when an RFP has been created.

In my experience, many healthcare engagements are initiated without an RFP, and from the consultant's viewpoint, that's OK. Consulting firms generally do not like putting together an RFP. Many firms will tell you that the RFP process is inefficient, especially if they have worked with the client before. It is common practice while completing engagements to inquire about add-on work ("Is there anything else we can help you with?"). The idea is to avoid the additional effort that would be involved in putting together another RFP. Assuming the current assignment is going well and trust has been established, you would hope to avoid the RFP process for the next assignment. Firms spend significant time and resources responding to RFPs. Ultimately, the client ends up paying for this as billing rates need to cover overhead (i.e., downtime). A far more efficient process for the consultant is when a firm has a retainer relationship that allows them to accept new work without having to go through the expensive and time-consuming RFP process. The client gains in such situations by hiring a firm that is already familiar with the culture of the organization, thus saving the time and expense necessary for orientation, and for whom a trust relationship has already been established.

When an RFP is not involved, it is vital that a scope of work (SOW) document and/or detailed proposal be developed at the outset of the assignment so that there is no misunderstanding of the scope, duration, and cost of the project.

Shoot-Out

When an RFP is involved, a few other things usually apply, foremost being the number of firms invited. Ideally, it should be limited. If the invitation is wide open, usually some firms will elect not to bid. As part of the RFP process, clients should attempt to reduce the initial number of firms to be considered to no more than two to three for final presentations. More than that and it becomes confusing and makes it harder to make a final selection.

Many RFPs involve an information phone call or session for firms that are interested in responding, especially for a complicated project. Consultants spend considerable time responding to an RFP, and clients should respect this and only select finalists that have a legitimate chance to land the engagement. If not, word gets out on this, and if one firm is used as a straw man not to be seriously considered, then fewer firms will likely bid on the next opportunity.

Shoot-outs are sometimes referred to pejoratively as "beauty contests," so the client should put some effort into creating a level playing field on which the consultants compete. One of the first questions that should be asked by any consulting firm is whether the client has worked with any of the firms before. The answer might cause some not to compete for the work, but this level of candor is important.

The presentations are an opportunity for the consultant and client teams to meet, and this can be invaluable. However, it can also be deceiving. The client might be suspicious of the potential bait-and-switch salesman who presents one team, but then substitutes another when it wins the work. Clients must be clear who will be on the consultant team. This is also why the next component of checking references applies.

Selecting a consultant always involves a subjective element. Chemistry matters. It is helpful at times to perform objective comparisons such as rates, time frame, experience, and so on, but in the end it is about a relationship. In my experience, quite a bit of hiring is done on a so-called *sole-source* basis. Such an approach begins with chemistry and ends with competence. For those competitive situations, it is important to defend the choice once it is made. Accordingly, a systematic approach is required that compares the options and justifies the decision. It is important to identify the stakeholders in making such a selection. A person or firm acceptable to the CEO is not necessarily the same one that is acceptable to the board of trustees or to other members of the C-suite who might be involved. Which stakeholders are involved is important from both the consultant's and the client's perspective.

This is particularly important in engagements where the medical staff is involved (employed or independent physicians), as well as the board of trustees (this could include multiple boards), and/or the community (e.g., in a community-needs assessment). A clear understanding of who the stakeholders are, how they are to participate, and how they will be affected by the results will help make this a consensus process. When this is done poorly, the consultant runs a greater risk of having the results of the work challenged.

CONSULTING IS BEING COMMODITIZED

The person hiring the consultant must have authority to enter into such an arrangement. This is particularly the case under a sole-source arrangement. As the healthcare industry has consolidated, there have been some dramatic changes to this contracting authority.

Most healthcare organizations are organized as nonprofit corporations, and the size of these corporations has grown dramatically in the past few years. Regional healthcare organizations routinely consolidate to the point where annual revenues are in the billions—thus, not your father's hospital. This consolidation includes not only hospitals but now also physician employees and diversification into ambulatory surgery, freestanding emergency rooms, community-based ambulatory care, and possibly provider-sponsored insurance. This is hardly the traditional experience of the past, where healthcare was represented mostly by the local 100-bed hospital just down the street, with an independent medical staff and an annual fund drive that would raise a few thousand dollars.

As these health systems have grown in size, purchasing consulting services has become far more complicated, involving multiple channels within the client organization and the bureaucracy that accompanies a typical capital equipment purchase.

There is an interesting trend evolving in consulting that is worth noting at this juncture. Thus far, we have emphasized that consulting creates a relationship for most engagements. However, an increasing number of functional assignments reflect more of a commodity status. Note that this pertains to the perspective of the client, not necessarily the consultant. This new form of relationship might not relate to the work involved as much as it reflects the consultant selection process. This becomes clear when such engagements involve the materials management department. When this occurs, the engagement is often treated essentially like any other product purchase. (Think medical supplies or equipment.) Furthermore, the consultant might be subjected to a standard purchase contract that can include more and more items over time, such as contracting as a "business associate" related to the Health Information Portability and Accountability Act, data privacy requirements covering personal health information, and other policy items as far-reaching as mandatory flu shots.

TIP FROM THE TRENCHES

Consultants are asked to fill out the same questionnaires as standard vendors and sign contracts that have similar language. While attempting to standardize the purchase or contracting function is understandable to a degree, it leaves a diminished feeling because it suggests that buying consulting services should be treated no differently than buying supplies or equipment. As further consolidation occurs in the industry and larger regional health systems are formed, it seems inevitable that more and more consulting will be subjected to this highly regimented, impersonal process.

Trying to close the sale of a consulting engagement through negotiations with the purchasing department is a far cry from the more traditional experience, where a conversation with the CEO and a signature on a written proposal document were all that was required to initiate an engagement. It is becoming more typical in CEO employment agreements to negotiate contracting authority where, beyond some approval limits (e.g., up to $5 million), some kind of oversight might come into play. This oversight might include the requirement to get competing bids, or board approval.

NICHE PLAYERS

Part of the attraction of consulting, in healthcare especially, is how specialized it has become. This expanding specialization leads to more niche players in the market. When accountable care organizations were developed as part of the latest component of reform in healthcare, there quickly developed a set of niche players focused on value-based care. Every new reform seems to bring about the formation of new firms focused on planning and implementing that reform. There is an innovation cycle that is linked to consulting services. However, it should be noted that some of these innovations can have short shelf lives.

For example, every major healthcare consulting firm quickly developed a group under a title similar to "population health." A few short years later, after some clients had been urged by their consultants to spend enormous amounts on such initiatives, there has been relatively little perceived return on this investment (i.e., a shift in patient volumes). As a result, population health has become less attractive as a label, replaced with other terms such as value-based care. While niche players abound, the niches can be quite fickle. Such is healthcare reform in this transitional era.

FIRING THE CLIENT

"The customer is always right" is a popular mantra in retail. If the customer feels in any way disrespected, you have lost their business. In retail, with relatively small margins requiring many sales to break even, one cannot afford to lose any business. This is not always the case in consulting.

Consulting is a relationship. Like all relationships, there is a risk that things could go wrong. The literature is rich with references to the "toxic client" and how to fire the client "nicely." Aside from the obvious, there really are important reasons not to prolong a process that simply is not working. While things might have deteriorated in a particular engagement, it could always get worst. This benefits no one.

From the consultant's perspective, there are four specific reasons to consider a change (Clark 2015):

1. When you're doing work you no longer want to do
2. When your client wastes your time
3. When you are locked into low fees
4. When your client is never satisfied

The interesting thing I have found is that it is never a mystery that an engagement is not working out. The client tends to feel the same way, perhaps for some of the same reasons. There have even been a few times when I gained the client's respect by suggesting that we terminate the engagement. As previously stated, consulting is a relationship. Personalities and styles do not always mesh, and it's sometimes better just to move on. In doing so, you are demonstrating an appreciation for the client perspective as well.

REFERENCES

Agwunobi, A. 2019. *An Insider's Guide to Working with Healthcare Consultants.* Chicago: Health Administrative Press.

Clark, D. 2015. "A Consultant's Guide to Firing a Client." *Harvard Business Review.* Published January 26. https://hbr.org/2015/01/a-consultants-guide-to-firing-a-client.

Maister, D. H. 1993. *Managing the Professional Service Firm.* New York: Simon & Schuster.

Maister, D. H., C. H. Green, and R. M. Galford. 2000. *The Trusted Advisor.* New York: Free Press.

Watkin, H. 2017. "What Makes a Good Retail Experience for Customers?" Zoovu. Published March 30. https://zoovu.com/blog/good-retail-experience.

The Firm Experience

CONSULTING AS A SKILL SET is not the same as the business of consulting. Part I focused on the personal skills required of consultants. Part II contains several chapters that focus on the business of consulting, which includes the firm experience. As much as people differ one from another, so do firms. To best describe the different types of consulting firms, we suggest a few different categories and offer some examples of each.

A number of things come into play when focusing on the firm experience. It is helpful to appreciate that managing highly energized and talented people was never an easy task. Expectations are a key consideration, which is why we explore different types of firms from a number of perspectives in this section. Furthermore, it is important to have realistic expectations when considering different consulting firms. Given the wide variation in numbers and types of firms, it is helpful to know what you are looking for (to the extent possible) before beginning the search process.

CHAPTER 8

What We Can Learn About Different Firms

WHAT DISTINGUISHES ONE FIRM from another? How does this apply to consulting in healthcare? These and other related questions are covered in this chapter.

While there are different types of consulting firms, there are also functions that all firms have in common. It is helpful to understand these functions as part of understanding the business of consulting. Where applicable, we will also point out some differences in the way these functions are approached. Getting with the right *type of firm* is as important as getting with the right firm. The differences can be dramatic and important. For purposes of this discussion, firms and practices are intended as the same thing.

SURVEY RESULTS

We begin this discussion with the big picture, looking at the macro environment for consulting firms by reviewing several surveys. The first survey we review is "America's Best Management Consulting Firms" (Valet 2019).

The survey suggests that consulting revenues have grown in lockstep with "economic uncertainty" to $241 billion (+3.6 percent over previous year) for the more than 708,000 firms they identified over the last five years. The survey covered a sample of 7,500 partners and executives, and 1,000 senior executives who worked with such firms over the previous four years. Consulting, the survey concluded, is clearly big business and has a bright future.

The survey was divided into 16 sectors, which included healthcare, and 16 functional areas, including strategy, sustainability, and digital transformation. The 216 firms that received the most stars in a rating system were then ranked. Bain & Company and Deloitte tied for the title of "most recommended consultancy," each earning "nods in all 32 sectors and functional areas." Accenture won the most five-star ratings.

The second survey is conducted annually by *Modern Healthcare* (2018). It focuses on just healthcare through the use of a self-reporting survey of the largest healthcare consulting firms. A global firm, Deloitte Consulting, led the pack in 2018 (the latest year available), at $2.35 billion in revenue, of which 39 percent was consulting to providers. This was significantly more revenue than the next closest firm. However, it is worth noting that some of the best-known firms did not participate in the survey (see the footnote below exhibit 8.1). A third survey is covered later in this section, focused on the global firms.

DISTINGUISHING DIFFERENT TYPES OF FIRMS

Before looking at the different types of firms that exist, it is worth examining the decision process from the potential employee's perspective. As will be discussed later, fit is the ultimate criterion worth considering. However, before fit can become an issue, what is it that you should look for? We discussed some of the things that clients look for when choosing a consultant, but that is not the same as what a potential employee would look for in a firm. Clearly, there are choices involved.

The choice of what firm to join might start with geography. If that is the most important factor, this will reduce the pool of potential firms, sometimes dramatically, depending on what locations qualify. For example, if you include most major metropolitan cities like New York, Dallas, Los Angeles, and Chicago, then the pool will be large; it will be less so for the secondary cities such as Miami, San Diego, and Portland, and rural areas.

If geography is not your driving factor, then we move on to the next criterion, which I recommend should be your functional areas of interest. If you have specialized in an area such as finance, IT, or nursing, then it helps to zero in on the firms that focus on these areas. On the other hand, if operations and/or strategy are of interest, these tend to be broader and don't necessarily add much focus.

There is only so much planning that can go into your decision-making. Some of this process is certainly circumstantial, such as which firms recruit at your school, or which ones you are familiar with through a friend. Your decision could also relate to how you might be recruited by a given firm, because recruiters know how to turn on the charm.

At the end of the process, and if you have the luxury of choice with few limitations, you want to be able to ask yourself, "Compared to what?" In other words, you want to have some clarity regarding why you chose firm A over firm B.

Exhibit 8.1: *Modern Healthcare's* 2019 Management Consulting Firms Survey

RANK	COMPANY	HEADQUARTERS	TOTAL PROVIDER CONTRACTS 2018	TOTAL HEALTHCARE CONTRACTS[1] 2018	TOTAL PROVIDER REVENUE 2018 ($ IN MILLIONS)	TOTAL HEALTHCARE REVENUE[1] 2018 ($ IN MILLIONS)
1	Deloitte Consulting	New York	—	—	$923.0	$2,351.9
2	Optum	Eden Prairie, Minn.	—	—	430.0	990.0
3	Vizient	Irving, Texas	817	817	336.4	336.4
4	FTI Consulting	Washington, D.C.	1,614	1,614	295.2	295.2
5	Gallagher	Rolling Meadows, Ill.	17,021	19,087	221.3	280.3
6	Berkeley Research Group	Emeryvillie, Calif.	242	589	126.5	203.5
7	Nordic	Madison, Wis.	163	998	18.0	190.0
8	Crowe	Chicago	1,970	1,970	172.9	172.9
9	West Monroe Partners	Chicago	180	400	20.0	100.0
10	RSM US	Chicago	—	—	56.0	93.6
11	GE Healthcare Partners	Chicago	66	66	90.0	90.0
12	Dixon Hughes Goodman	Charlotte, N.C.	2,979	2,990	56.7	57.2
13	PYA	Knoxville, Tenn.	3,311	3,311	57.2	57.2
14	BKD CPAs & Advisors	Springfield, Mo.	7,555	7,685	53.3	53.3
15	Huron	Chicago	—	—	42.7	42.7
16	CLA (CliftonLarsonAllen)	Minneapolis	3,343	3,343	42.5	42.5
17	Baker Tilly	Chicago	790	1,021	15.7	36.0
18	Point B	Seattle	190	296	25.8	33.9
19	Cope Health Solutions	New York	110	110	22.2	22.2
20	Clarity Insights	Chicago	7	19	1.0	22.0

Note: Information is self-reported from companies responding to *Modern Healthcare*'s 2019 Management Consulting Firms Survey. Accenture, Alvarez & Marsal, ECG Management Consultants, Ernst & Young, KPMG, McKinsey & Co., Oliver Wyman, PricewaterhouseCoopers, and Quorum Health Resources did not participate in the 2019 survey. Healthcare IT firms and revenue-cycle management firms are omitted from the above ranking.
For more charts, lists, rankings and surveys, please visit modernhealthcare.com/data.
[1]Total healthcare contracts and total healthcare revenue represent consulting work with providers as well as other sectors of the healthcare industry.
Source: Modern Healthcare (2019). Used with permission.

Realistically, this can only occur when you are knowledgeable of what is out there and how one firm compares to the other. Additionally, it brings into play the many variables that we discussed earlier regarding how consulting in general aligns with your career goals. Circumstances also include situations that are beyond your control—for example, not all firms are hiring all the time.

Firms function differently according to size and scope; it is important to understand some of these differences. How do they hire, determine who works on each project, seek new business, and run their business are all important considerations. How they treat their people, both before and after they leave the firm, is important. What is the firm's focus? How does the leadership interact? What values do they espouse and also live up to—in other words, are they authentic? These are all factors that should be considered.

To get a handle on this, it is helpful to better understand the different types of firms. For our purposes, we have divided firms into the following categories:

- Solo practice
- Small and medium specialty and general practice firms
- Global firms
- Virtual practices

SOLO PRACTICE

Solo practice is one of the more popular forms of consulting and, even though it is not generally practical for the new careerist, it is worth knowing about. Solo practice is more relevant for midlevel or senior executives looking to leverage their knowledge and experience. Some enterprising individuals have been able to enter the industry as solo consultants, but that is more the exception than the rule. Those who have done so have had a high tolerance for risk (I know because I was one), have had some previous exposure to consulting, and have been highly motivated. Solo practice can include a high dose of interim staffing along with legitimate consulting.

The major appeal of solo practice is simplicity and self-determination. Obviously, a solo practice reflects the personality of the individual, and this is part of the appeal. Additionally, this is *self-employment*, and so you are able to avoid employment law, which can be very oppressive. Since you are effectively the corporation, you will likely avoid most conflict. It's still possible, of course, because you will likely work with others if your clients' needs exceed your skills and/or time limitations. These others are generally referred to as *independent contractors* or *stringers*. Whether they are used for support services or as consultants, I recommend that you execute a formal agreement, making clear what they are being asked to provide and how they will be compensated. Support can often be provided by temporary workers who can be hired on a daily, weekly, or monthly basis.

For a new careerist, it is possible to contract with a solo practice to complete certain tasks (i.e., gigs). An effective way of contracting with a stringer is to have a general agreement that covers the relationship with authorization provided for specific help with a specific client engagement. For example, the agreement could be *for marketing assistance with client A, authorizing up to 40 hours of billable time as required to complete work in section X of the proposal dated Y.* It is quite common for solo firms to band together to respond to an opportunity that exceeds the capacity of one firm to fulfill. Most solo consultants have a high IQ for collaboration. An internship is not out of the question, either.

SMALL AND MEDIUM SPECIALTY PRACTICES

Small and medium specialty practices are among the most popular and best-known consulting firms serving the healthcare industry. For most new careerists considering consulting, it is likely that you will be interviewing with one or more of these firms. Size is certainly a key variable. For our purposes, small is defined as 2 to 15 consultants, and medium will range from 16 to 300 consultants. Obviously, such a range in size makes for much variation among firms in this category, so some of what is offered in this section is a generalization that might not always apply. Variation is both the attraction and the risk in considering firms in this category.

The smaller firms are usually built around one or a few key founders who have some name recognition in the area in which they practice. Defined as a specialty firm for our purposes, we are assuming that these firms focus only or mostly in healthcare. However, this still leaves a wide range of functions that can be offered (e.g., IT, human resources, executive and physician search, facilities, finance), as well as core client groups within the healthcare industry, such as insurance companies, hospitals, physician groups, and life sciences, to name a few. Smaller firms built around one or two founders can be high energy and exciting, depending on the personalities of the founders.

It is worth remembering that most name firms started out this way. In the examples of the Hunter Group and Studer Group, shared earlier, each started out as a small firm. Of course, these firms can also be classified as high-risk startups, since they are dependent upon one or two individuals as the "rainmakers" to find client business. For the new careerist working in such a firm, this is more akin to an apprenticeship. Being small, there is likely limited hierarchy at the firm. Also, depending on how small and specialized it is, the firm could have a limited number of skills represented, since most smaller firms focus on specific services.

There is nothing wrong with this approach, however. Under the right leadership, this can be an excellent learning opportunity for you. If the founder or key leaders enjoy teaching, you gain exposure to consulting from those who know their craft. Another advantage is that you are better able to progress at your own pace, rather than being dependent upon some kind of elaborate points system used at the larger firms for awarding promotions. It is also likely that the founders will be more willing to roll up their sleeves and help with some of the more mundane tasks that in larger firms are relegated to junior staff. Remember, management of such firms revolves around the founders. It functions like a family, and this level of intimacy is not necessarily right for everyone. It is, however, somewhat unavoidable in such a small setting. Generally, these smaller firms will be more formalized than a solo practice, with more standardization. They still tend to exhibit a high level of energy and are quite entrepreneurial in nature.

Be sure to recognize that such a small environment can change dramatically when someone leaves the practice and may depend on the health and energy of the founders. Again, almost all of the specialty firms started out with just a handful of employees, and have since grown to tens or hundreds of employees. But there can also be a high attrition rate, because smaller firms are gobbled up by larger firms, or go out of business when the founder moves on or retires.

For the medium-sized firms, it gets more complicated. They are potentially more stable due to a reliable group of repeat clients. These firms tend to function as partnerships, whether or not they are legal partnerships *per se*. The unfortunate phrase that is used to describe the business model of these firms is "eat what you kill." They tend to have more of what some consider pure consulting, where the person who sells the work does the work. Few professions other than consulting work this way. For example, the larger service firms usually have dedicated sales staff who have little or nothing to do with delivering the service. Most medium-sized consulting firms operate through different divisions or practices, where senior partners generate the work and use junior staff as needed. Junior staff can be assigned to a specific division or be part of a pool that gets allocated as business is brought into the firm.

Out of necessity, these firms have more hierarchy than smaller firms, and include more standardization, often with elaborate employment policies and staffing structures. They also have an identifiable segment of the team that is dedicated to management. Depending on the firm, this could be done by full-time executives or by a combination of dedicated staff and hybrid staff (i.e., part management and part consultant who is billing hours). Usually in these firms, the practices are led by hybrid staff. In the smaller practices, management is all hybrid and is responsible for virtually all of the sales. The key in this model is to help staff their engagements and allow them time to continue to sell. This model has survived well over time.

In some larger firms, the hybrid staff might better be described as using a player-coach model, to use a sports analogy. It is important to understand this model as it can have important implications. Where some senior partners have dedicated management responsibility, they might also have sales goals and some related billing targets. Every hour of their time not covered by billings is considered overhead. Firms work hard to keep their overhead down. The essence of the player-coach position in consulting is either administrative- or sales-oriented. The billable hours ratio[1] might be down to 25–40 percent versus 80–90 percent for a new consultant. The rest of their time is focused either on sales or such administrative functions as running a practice or division, including hiring and recruiting, and staffing engagements. This role is more operational in nature.

It is common for partners to charge some time to client engagements, especially when they were involved in the sale. Where they have specific skills to contribute to the engagement, notably with oversight or client management, billing some time to the client is obvious. But it is also common that partners can charge clients for some of their time relating to the original sale, even though the partner is not contributing to getting the work done. Sometimes, this is called the *partner's tax* (not a compliment), and it can be controversial and annoying to the consulting team, especially when the project has a tight budget. (When is this *not* the case?)

The player-coach model can get really dicey when that person was not involved in selling the engagement, but the firm needs to cover some of the cost, so it is allowed to charge the client for some of that person's time. The whole situation is complicated and can get very political.

More complications arise with the player-coach model when that person displaces someone on a team who otherwise would provide that skill set and/or who sold a specific engagement. Said differently, a conflict of interest can arise when the player-coach is under pressure to cover their minimal billing goals, but does so at the expense of another consultant who might normally offer the same skill set to the team. Where the player-coach "pulls rank" and displaces the other consultant, there can be sparks. I would like to tell you that this never happens, but it can and does.

Client engagements are completed by consulting teams directly involved in the client's work. These teams can be fixed (used for multiple clients) or variable (brought together for one client). In my experience, consulting teams are one

---

1. Hours that can be charged to a client versus unbillable hours expressed as a percentage of total. Usually relates to 2,080 hours per year.

of the most exciting aspects of consulting. When they work well, they can be incredibly productive, creative, and energizing, especially when teams get used to working with each other. When they don't work well, they can be very difficult to tolerate and uncomfortable. Partners, including player-coaches, are responsible for putting these teams together for specific assignments. For those who are interested, the medium and larger firms also have the ability to scramble teams and encourage individual consultants to work with different people. *(It should be noted that the ability to work with different groups is a skill that is highly valued in such firms.)*

GLOBAL FIRMS

General versus *specialty* is perhaps the biggest differentiator among consulting firms, where general means any type of consulting and specialty involves a functional specialization, an industry focus, or both. Over time, general has really morphed into global. As used here, *global* refers to both reach (think "international") and a broad range of industries served. Specialty, for our purposes, refers to healthcare (or related) and can be domestic. Specialty can also refer to a more limited focus of the practice, such as facilities, finance, or IT versus general ("we do everything"). Legal structure tends to be either public or private, with partnerships noted where appropriate.

According to Vault (2020), the top 20 best consulting firms, even for healthcare consulting, are dominated by global firms (exhibit 8.2).

The global firms generally look to new graduates—undergrads or grad students—to fill their ranks, and it is rare that global firms recruit from outside the consulting industry. Virtually all of the global firms have extensive internal training programs that can be quite elaborate (e.g., Deloitte University) and tend to be highly regarded. Their offerings can be extensive and cover many industries. These global firms do a thorough job of helping the individual gain the necessary skills at each level of practice, with the ultimate focus on leadership and innovation. New careerists are well taken care of in terms of training, support, and feedback. The performance evaluation systems of the global firms are intensive and are closely linked to training programs.

All of the global consulting firms actively recruit from major colleges and graduate schools. The more selective ones tend to focus on upper-echelon programs. Some of these global consulting firms have, as one of their benefits, sponsorship programs in which loans or grants are given to the best consultants with an interest to attend a top graduate program (usually an MBA program). Such sponsorships require the student to then return to the firm for a specified period of time to offset the grants or forgive the loans.

Exhibit 8.2: Vault's Top 20 Best Consulting Firms for Healthcare, 2020

Rank	Firm	% of Votes	Global or Specialty	Legal Structure
1	McKinsey & Company	34.47	Global	Private
2	The Boston Consulting Group, Inc.	25.89	Global	Private
3	Deloitte Consulting, LLP	15.75	Global	Private Partnership
4	Bain & Company	15.66	Global	Private
5	GE Healthcare Partners	15.62	Global	Public
6	ZS	12.74	Global	Private
6	Huron	12.74	Global	Public
8	Clearview Healthcare Partners	10.82	Specialty	Private
9	PwC Advisory Services	10.59	Global	Private Partnership
10	L.E.K. Consulting	10.55	Global	Private
11	Accenture	9.86	Specialty	Private Partnership
12	IQVIA (formerly IMS Consulting Group)	9.41	Global Bio	Public
13	Kaiser Associates	9.36	Global	Private
14	Navigant Consulting, Inc.	7.81	Global	Public
15	The Advisory Board Company	6.71	Specialty	Part of Optum/ UnitedHealth
16	Oliver Wyman	5.84	Global	Part of Marsh & McLennan Companies (MMC)
17	Putnam Associates	4.98	Global Bio	Private
18	Mercer, LLC	4.93	Global HR	Public part of MMC
19	EY LLP Consulting Practice	4.47	Global Accounting	Private Partnership
19	Health Advances, LLC	4.47	Specialty	Private

Source: Adapted from Vault (2020).

Most of the career consultants I have encountered have spent some time in a medium-sized or global firm, with some exposure to these advanced training programs. This experience especially applies to those who have later established their own firms.

THE VIRTUAL FIRM MODEL

Virtual care is quickly becoming mainstream in healthcare (think *telehealth*), and technology is allowing many consulting pursuits to be more virtual. In consulting, the term *virtual* is generally used when small or solo practices team up for larger client assignments and tend to involve multidisciplinary teams, which are increasingly required by healthcare clients. As healthcare organizations get larger and more complex, consulting firms that serve these clients will be required more and more to bring together diverse skills to address important issues.

Healthcare is complicated. The result is that specialists are an integral part of the landscape, whether the issue is clinical or administrative. Many consulting engagements need to employ a variety of specialists to address such issues as physician engagement, information systems, capital planning, facility design, governance, and strategic planning, to name a few.

Virtual firms are interesting from many perspectives. The advantage to this model is flexibility. Virtual firms can adjust staffing up and down depending on the needs of a particular client. The model routinely employs special talents for brief assignments, and they can do so without the need to compensate idle staff. Downtime of full-time staff is expensive, something the global firms can cover given their scale and billing rates. Certain specialists can also be expensive because of their high demand. At times, this results in consultants remaining as independent contractors because they can be picked up by all types of firms for specific engagements that require their specialized skills.

Being "networked" is one of the key elements of the consultant value chain reviewed earlier in chapter 2, where it was noted that consulting is a team sport, requiring both group and interpersonal skills. The virtual firm model in some ways represents the ultimate in professional networking. Usually, one consultant takes the lead with a client and assembles a team from among other solo practitioners or small firms. In support of this model, firms will represent themselves as "virtual firms," with the understanding that they really represent a network of talent that can be assembled to meet an array of client needs. This can involve a solo firm or even one of the Big 4 accounting firms, where each represents itself as a "network" of talent. It increasingly takes a broad network to respond to a request for proposal (RFP). Sometimes the client actually takes on the responsibility to put such teams together. The client might know a few consultants from previous work and ask them to combine their specialized talents in order to address a particular issue. One time I had a client interview both my firm and one other, and, finding it hard to select among us, asked if we could find a way to work together on that particular assignment (which we did).

The major challenge of such virtual firms is accountability. Someone must take the lead, even though each consultant tends to be quite capable of completing the assigned portion of the engagement. I have found such work to be particularly invigorating as it involves experts sharing their insights, and there can be significant synergies within such engagements. The client is usually eager to have an identifiable lead to the consulting team to help coordinate the work from the different consultants. Contracting can be a bit of a challenge because everyone must be committed to their portion of the engagement. Depending on the preference of the client, billing is centralized in the lead firm or can be done separately.

CONSULTING AS A SUPPORT SERVICE

Many small and solo consulting firms are content to remain as they are. Being small, such businesses can be very focused; they know what they do and what they do not do. But some of these smaller firms might also have an *exit strategy* to be purchased and/or "rolled up" into a larger company that has a different business model. Such rollups are also typical of software and product firms. I made a stock sale of my first consulting firm, National Health Advisors, Inc., to Apache Medical Systems, which had just gone public. As a result, consulting went from being the core business of my consulting firm to a support division of the company. Apache created an innovative algorithm that calculated the physiologic reserve of individual patients as an aid in determining how best to work with patients and the likelihood of success of certain treatments. Why would such a firm be interested in consulting?

The strategy behind such an acquisition is that consulting is widely perceived as opening doors for other products and services. Since consulting often involves entering a healthcare organization through the C-suite of decision-makers, the acquiring firm views the addition of such services as a way to gain traction in these organizations to other services they offer.

A dramatic example of this occurred some years ago when Cross Country, a temporary nurse staffing company, rolled up several firms to gain traction for their core business (Krentz 2019). These acquisitions included at the time Gil Balsano (physician practice management), The Bristol Group (facility program planning), and Jennings, Ryan and Kolb (general healthcare and finance). The acquisition effectively relied upon the ability of these consultants to do cross-selling to help grow the core staffing business of Cross County. A few years later, after not being able to achieve these cross-selling synergies, Cross Country ended up selling these businesses as a group to MitreTech (now Nobilis).

A critical idea to take away from these examples is the change in culture involved, where consulting shifts from being the core business to being a support business. Occasionally, the shift might be minor, where a great deal of autonomy continues to reside with the consulting practice. But this seems to be more the exception than the rule. A product or software company has a fundamentally different culture than a consulting firm, and mixing the two can be quite challenging. While viewed strategically as a form of "diversification," it is not necessarily related to diversification in the textbook sense. The result can be disappointing for firms that previously had infrastructure to drive growth of consulting services versus being part of another business that now supports infrastructure with a different focus. The consulting piece can quickly be perceived as less important or secondary to the core business.

Perhaps the most visible example of consulting being viewed as a support business comes from accounting firms. Clearly, there are consultants who are unwilling to report to accountants because that can be viewed as quite limiting of innovation and other interests. This requires more explanation.

ACCOUNTING VERSUS CONSULTING

When I first started in the business, there were the Big 8 accounting firms that dominated professional services worldwide. These firms all boasted of having a consulting arm. It is somewhat remarkable what has happened since 1989, as shown below in exhibit 8.3.

In June of 1989, Arthur Young merged with Ernst & Whinney. Deloitte Haskins Sells also merged with Touche Ross. After these mergers, the Big 8 accounting firms became the Big 6. Then in 1996, Price Waterhouse merged with Coopers & Lybrand to form PricewaterhouseCoopers (PwC), and have since

Exhibit 8.3: The Big 8 Accounting Firms

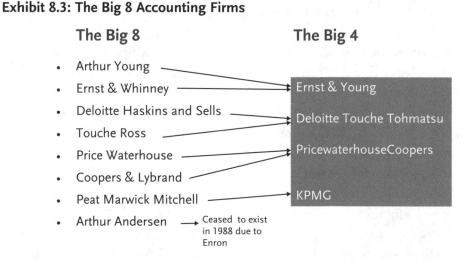

Source: Adapted from Accountingverse.com (2020).

Exhibit 8.4: The Big 4 Accounting Firms

Firm	Revenues (in billions)	Employees	Revenue per employee	Fiscal year	Headquarters
Deloitte	$46.2	312,000	$148,077	2019	United Kingdom
PwC	$42.5	276,000	$153,794	2019	United Kingdom
EY	$36.4	284,000	$128,169	2019	United Kingdom
KPMG	$29.8	219,000	$139,870	2019	Switzerland

Note: Each of these accounting firms has a consulting arm.
Source: Adapted from Accountingverse.com (2020).

rebranded as PwC. After this merger, there were the Big 5 accounting firms. Then, in 2002, as a result of the Enron scandal that began in 1988, Arthur Andersen was forced to close its business worldwide (Abelson and Glater 2002). The consulting practice from Arthur Andersen survived as Andersen Consulting. Thus, the Big 4 was born. As shown in exhibit 8.4, these firms or professional networks of the surviving Big 4 are remarkably large.

TIP FROM THE TRENCHES

For many years, people thought that the global accounting firms had an unfair competitive advantage over other consulting firms because many companies required an audit from one of the Big 8 firms. Audits got a foot in the door that could subsequently lead to very lucrative consulting engagements. Many people believed that this represented an inherent conflict of interest. This remains unresolved, although in 2018, KPMG became the first of the remaining Big 4 accounting firms to publicly pledge to stop offering consulting services to large audit clients in the United Kingdom following a series of high-profile scandals.

It has always been clear that in order to meet external standards, accounting firms had to remain independent—that is, accounting firms cannot be owned by law firms or consulting firms. However, this same standard has not been required of consulting firms. The Enron scandal definitely changed things for professional services firms. In 2000, Arthur Andersen received slightly more than half of the $52 million of consulting work from Enron (Abelson and Glater 2002). The scandal uncovered significant violations by executives at Enron and Arthur Andersen, resulting in bankruptcy for Enron and dissolution of Arthur Andersen accounting because of the destruction of audit-related documents and other crimes. Some of the scandal clearly revolved around inappropriate interaction between audit and consulting activities.

Exhibit 8.5: Comparison of Audit to Consulting Revenue for Big 4 Firms

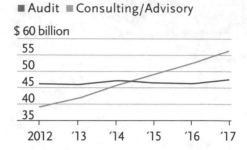

Note: Consulting/advisory includes revenue from risk, financial, and transaction advisory services.
Source: Adapted from Ernst & Young, Deloitte, PwC, and PBMG annual reports.

By 2017, the Big 4 generated $17 billion in consulting fees and, "since 2012, the firms' combined global revenue from consulting and other advisory work has risen 44 percent, compared with just 3 percent growth from auditing" (Rapoport 2018). This represents a dramatic change from when auditing dominated the revenue streams of such firms, as shown in exhibit 8.5.

The article continues: "While consulting can be lucrative—it tends to be more customized, creative, and driven by corporate clients than auditing is—the presence of the business at audit firms has been a concern for years. Investors fear it could cause the firms to take their eyes off the ball when it comes to their core auditing responsibilities and that it would be harder for an audit firm to be impartial if it is also reaping large consulting fees from the same client."

The result is that the potential for conflicts of interest has increased dramatically.

It is not the purpose here to prosecute this issue. Rather, it is important to differentiate between the pure consulting firms and those that are part of accounting firms. Since Enron, the consulting arms for the most part tend to operate independently in order to avoid such conflicts.

INTERNAL CONSULTANTS

Another category of consulting worth noting refers to internal consultants. The name consultant often has "independent" in front of it, indicative of the fact that the consultant is external to the organization to which they consult. In contrast to the independent or external consultant, the internal consultant is on the organization's payroll (i.e., a dependent) and is exclusive to the employing organization. Otherwise, internal consultants can function in all areas similar to external consultants but with different incentives.

Exhibit 8.6: Comparison of Internal and External Consultants

Internal Consultants	External Consultants
Cheaper (one study found that internal strategy consultants could be four to six times cheaper)	Considered more independent
Better understanding of the culture of the organization	Trusted to offer objective advice
More likely to play a role in implementation	Draw from a broader client base
Teams remain internally focused	Broader choice of consultants for a project

Source: Adapted from Consultancy.uk (2020).

The reason that firms support internal consulting teams usually revolves around the desire to save money over the significant fees that are charged by external consultants. Sometimes, there is also a fear of a growing dependence on external advisors that can be at least partially offset by a cadre of internal consultants. One interesting article compares internal to external consultants, as noted in exhibit 8.6.

Clearly, internal consultants can play an important role. Many healthcare engagements have the look and feel of an external consulting team working with an internal team or task force. While this model has proven successful, it is clearly different from working with the independent consultant, which is what we are focused on in this book.

REFERENCES

Abelson, R., and J. D. Glater. 2002. "Enron's Collapse: The Auditors: Who's Keeping the Accountants Accountable?" *New York Times.* Published January 15. www.nytimes.com/2002/01/15/business/enron-s-collapse-the-auditors-who-s-keeping-the-accountants-accountable.html.

Accountingverse.com. 2020. "Big 4 Accounting Firms." Accessed September 14. www.accountingverse.com/articles/big-4-accounting-firms.html.

Consultancy.uk. 2020. "External vs. Internal Consultants." Accessed January 20. www.consultancy.uk/consulting-industry/external-vs-internal-consultants.

Krentz, S. 2019. Interviews with the author. October.

Modern Healthcare. 2019. "Largest Healthcare Management Consulting Firms, 2019." Published August 26. www.modernhealthcare.com/data-lists/40389/largest-healthcare-management-consulting-firms-2019-pdf-and-full-survey-results.

———. 2018. "Largest Healthcare Management Consulting Firms, 2018." Published August 27. www.modernhealthcare.com/article/20180825/DATA/500039366.

Rapoport, M. 2018. "How Did the Big Four Auditors Get $17 Billion in Revenue Growth? Not from Auditing." *Wall Street Journal*. Published April 7. www.wsj.com/articles/how-did-the-big-four-auditors-get-17-billion-in-revenue-growth-not-from-auditing-1523098800.

Valet, V. 2019. "America's Best Management Consulting Firms 2019." *Forbes*. Published March 19. www.forbes.com/sites/vickyvalet/2019/03/19/americas-best-management-consulting-firms-2019/.

Vault. 2020. "Vault Consulting 50." Published January 20. www.vault.com/best-companies-to-work-for/consulting/vault-consulting-rankings-top-50.

CHAPTER 9

Administrative and Operational Functions Common to All Consulting Firms

MOST CONSULTING FIRMS PROVIDE management services, although this does not necessarily translate into how well they manage themselves. In general, traditional consulting firms make three mistakes (Sortwell 2014):

1. They "sell" instead of "solve."
2. They don't reinvigorate their assets.
3. They don't pay enough attention to existing clients.

Practice management is truly an art and some firms simply do this better than others. The global firms enjoy a very positive reputation when it comes to developing their future leaders to manage practices and the firm. That is why they have been in business for so long in a highly competitive industry.

Part of recognizing how firms are different is looking at their internal operational and administrative functions. Having an appreciation for them can help you better understand the business of consulting. These functions can be approached very differently, and they become a reflection of the corporate culture that we hear so much about (more on this in chapter 11). In this section, we will compare and contrast the information that is available on some firms, recognizing that the best information is uncovered by discussions and visits with people from the different firms.

RECRUITING AND STAFFING

For some people, how firms recruit on campus is a big deal. Year after year, firms focus their attention at a limited number of select colleges. This might be driven by alumni who are leaders of the firm. Global firms have a long history of recruiting from some of the best colleges and business schools in the United States. This can shift over time, but many colleges brag about their attractiveness to such recruiters as part of their marketing. You are clearly ahead of the game if you attend one of these colleges where the best firms recruit.

Even if you are not at one of these campuses, that's OK, as I can share from personal experience. When I was in graduate school (not among the top ten), I sent copies of my resume to a long list of consulting firms I found in the Yellow Pages of the Washington-area phone book. I was almost a year out of graduate school when I got called by a Booz Allen recruiter (nowadays referred to as a "talent acquisition team") for an interview. It happened that they were interviewing kids at Harvard but I was not a Harvard grad. I was added to the list of people to be interviewed when Booz Allen visited the campus. Perhaps I ended up being compared to the other candidates from that school. Somehow it all seemed to work out, and it did not hurt that I had a year's experience under my belt, in comparison to some of the other candidates who were undergraduates or still in graduate school.

It should be noted that formal campus recruiting generally occurs with only the medium- to global-sized firms. For the smaller and regional firms, you're better off networking with your alumni association and other contacts to pursue local postings.

Recruiting and staffing seem to go hand in hand. The medium and larger firms tend to have dedicated full-time internal resources accountable for recruiting and staffing. The smaller firms must rely on outside recruiters and internal staff referrals, and some of these firms offer generous "bounties" for referrals who end up getting hired. The smaller firms might also use internships as a more practical way to identify potential staff.

COMPENSATION AND BENEFITS

Clearly, compensation and benefits are two of the main attractions in consulting. These factors can also be differentiators among firms, so management generally spends a great deal of time and effort addressing compensation packages. Most studies suggest that compensation for employees in general tends to be a neutral element (neither a pro nor a con). However, in recruiting, compensation is important, along with benefits. Benefits are an area where significant innovation can occur. Perks such as parental leave, tuition reimbursement, and legal and travel assistance are becoming more common.

Clearly, larger firms have advantages when it comes to compensation and benefits, using creative approaches such as giving employees personal travel credits for client-reimbursed business trips. Some of the larger firms will even help consultants get into a top graduate school program and then pay for it, with a corresponding requirement that they return to the firm for a certain period of time after earning their degrees. These same firms typically leverage this benefit as a particularly attractive component in their recruiting efforts.

Compensation is often a key draw that can be even more attractive when a candidate has some school debt that they carry after graduation. Consulting firms offer some of the highest-paying jobs when one gets out of graduate school, which makes consulting one of the sought-after jobs. It is no coincidence that one of the measures by which recruiters compete for new graduates (especially at the top business schools) is based on average starting salary, which can include an element of loan forgiveness.

There are two general philosophies when it comes to compensation in consulting. The first is to offer a relatively high base salary (often with a signing bonus), and then tie that to performance-based bonus potential. Performance is a way to inspire the consultant involved to have some "skin in the game." The second approach is to offer a smaller base salary, but to then dangle an even more lucrative upside based on performance bonuses. While either approach can be successful, cash is king. In weighing these approaches, you must consider how and when you accumulate cash, and the risk involved. Most firms now include a signing bonus when hired, indicative of the importance that new hires place on cash. Some firms also supplement compensation with such things as "award payments" that recognize individual efforts (e.g., one firm pays "applause awards" of approximately $500 each for outstanding performance and for efforts that demonstrate special initiative).

Nonmonetary benefits, such as those listed below, appear to have significant appeal to millennials (Woodrum and Woodrum 2019):

- Flexible work arrangements and telecommuting
- Family friendly hours, half-days off in the summer, and casual Fridays
- Open floor plans with flexible workspace, formal job sharing/swapping programs, and periodic happy hours
- Formal mentoring programs and professional seminars
- Payment of professional organization dues
- Health savings accounts, health education, and healthy eating initiatives
- Company award programs

While these benefits might not appeal to all generations, firms pay close attention to these surveys.

FINDERS, MINDERS, AND GRINDERS

One of the more important ways of understanding consulting is related to the different tiers in the hierarchy of a traditional consulting firm. Briefly, these are defined as follows:

- **Finders.** These are the people responsible for sustaining the business and managing growth.
- **Minders.** Minders take responsibility for the management of these engagements and act as the primary client liaison.
- **Grinders.** Traditional entry-level position for consultants; those who do most of the analytics and groundwork.

As part of a firm, there is a progression that applies to these positions, as noted in exhibit 9.1.

When I first got involved in consulting with Booz Allen, the word on the street was that the average grinder would stay approximately two years, after which only one in five would rise to the next level of minders. Likewise, the minders would only stay on average another three to five years, after which they were either promoted to finders or they were out. No one said this was an easy business.

TIP FROM THE TRENCHES

The larger, more global firms generally like to develop their future leaders from within. Global firms employ a traditional model that seeks candidates from the top business schools, trains them, and then culls from their ranks the future leaders of the firm. Similar to law firms and accounting firms, they try to recruit the best, recognizing that the rate of attrition moving up the ranks is high.

Exhibit 9.1: Finders, Minders and Grinders

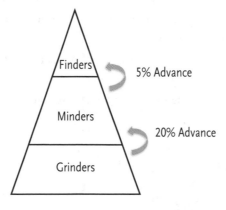

Grinders, as the name implies, do most of the analytics and groundwork, although some of the more sophisticated analytics are being delegated to a specialized internal division devoted to these efforts. Grinders tend to gather the data, analyze it, participate in the interviews, draft the reports, and develop original drafts of the deliverables. They have client contact, at least at the lower levels, but they can stay entirely in the background for certain engagements. They might be assisted by research associates or others with similar positions. These employees have specific tools at their disposal and are well versed in the formats used for various types of studies.

Grinders work with a minder (manager) on a given engagement and might be involved in two to five different engagements at the same time, each with a different pace. Grinders keep track of their time with expectations of anywhere from 75 to 90 percent billing targets. For 220 billable days a year, this keeps people busy, to say the least. One learns quickly in this profession to stay billable and raise your hands when work starts to wane. The culture in these bigger firms, if you want to get ahead, is not to stay long "on the beach" (unbillable). The most productive grinders generally have no problem staying busy because savvy minders tend to go after the most productive grinders, who in turn make them look good.

The primary skills for grinders include writing, analysis, problem-solving, interviewing, and presentation prep. Tables and exhibits are their currency, along with presentations and reports. The training they receive is commensurate with these skills. Generally, grinders are not involved so much in the sales process, other than perhaps contributing to writing proposals and related presentation materials. Of course, this varies by the size of firms; grinders at smaller firms tend to get involved in more activities earlier. Some firms invest very serious time and resources in training their entry-level consultants through initiatives such as the Deloitte Farm (see the later section on training). Some people clearly wash out at the grinder level after about two years because they lack writing or analytical skills, but usually the vetting process identifies these skills during the recruiting period. A self-selection process usually takes place after two years based on feedback from the firm and/or experiences that the consultant has had.

Those who are promoted to minders take on more responsibility as the managers of engagements. Their currency is a job done well, on time, and on budget. Minders also mentor grinders and keep the clients happy, in addition to keeping their finders happy. With clients, minders are involved in higher-level interviews and provide guidance to the overall results (findings, conclusions, and recommendations). Along with finders, minders might be involved in the initial sales effort. They will always be asked by their finders to identify add-on potential with clients—that is, any additional work that might be warranted upon completion of the current assignment. The add-on work might not be related to the current assignment, but something the minder identified while on-site. Minders may be involved at some level as a liaison with the client. They may not always be the primary contact, but sometimes they are.

Note that only one in five grinders are expected to rise to this next level. Some attrition is natural, because consulting simply isn't for everyone. Many leave due to consulting's lifestyle (lots of travel and long hours), added responsibility (do not want more), disinterest in sales or inability to sell (truly a different skill set from analytics), poor management and mentoring skills, or low productivity (inability to manage tight budgets). Other grinders impress their clients and get hired away from the firm. This is not uncommon.

Gaining a promotion to the minder level is a big achievement that is widely recognized in and out of the consulting world. Minders are fungible, having acquired skills that are easily transferable into line management positions at client sites. What keeps minders in the consulting world is high salaries, stimulating client work, and the prospect of a future promotion to full partnership (or ownership).

Finders represent the pinnacle of the profession. For those few lucky enough to make the cut to the highest level, the skill set changes dramatically with a specific emphasis on sales and growth. This is a truly difficult transition for some people because the requirements, while cumulative in some respects, are also quite distinct from the grinder and minder stages. It is for this reason that only a small percentage (about 5 percent of those who started as grinders) will rise to this level. As finders, it is necessary to grow the business, and those who do are known as *rainmakers*, although not all finders are rainmakers. Rainmakers more accurately describe the few people within each firm that are most prolific in their ability to generate client-based work.

To be a finder, experience is critical, as is the ability to sell both your personal brand and the firm's brands. At this level, consultants usually have developed an area of expertise and a strong network of clients and contacts. They have published articles or books, given numerous speeches, and have a list of clients who will vouch for their talents. Their practice has reached critical mass in which their experience speaks for itself and they enjoy some name recognition (i.e., their personal brand). In the larger firms, these practices are linked to firm capabilities.

Not all finders are partners/owners. Many firms require finders to generate a certain level of growth. Often, attaining ownership level involves a financial buy-in that then provides access to a compensation pool[1] that is not available to non-owners. There might be other benefits as well, including pension enhancement, expense accounts, and so forth.

---

1. Calculated by what remains after accounting for normal operating expenses and capital investment.

It is also at the finder stage that some individuals realize that they have built a sufficient personal brand to the extent that they become interested in striking out on their own as a new firm or solo practice. Noncompete clauses often require that a person leaving the firm be prohibited from calling on a client of that firm for a year or two after leaving. As a result, those leaving established firms often have to find new clients with whom to launch their independent practice. Firms try hard to make this a genuine hurdle that inhibits consultants from leaving, but it has proven difficult to legally enforce noncompete clauses for more than a year or two in most states.

MARKETING AND SALES

Marketing and sales are such important functions to any consulting firm that they are given special treatment in this chapter, and they might be among the biggest differentiators among firms. David Maister (1993) sets up this challenge nicely in describing the wary purchaser of professional services:

> I'm skeptical. I've been burned before by these kinds of people. I get a lot of promises: How do I know whose promise I should buy? I'm concerned that you either can't or won't take the time to understand what makes my situation special. In short, will you deal with me in the way I want to be dealt with?

The function of marketing and sales might be the single most important influence on the characterization of a firm's culture. The core business model of consulting firms is completely dependent upon how future business is generated. In chapter 6, we discussed RFPs and the shoot-out process from the client's perspective. Accordingly, we spend some time in this chapter delving into some of the mechanics of marketing and sales to gain more insight into the different components that go into marketing and sales from the firm's perspective.

Before getting into this, however, there is another way of looking at sales that is important to discuss, given its relevance to consulting. Business professional and motivational speaker Dr. Nido Qubein (2011) has written and spoken extensively about how sales is misunderstood. He emphasizes that sales as a basic life skill is part of "positioning ourselves for success," and he likes to refer to sales as "building relational capital." He distinguishes between positioning and sales. Sales, he says, is really about a progression of key questions:

> Why should this person do business with me?
> How hard is it for another person to imitate me?
> If I am in the market to buy what you are selling, why would I think of you first?

He stresses that we must shift from "training to educating." We must understand the "why" of a particular offering (e.g., why we added this feature to a piece of equipment) and not just learn the talking points related to the "what" (e.g., you activate it by turning this switch). It is with this broader concept of positioning that we discuss how firms try to differentiate themselves when it comes to marketing and sales.

PROPOSAL WRITING

How a firm develops and submits a proposal is clearly an extension of its brand. Not all firms embrace competitive proposals. McKinsey, for example, has created a culture built around the tenet that those in the company "don't sell." Instead, they position themselves through elaborate means of marketing their intellectual property for clients who face a challenge. Other firms are able to rely on sole-source opportunities that have been cultivated over time through their brand. But most firms must go through a competitive process for future business. Who writes proposals? When? How many? How are they organized? How do they appear? Are the writers also the people responsible for delivering the end product? These are among the important questions related to proposal writing. Most proposals are organized in a similar fashion:

- Our Understanding of the Situation
- Proposed Scope of Work
- Staffing, Cost, and Timetable
- Qualifications to Do This Work

Some parts of the proposal are clearly boilerplate, like the firm's qualifications, while others are highly customized, such as understanding and budget. Staffing includes the resumes of those with relevant experience. The proposal should also convey how the team is organized (budget will include hours by staff level by billing rate, which may or may not be shared as part of the proposal) and who is in charge. Finally, references from similar client work are usually required. Sometimes selections will be made on the basis of the proposal alone. For the larger jobs, the proposal is used to select the finalists, who will be asked to attend a shoot-out.

SHOOT-OUTS

Because consulting is a competitive business, consulting firms are often required to make presentations to the prospective client in addition to submitting a proposal. Presentations can vary considerably depending on the client and the engagement.

For example, for strategy work, which tends to be quite involved, I would generally insist on meeting with the client before submitting a proposal. Obviously, this is not a practical approach to every type of consulting. The most common approach is to submit a competing proposal with the hope that you get selected among the finalists to meet with and present to the prospective client. In other words, the purpose of the proposal is to get to the next level of making a presentation. Some RFP processes involve *bidder conferences*, during which questions can be asked and additional information is shared. This can be a conference call or a meeting in person, and such meetings can be individual to each bidder or for all bidders at the same time.

The proposal tends to be rather static and not very interactive. This is the opposite of the presentation, when the team presents and the clients can see the whites of your eyes, and you can see theirs. There is really no substitute for the shoot-out in that it truly allows for a more intimate interaction. How does the team from firm A *make you feel* in comparison to the team from firm B?

Firms make significant investments preparing for shoot-outs because this is the opportunity to shine. Often, it is *the* differentiator for the client in deciding between Firm A and Firm B. To illustrate this point, I offer a recent story from James McCraigh of The One Page Business Plan Company:[2]

> A few years ago, I had the opportunity to make a presentation to a small group of consultants; a couple of them worked for Chevron. They had just completed a screening process for a multi-million consulting project. In brief . . . here's what they shared with me:
>
> 1. First consultants eliminated were ME CENTERED. . . . They dominated the conversation, told all about their processes, products, past clients. It was all about them. They asked few questions.
> 2. Second set of consultants eliminated were CONTENT or FACT CENTERED. . . . They knew everything about everything. They quoted all of the latest management books, they were able to quote facts from all of the top surveys and analysis, they had a quote, a fact, and the references to back up everything they said. They were undoubtedly very knowledgeable . . . but without a doubt, they were not going to work with this client.
> 3. Third set of consulting firms eliminated were PRODUCT CENTERED. . . . These firms offered their product solutions long before they understood the underlying problems. My friend indicated that these firms were outstanding at demonstrating their products and espousing the features of the products . . . but nobody cared. These firms took no time to understand the real underlying issues.

---

2. Shared with permission from James McCraigh.

4. The final two firms were CLIENT ORIENTED. . . . They took time to fully interview the prospective client and understand the underlying issues. They asked tons of questions. . . . Finally my friend asked them if they thought they had a solution to the problem. They said not quite . . . and then asked another question!

Take time to get to know your prospects . . . and, just about the time you think you are ready to offer a solution, ask another question! As my friend was wrapping up, I told him I frequently say to prospects that The One Page Business Plan is not for every organization (which is the truth). He said, when you come to present One Page Business Plan at Chevron (which he did), make that your first statement. He said the executives will then listen to the rest of what you have to say!

Of course, not every client is looking for the same thing in a consultant. Attempting to understand specifically what the client is looking for certainly is part of the competitive landscape. Too many firms spend the whole shoot-out touting their wares instead of taking the opportunity to better understand the client and its needs. Indeed, better listening is an integral part of most sales training programs, where the simple test after such a presentation is "Who did the most talking?" (Rackham 1988). If it is the consultant, the sale is not likely; if it is the client, you likely connected and have a better chance of gaining their business.

SALES MANAGEMENT/CUSTOMER RELATIONS MANAGEMENT

Because securing client engagements is the lifeblood of consulting, it is understood that how someone gets credit for such sales is very important. For the senior consultant or partner, much if not the majority of their compensation will be linked to sales. In smaller firms, where the contacts are personal and most of the business that is generated can be traced to a single rainmaker, such credit is straightforward and easy to manage. But as the firms get larger and the engagements involve multidisciplinary teams, it becomes far more complex. Key people can devote significant time and sweat equity in the generation of a client opportunity, only to have to share the credit to the point that they receive relatively little reward for this effort. This can very be frustrating. More to the point, it can have significant monetary implications and can be demotivating.

While the monetary implications are important and very clear, it is the psychological cost of this culture that is of more concern. If such situations adversely affect the compensation of some key executives, this becomes a serious challenge.

The firm will certainly benefit from the successful completion of such large and complex engagements, and it will likely lead to future growth. But an unintended consequence will be that executives get frustrated and feel they have been treated unfairly. Over time, this frustration can cause people to migrate away from such engagements in favor of a more individualized practice in which they will get more of the credit for growth. Or they will leave the firm outright.

Elaborate systems have been developed by firms to help deal with these issues. Initiatives such as parsing the sales process into "referral credit" and using a shared points system can help create an improved sense of fairness. Yet, it takes effort and a transparent arbitration process to make such a system work well. You should understand that this situation is nearly unavoidable. It simply comes with the territory as firms grow. It is not an exaggeration to suggest that this issue alone is as responsible as any other for why many new firms are formed when key executives decide to leave and create their own practices. Many of the better-known firms today were founded by displaced executives from larger firms.

TIP FROM THE TRENCHES

Credit for sales is one of the trickiest elements of consulting, especially in its impact on overall compensation and promotions. More than any other factor, it is probably responsible for why people leave a firm and/or why firms break up. Stories are told about the importance of getting sales credit from accounting, especially in the larger firms, even to the point of fights breaking out in the corridor that leads to the accounting office as senior members argue over credit for a sale. Most firms have some form of arbitration to deal with disagreements. It should not be taken lightly.

Sales management is foundational for firms on a growth trajectory. These firms tend to devote considerable resources to systems and training that foster new client generation. Clearly, this is a valuable skill to any consulting enterprise. It is noteworthy that many firms now invest in customer relations management (CRM) software. Oracle and Salesforce, for example, have become some of the fastest growing companies in the world focused on fostering sales growth. These are complicated subscription programs that integrate with other office functions such as email, and help to track and capture potential leads that can grow the business. Anyone who has been through the process of integrating CRM software into the daily routine will tell you that these are powerful programs that require an enormous amount of time to learn and integrate into your work routines.

SPONSORSHIPS

Many consulting firms rely on paid sponsorships to generate visibility and name recognition. Sponsorship comes in different forms. A consulting firm can provide sponsorship through a professional association (e.g., the American College of Healthcare Executives) or a private group like Becker. The consulting company pays for recognition during the year or at conferences by providing speakers or sponsoring sessions. Some sponsors provide letterhead and other related marketing materials. The idea is to get the company's name in front of key buyers.

Generally, smaller firms have limited resources for this form of marketing. They are more inclined to provide speakers, write articles and white papers, and find other ways to gain recognition. The larger firms will spread the wealth with key groups that prove to be helpful in generating leads to result in new business. They will also track these investments very closely.

Some firms have aggressively sponsored charity events as more of a socially conscious way of endearing them to potential clients. These events have been particularly successful in giving employees an opportunity to express their views in tangible ways that bring benefits to a particular charitable cause.

CLIENT REPRESENTATIVES

The bigger firms have found that a client representative approach works well for them, both for generating business and for securing long-lasting client relationships. Under this model, seasoned executives who have strong relationships with leaders in a given industry are hired by major consulting firms and other healthcare firms, such as private equity, suppliers, drug manufacturers, and others, to help get the firms in front of key executives in an effort to grow their business. This approach has proved to be an effective door-opener.

CROSS-SELLING

Cross-selling is truly an enigma in healthcare consulting. The assumption is that if you can sell product A, then you can also sell products B and C. While this can certainly work when selling services from different practices (e.g., strategy, finance, operations), it gets more complicated when trying to sell unrelated services (e.g., staffing) and products (e.g., pharmaceuticals). Virtually all of the big firms spend considerable time discussing how to successfully practice cross-selling.

Part of the challenge is defining what cross-selling is. Is it cross-selling if I create an opportunity to bring to my client another partner who offers a different set of services? Sure. Is it cross-selling if I am able to get the client interested in a different service that the firm offers? Yes, but these are not the same.

What they have in common is knowledge about the other service. You must understand this other service—what is recommended, what it can accomplish, and how it is approached. Ideally, there is also some knowledge about the "hooks" that are needed to gain traction with the client related to the service.

The challenge is subtle. Understandably, consultants become most associated with the particular service that they offer, less so with services offered by others.

When I first got involved in consulting, a generalist approach was favored, and this approach continues to thrive among some of the global firms. The client today tends to have more specialized needs, and a consultant becomes associated with the engagement that they completed for that client. The client sees the consultant as an expert in that area, but not necessarily in others. It therefore becomes more difficult for that same consultant to sell service B or C. I have been with several larger firms, and I learned that a common frustration is that when we completed one type of project, the client hired a competing firm for another service that we also offered. The client did not realize that our firm also had expertise in that area.

What happened? Sometimes, we simply did not know that the client was in the market for such a service. Just as important, the client did not realize that our firm offered that service. Other times, while we successfully completed one type of service, the client finds it difficult to believe that the same consultant or firm is capable of providing the other service. Sometimes, the client wants to hire the specialty or niche firm that *only* does that service. There is certainly a robust market for niche firms in certain services (e.g., fair market value, facilities planning, equipment planning).

TRAINING

Several of the bigger firms train new consultants using a cohort approach. In this way, people "share a foxhole" together, as they say in the military. The new consultants receive training together, they help each other, they put in long hours together, and they share the impact of the new consultant experience.

I believe that training is a fertile area in which firms can genuinely differentiate themselves. The global firms have invested significant resources in the development of their people. This is perhaps a result of Jack Welch's well-known investment in GE's training center at Crotonville on the Hudson River in New York. "GE spends more than $1 billion annually on employee development around the world, and this training center is the focal point. Every year, as many as 12,000 employees trek to the woods in Westchester to visit. . . . If the Boston headquarters is GE's head, then Crotonville is its heart" (Chesto 2017).

In another example of consultant training, Deloitte now has Deloitte University (the old Perot Ranch outside of Dallas), which it describes as "The Leadership Center." This is where Deloitte consultants are sent for training. The subheadings on the web page read, *Growing the World's Best Leaders*; *Where Ideas Prosper*; *Work That Really Matters*. The page also boasts that Deloitte is able to "maintain a robust pipeline of promising new talent" by identifying candidates *at the college level*. Think they take training and recruiting seriously?

SOURCE OF FUNDING

In my experience, the culture and feel of a consulting firm have a lot to do with its revenue cycles. Unlike many other businesses, consulting businesses' revenue cycles correspond to the typical length of their engagements. Some focus on shorter-term engagements and some are longer, and the cash flow follows that pattern.

Specialty firms, like those that specialize in IT, tend to tie their finances to a revenue cycle corresponding to the typical client engagement of 12–18 months. Facility firms focus on the duration of the project, whether it relates to design (e.g., architectural and engineering) or construction (e.g., construction management). Strategy firms tend to focus more on the four- to eight-month strategic planning or business plan engagement cycle. Every type of engagement has its own typical cycle. This is why most larger consulting firms offer a diversified portfolio of services having differing revenue cycles. The result is that risk mitigation is based on the diverse cash flows of different engagement cycles.

Growth requires access to capital. In some cases, consulting firms partner with equity firms to invest in growth. In other cases, consultants went to the public markets for funding. In one rather unique case, the user groups (hospitals and health systems) formed their own membership organization to share best practices. This firm—Premier Inc.—ultimately went public, thus benefitting the original founding organizations that continue to buy services from Premier, largely on a subscription basis.

Ownership comes into play with respect to financial accountability. While the differences might seem inconsequential at the lower levels of the firm, they become more apparent at higher levels, and crystal clear when reaching the partner stage. It is about accountability and risk. Cash flow affects the company's ability to meet ongoing obligations in addition to influencing future-oriented decisions like hiring. Understanding the financial nuances of ownership can be important as you consider what might be a compatible home for your practice. The levels of financial investment in ownership are summarized in exhibit 9.2.

In its simplest form in a solo practice, the mission of the consultant can be reasonably assumed to be serving clients in order to make a living. The mission gets more complicated as more people are added and the firm takes on a more sustainable business persona. It is at this stage that the dynamic between serving

Exhibit 9.2: Alternative Ownership Structures of Consulting Firms

Dimension		Type of ownership			
	Sole proprietorship	Private partnership without financial partner	Private partnership with financial partner	Public partnership	Public corporation
Access to capital	Limited to funds of owner and secured lines of credit	Limited to joint partner funding and secured lines of credit	Combination of joint partner funding and equity/loans provided by private equity	Access to public equity markets	Access to public equity markets
Risk	Moderate to high	Moderate to high	Moderate to high	Moderate	Moderate
Accountability	Limited to owner	Limited among partners	High, depending on culture of financial partner	High	High
Operating focus	Sustainability	Growth	Cash is king and focus is on maintaining steady flow of work	Focus on divisions and rainmakers generating future business	Similar to public partnership with more focus on acquisitions of smaller groups
Growth potential	Limited	Focus on partners with limited access to capital	Focus on partners with access to capital	Good	Good
Structural implications	Simple	More formal	Significant	Significant	Significant

clients and making owners wealthy can be noticed. Values matter, and they influence how services are delivered. What is the firm's attitude toward clients? When there is a conflict between revenues and client services, what wins out? Sometimes this conflict can be subtle. Other times it seems black-and-white.

Firms that carry outside investors along with them (either private equity or publicly traded firms) experience more pressure to generate a sustainable revenue stream. How do these firms put clients first? Some seem to have been formed merely to be able to amass wealth by focusing on a lucrative exit strategy (e.g., sale).

Many years ago, one such firm brought me to New York City to discuss the potential acquisition of my firm. At a $50-per-person lunch with one of the partners at an upscale restaurant, I was told that they had just finished a weekend in the office with more than 20 people involved in a rush job for a specific client. Little did they know that I had just completed an internal retreat with my small firm (15 people), where the main topic was work/life balance. Talk about a clash of cultures! It was a short courtship. (See chapter 11 for more discussion on culture.)

BILLING

Not all firms bill their services on a time-and-expenses basis, because there have been some innovations in how consulting firms charge. Alternatives have developed evolving from this traditional approach, as noted in exhibit 9.3.

The newest forms of contracting are risk-based and subscription. Risk-based contracting can be controversial. Many firms have embraced this approach but on a selective basis. Some firms, like Berkley Research Group, use this as their primary form of compensation. They have built their business working with organizations that are experiencing financial stress, many of which get into technical default on their bonds. Bond counsel, who provides oversight on the borrowers for the bond holders, contracts with these firms to intervene and quickly reverse financial performance to be in compliance with key bond covenants. The consulting firm can then include a performance component with its fees tied to the "savings" that it derives. It is an understatement to suggest that this can be controversial, as there are many potential reasons for savings and ways to interpret the results of such practices.

Other firms that have used this approach have tried to restrict its application to areas that are less subject to dispute, and where they might offer interim management. This adds transparency to the claim that they can take credit for a piece of the savings.

Exhibit 9.3: Alternative Billing Approaches for Consulting Services

Billing method	How it works	Mostly used for . . .	Advantages	Disadvantages
Time and expenses	Hours × rate	Open-ended engagements	Tends to involve shared risk with the client and a "not to exceed" component	Harder to budget for; more subject to disputes
Fixed fee	$X	Well-defined projects; repetitive work	Easy to budget for; no surprises	Lack of flexibility
Risk-based	Usually involves a base fee with incentives for performance	Quick-turnaround engagements that improve cash flow	Firms share risk of performance and are rewarded based on results	Challenging to determine measurable level of improvement with precision
Retainer	Usually monthly fee that "reserves" a certain amount of consulting time	Process-type engagements over extended periods with many moving pieces	Easy to budget for; provides for an ongoing level of effort	Can be hard to terminate
Subscription	Usually annual fee for set of services	Research-related studies	Reserves time to devote to issues as they arise	Commitment is made, but need might not exist or be greater/less than needed

The subscription model holds significant interest for many consulting firms. This type of pricing is generically known as *flexible consumption*. Flexible consumption includes both subscription and usage-based monetization models. It actually traces its origins to the telecommunications industry, where pricing was historically based on usage (remember when the cell phone bill allowed for up to X hours of time?). While the usage-based model went away with the advent of "unlimited" plans, the perks of customer loyalty remained. Amortized deals on new expensive phones locked in the user for multiple years. Likewise, the purpose of subscription for consulting is to lock in the client to contracting for future services, rather than incurring unnecessary time and expenses to foster competition among multiple firms.

The challenge of consulting is to provide an ongoing revenue stream, and the nature of consulting makes this difficult because most work is of a relatively short duration and with different clients. The ability to capture a steady revenue stream using a "membership model" (i.e., a subscription) helps to smooth out the seasonal ebbs and flows of consulting. A good example of the subscription model of billing in healthcare is Advisory Board (now part of Optum).

Advisory Board can be characterized as a major disruptor to traditional healthcare consulting. In many respects, it has worked to displace other consultants in the industry by providing more research rather than consulting. Advisory Board was founded in 1979 by David Bradley with only five employees. Its purpose was to provide targeted research in key industries, including healthcare. It is a "best practices firm helping healthcare organizations worldwide to improve performance using a combination of research and data" (Advisory Board 2020).

Advisory Board went public and reached several thousand employees before the company split and sold for $2.58 billion many years later. A "consulting and software company" at the time of the sale, the healthcare business was sold to UnitedHealth (Optum) and the education unit was sold to Vista Equity Partners in 2017.

At its apex, Advisory Board was able to penetrate a remarkable percentage of community hospitals and health systems in the United States by providing insightful research publications based largely on interviews and literature searches. Through a proven method of training young, energetic college graduates, it was able to leverage this research into regular, highly scripted presentations and research papers regarding key trends and innovations, which were presented to healthcare executives at many meetings conducted at attractive destinations.

Advisory Board's market penetration was so successful that many of the interviews conducted by its staff were with member organizations. To some extent, its business model could therefore be characterized as interviewing its members, then packaging collective best practices and selling them back to those same members. The importance of the subscription business model, at least in part, is in eliminating the costly and time-consuming process of competing for consulting work. Advisory Board already had a relationship with many hospitals throughout the United States as a result of its educational subscription programs. Leveraging consulting was simply a matter of adding at the end of an educational presentation, "*And we can help you with this.*" Unbundling packets of commodity-based consulting was relatively simple and lucrative considering the sales price of the firm.

As noted before, most of the work of Advisory Board might more accurately be characterized as research rather than consulting. The subscription fee applied mostly to the research part, where a certain number of reports were routinely issued in key subject areas. Members could subscribe to the complete offering or to select components. Then there were some "customized" studies. They also offered some highly regarded training programs ("higher education membership programs") for key executives.

After several attempts to launch a consulting practice, the consulting segment of Advisory Board was vested in a few limited prepackaged operational studies (H*Works) that focused on specific areas for performance improvement such as imaging, as well as physician integration studies and related business intelligence and data analytics programs. The physician integration part of the practice was added when it acquired the Southwind Health Partners practice (founded in 1998 by John Deane). The practice was located in Nashville, the mecca for hospital equity firms like HCA and CHS (Wilde Mathews and Cooper 2017). Part of the reason for this acquisition was likely the potential linking of this firm with those hospital equity firms in Nashville, where Advisory Board had little penetration prior to that time. After five years, the Southwind name was dropped in a rebranding effort that labeled the firm as Advisory Board Consulting and Management. Southwind had also worked out an innovative marketing deal that placed its physician practice work in front of all member organizations of Voluntary Hospitals of America, a nationwide consortium of major hospitals and health systems.

Other consulting firms have used a subscription approach for such services as financial planning, like Kaufman Hall, and affinity membership meetings, such as Voluntary Hospitals of America. It is expected that future consulting firms will continue to standardize some services under a subscription model, much the same way that Apple is growing its service components to its users.

WRITE-DOWNS AND OVERRUNS

Financial management of consulting firms is relatively straightforward. Revenues come in and expenses are paid. The vast majority of revenues are consulting fees, with expenses that can be reimbursed and administrative fees on top. Reimbursable fees cover the usual travel expenses, charged at cost. Some firms also charge an administrative fee that can be used to cover a variety of costs, including office support. It is also a technique that can be used to charge an add-on fee for stringers (e.g., cost plus 10 percent) when assembling virtual teams. The bulk of expenses for consulting firms are focused on salaries and benefits.

Write-downs—where fees charged turn out to be less than budgeted—and *overruns*—where time and fees allocated to a project exceed budget—can easily be overlooked as a challenge. I can remember virtually every write-down and overrun I have ever had. They are memorable not because they have been frequent but because they have been consequential. Of the more than 400 clients and thousands of engagements I have had, I have had fewer than ten major write-downs and overruns over the years. They were expensive, though, and disappointing to say the least.

Write-downs and overruns can occur for a number of reasons. For example, sometimes the budget is inadequate or there is a disagreement over a portion of an engagement. Discrepancies can also come up at the end of an engagement when there was "scope creep" that involved some additional services that the client requested but exceed the original scope of the engagement. Even though this additional work might have been accounted for separately by the firm, failure to gain prior agreement with the client runs the risk of not being able to collect for the extra work. In another case, there was disagreement about how to approach an engagement after completing much of the work. In yet another situation, the engagement was terminated early before some back-end tasks were completed. So the work was booked but only partially completed. Finally, sometimes a consultant on the team turns out to be less than competent, and the client insists that the portion of fees associated with this individual be backed out of the final fees.

Turnaround engagements can be particularly dicey because there is often turnover, and CEOs can be very vulnerable. In one case, a CEO was terminated toward the end of an engagement and an interim CEO was charged with reducing expenses immediately, including negotiating write-downs with all vendors. That was not a pretty picture. It is easy to understand why this is a part of the business that no one likes to discuss, but it is a reality of consulting.

REFERENCES

Advisory Board. 2020. "About." Accessed March 31. www.advisory.com/about-us/our-history.

Chesto, J. 2017. "GE's Secret Weapon Is Its Training Center on Hudson River." *Boston Globe*. Published February 13. www.bostonglobe.com/business/2017/02/13/hudson-river-secret-corporate-weapon/Iu2txUamtMMT94HZ38ztNM/story.html.

Maister, D. H. 1993. *Managing the Professional Service Firm*. New York: Simon & Schuster.

Qubein, N. 2011. "10 Crucial Factors in Positioning Yourself for Success." SpeakersOffice. Published March 28. www.speakersoffice.com/10-crucial-factors-in-positioning-yourself-for-success-by-dr.-nido-qubein.

Rackham, N. 1988. *Spin Selling*. New York: McGraw-Hill.

Sortwell, A. 2014. "The 3 Common Mistakes Traditional Consulting Firms Make." *TrustedPeer Blog*. Published December 8. www.trustedpeer.com/blogs/3-common-mistakes-traditional-consulting-firms-make.

Wilde Mathews, A., and L. Cooper. 2017. "Advisory Board Co. to Be Split and Sold for $2.58 Billion, Including Debt Consulting and Software Company to Sell Health-Care Business to UnitedHealth, Education Unit to Vista Equity Partners." *Wall Street Journal*, August 29.

Woodrum, S. C., and D. L. Woodrum. 2019. "Designing a Nonmonetary Compensation Program." *Healthcare Consultants Forum Newsletter*, Summer.

CHAPTER 10

Specific Examples of Healthcare Consulting Firms

HERMAN SMITH, AMHERST ASSOCIATES, McManus Associates, Ryan Advisory, APM Management Consultants, Gordon Friesen, and James A. Hamilton Associates are among the many well-known firms that were around when I first got in the business. Today, none of them exist. What happened?

Some firms had a relatively short shelf life and were sold outright, with the founding partners retiring shortly thereafter or after satisfying an earn-out requirement. Other firms that had sustainable size and expertise merged or were "rolled up" to achieve critical mass. Still others folded due to lack of business or the founders simply retired. Consulting to healthcare organizations has been a fluid business.

Yet, out of this era of transition, as hospitals grew and expanded while Medicare and Medicaid were implemented in the 1970s and '80s, a number of firms grew to the point where they are well established today. Among those names are Kaufman Hall, The Chartis Group, ECG Management Consultants (formerly Executive Consulting Group), and Navigant and Huron, to name a few. Each one has their own story to tell and a somewhat unique approach to the business, and we will examine a few of these to illustrate some of the differences that exist.

SOLO PRACTICE AND VIRTUAL FIRMS

In solo and virtual firms you are creating your own business. This means that you possess the acumen to run your own firm instead of relying on others (i.e., outsourcing the function to another existing firm). There were two different times in my career in which I qualified as a solo practice. Initially, I was in solo practice at the age of 30. I could only take on smaller engagements that I could complete on my own. My business grew to the point where I needed to outsource some of the work and/or add some expertise, or supplement my limited time with other personnel. Initially, this outsourcing was limited. Over time, it became apparent I needed to pick up some full-time staff, which I did.

I sold my first firm and then went to work for the company that purchased it. The second time I was technically in solo practice was when I left that firm. I did so only after meeting the required transition period as a condition of the sale (three years). This second time, I made a conscious effort to employ the virtual firm model by taking a "best in breed" approach, where I would bring in seasoned veterans from other firms to supplement my capabilities. This worked particularly well in strategic planning engagements, where I liked to set up smaller work groups. These groups drilled down on key issues to gain insight and commitment that would then form the core strategies of the plan. Areas such as quality improvement and physician engagement benefited from other experts who were well versed in the many breakthrough strategies of the time.

In another example of a solo practice, some years ago Matt Steiner broke away from CHI Systems as he was getting closer to retirement, but for several years he continued to provide operational support on a regular basis to a small group of steady clients. His model was created around a dashboard of operational and strategic measures. Today, it might be referred to as *coaching*. The dashboard was simply a device used to manage a regular meeting agenda in which Matt acted as a sounding board for issues and ideas. CEOs from these smaller organizations often complain that they have no one to talk to or share ideas with. Given their relatively small staff, there is immense value in having an experienced person with whom to interact. Steiner performed this service. His clients were longstanding and already trusted his capabilities from many prior engagements. He was not looking to grow his practice, but rather to support these clients until he ultimately decided to retire. More than a few people would envy this approach to consulting as a nice soft landing into retirement. I dare say his clients might agree with that as well.

A nuance of solo practice, especially involving a more experienced consultant, is the ability to be more selective about taking on clients and engagements. While not all such practices do things this way, I essentially avoided competitive bid situations through the virtual practice because I had a relatively loyal set of clients. I liked to say that I no longer wrote proposals, I wrote engagement letters. Most solo firms have neither the resources nor the inclination to get involved in lengthy competition for clients.

REPRESENTATIVE SMALL AND SOLO FIRMS

Because this is a particularly important category, I have selected several firms to illustrate how such practices work and can be differentiated from one another. These small firms include both general and specialty firms. One obvious attribute they share is the limited capacity to complete work without assembling a larger team or collaborating with other firms.

Most consultants have a story of how they came to the business, and many have a story about how they got out as well. Solo consultants tend to stay in it for the long run. As you read the stories below, note how many different firms they had been with before they went solo. It is also interesting to note what keeps them excited about consulting. We have selected a few different examples, where some practices were more general in scope and others were more specialized, as noted in exhibit 10.1.

Exhibit 10.1: A Snapshot of Three Solo Firms

Firm/Founder	Lifton Associates James Lifton, LFACHE	Krentz Consulting, LLC Suzie Krentz	Nutter Group, LLC Roger Nutter
Focus	Strategy consulting focused on medical staff and growth	Business strategy for hospitals and healthcare systems, with particular expertise in children's hospitals	Executive search for healthcare organizations
Structure	Limited liability company	Limited liability corporation	Limited liability corporation
Services offered	Medical staff development planning	Strategic planning, service line planning, market and geographic strategies	Executive coaching, compensation studies, executive search, succession planning, board development
Example of clients	Mercy Health, Parish Medical Center	Akron Children's Hospital, Nemours, Vizient	Memorial Health System, Ozarks Medical Center, Wood County Hospital, Thomas Heath, Davis Health System, Deaconess, associations

(continued)

Exhibit 10.1: A Snapshot of Three Solo Firms (*continued*)

Firm/Founder	Lifton Associates James Lifton, LFACHE	Krentz Consulting, LLC Suzie Krentz	Nutter Group, LLC Roger Nutter
How they came to consulting	Joined TriBrook on a chance interview through the University of Chicago	Sister's college roommate called to see if she had an interest in joining a firm she worked for	Interviewed as candidate for human resources position and, though not selected, was offered job as executive search consultant
Firms where they worked	TriBrook; Medicus Systems; Ernst & Young; Chi Systems; Superior Consulting; Arista	Amherst Associates, Inc; Jennings, Ryan and Kolb; Noblis	Witt Associates; Kieffer; Ford; Hadelman
Typical duration of client engagement	1–3 months	2–6 months	3–4 months
About consulting	Grateful to have gone through "Charm School" with Ernst & Young	Grateful to have worked with some really exceptional people early in her career	Who you know helps, but how you serve is what sustains repeat business and referrals
Other	During his more than 40 years of consulting, Jim and his wife have lived in the same house in Park Ridge, Illinois	Works with one other staff member with whom she has worked for 32 years	With family as a priority, Nutter Group was an early firm to go remote/virtual; firm was cofounded with Vikki Bowen Nutter; long-term relationships with clients, candidates, and professional colleagues

Source: Information from interviews conducted in October 2019.

Each of these firms is profiled to demonstrate the careers paths taken by others. As their stories show, it requires some experience to successfully operate a solo or small consulting firm. A client of mine adopted the strategic mantra of "no straight lines," indicative of the lack of predictability and standardization in healthcare. Likewise, the way people come to consulting can vary dramatically, as can the reasons that people make career choices along the way.

THE KRENTZ CONSULTING STORY

Susanna Krentz refers to herself as "The Accidental Consultant." One of six children, Suzie grew up in St. Louis in a family of pastors and academicians. She has three siblings who are college professors. A graduate of Yale University in Art History, Suzie gave little thought to how she might be employed. After graduating in 1980, she returned home and began to wrestle with how to get a job. She ended up spending time with an older brother who lived in Chicago and was a church musician, in addition to pursuing a graduate degree from Northwestern University. A parishioner in his church mentioned that they were hiring people do some temporary work for the American Hospital Association on a CEO survey. After working on this two-week temporary job, Suzie was offered full-time employment on Panel Survey, which was done manually at the time. Self-reporting monthly surveys by 2,000 participating hospitals had to be vetted for accuracy before they were included in the published reports. Not exactly exciting work, but it was her introduction to healthcare.

Suzie became convinced that she should go to business school. She applied and was accepted at the University of Chicago, and began attending school at night. It was around this same time that her sister's roommate from Harvard University called. She mentioned that she was in Chicago and working for a firm, Amherst Associates, that did consulting and was hiring a research associate. As Suzie tells the story, she interviewed with several people and although she felt that she did not impress, she turned out to be the best. Marian Jennings was the leader of the Chicago office for Amherst and later told the story that she feared Suzie was a "poor hire." Suzie interjects that she had no interview experience so that feedback was not surprising. Little did they know, however, that they had hired a career consultant.

Suzie stayed with the firm for four years and split off from them, along with Marian and others, after Amherst went public and was then purchased by HBO (which became HBO/McKesson). After other sales and mergers, Suzie found herself consulting to private sector healthcare organizations at Noblis. Suzie stayed with this firm for almost eight years, serving as the deputy director for health innovation at the time of her departure. It was then that she founded Krentz Consulting with one other employee, who had been with her since 1987.

Leaving big firm life behind, Suzie practices out of a home-based office, as does her longtime colleague. Having now been in solo consulting for 11 years, Suzie appreciates the freedom from many corporate duties such as meetings and performance reviews, and the flexibility afforded by a smaller, nimble practice. She says that technology now makes solo consulting much easier than it used to be: You can provide excellent client service and deliverables without a big infrastructure. As a very small practice, Suzie does her own billing, scheduling, travel, and development of work products. After 32 years working together, Suzie and her colleague have such a seamless working relationship that clients sometimes aren't sure who is talking on a conference call. While Krentz Consulting provides services to a broad range of hospitals and healthcare systems, they have deep expertise with children's hospitals, some of which she has been working with for close to 20 years.

THE LIFTON ASSOCIATES STORY

Jim Lifton refers to himself as a "career consultant." During his more than 40 years of consulting, he has worked mostly with nonprofit hospital clients. At one point, he was offered a partnership at Ernst & Young, but he has spent the bulk of his career in small firms, and operated out of his own solo firm since 2006.

His story is rather unique and colorful, which will not surprise anyone who knows Jim. He graduated from the University of Illinois Urbana-Champaign in 1968 with hopes of going to medical school. Instead he went on to Wayne State University in Michigan for a graduate degree, but that was interrupted by a draft notice from the Army, and he was assigned to the Medical Service Corp at a post near Boston. Upon his honorable discharge, Jim returned to his native Chicago and applied to the vaunted University of Chicago Graduate School of Business. Jim admitted that he was never the best student, but he tested well. This helped him gain acceptance there, during which time alumnus Dick Johnson was interviewing candidates for a program called "hospital administration." With his service in the Army, Jim seemed like the ideal candidate for the program. The interview took place in Dick's new offices where he had just founded TriBrook Group—a healthcare consulting firm. Jim tells the story: "At the time I had the world's worst Fu Manchu mustache," and after the interview Dick said, "If you lose the mustache, I'd like to hire you."

Jim shaved and was on a plane the next day to help with one of TriBrook's first clients in Davenport, Iowa. Jim continued to work part-time for TriBrook for the two years it took him to complete his MBA. After graduating, Jim followed a colleague to Medicus Systems Corporation, where he worked with a variety of healthcare clients. He was assigned about half-time to do work in Chicago on operational and strategic studies at Rush Presbyterian St. Luke's Hospital. He speaks well of his experience at Medicus, from which quite a few people eventually spun off a number of small consulting firms like Lammers & Gershon. Jim then followed a colleague to Ernst & Young, where he stayed for almost 10 years and ended up with an offer to become partner, but this required that he move. Having been based most of his life in Chicago, he decided this was not what he wanted to do.

Like Suzie, Jim was involved in a few acquisitions before he landed with PSI, until it too began to disassemble. It was then that Jim decided that he would venture out on his own as Lifton Associates.

Since 2006, Jim has worked as a solo consultant out of a small office in Park Ridge, Illinois, over a jewelry store near the railroad station. He has maintained a modest practice with clients with whom he does mostly medical staff planning and strategy development. Jim notes that his wife has been gainfully employed during his career (most recently with the American Hospital Association) and has, at times, been the primary breadwinner. He plans to remain in consulting for another five years, when he will reassess the situation—and might reluctantly fold his tent.

THE NUTTER GROUP STORY

Roger Nutter's story begins in West Virginia, where he grew up and graduated from Marshall University in 1975. He started working in Cabell Huntington Hospital at a time when the medical school was being founded, and healthcare captured his interest. He subsequently went to graduate school there while working as a nurse assistant and director of volunteers. His graduate studies started out in clinical psychology, but then shifted into counseling and guidance. What Roger found was there were synergies between what he encountered at the hospital and what he was studying in graduate school. Then a few years later, as funds were reduced from behavioral health during the Carter administration, he needed to rethink his counseling career. He first worked in human resources at a hospital, and then later was hired as a search consultant by Witt Associates. Roger enjoyed the search business but travel was a problem; he was gone four to five days per week. In addition, he was also expected to put in some office time, which proved to be a challenge. He and his second wife, Vikki, decided they could manage their schedules better if they struck out on their own.

By starting Nutter Consulting, Roger and Vikki felt better able to practice their corporate values and still put family first. This worked well for them, and some years later, after they had grown the firm to 15 associates, they sold the business in a full-asset merger to Raymond Karson Associates, located in New Town, Pennsylvania. The core of this new business was sales and staffing with contingent search. Prior to this, Roger worked exclusively in retained search, and it became clear that this was not going to work for him. They eventually repurchased their assets and rebranded as the Nutter Group. Since then they have worked with a few more people, mostly as independent contractors (i.e., virtual firms), attempting to expand into Chicago and Nashville. Roger is quick to point out that the search business is a lucrative part of the staffing industry, but that it is highly competitive, with some of the large firms generating over $1 billion in assets. Because the business is built around relationships, Roger has found a preference among some clients for small firms that they can rely upon for their search needs. Recently,

Roger ended up transferring the firm to Vikki as a minority business to allow her to meet Social Security qualifications. Eventually, Roger plans to migrate to executive coaching with some of his clients. They may also get a few people to start a local search business using their infrastructure. Roger is a fellow of the American College of Healthcare Executives.

REPRESENTATIVE MEDIUM FIRMS

In comparing medium firms to the smaller solo firms, it is interesting to note that most of the medium-sized firms seem to offer many of the same services, but in different ways. These are among the best known firms in healthcare consulting, indicative of just how competitive healthcare consulting has become:

- KaufmanHall
- The Chartis Group
- ECG Management Consultants

Please note that we have relied on the information provided on websites for each of these firms. We have not attempted to offer any qualitative comparisons, other than a reference to awards and Glassdoor ratings. (Full disclosure: I worked for several years as a Principal with ECG Management Consultants.) An overview comparison of these medium-sized consulting firms is outlined in exhibit 10.2.

REPRESENTATIVE GLOBAL FIRMS

The global firms tend to have a more recognized brand (i.e., name recognition) than the others. While most global firms are somewhat involved in healthcare, we have attempted to focus on the ones that stand out as active firms working with providers and not just life sciences—a popular area for the larger firms. The ones we present here are:

- Deloitte Consulting[1]
- PWC
- Navigant

Obviously, extensive information can be found for each of these firms on their websites. We offer a brief profile, as noted in exhibit 10.3.

---

1. Disclosure: I have a daughter who is employed by Deloitte Consulting.

Exhibit 10.2: Comparison of Medium General Healthcare Consulting Firms

Variable	KaufmanHall	The Chartis Group	ECG Management Consultants
History	For over 30 years, we have focused on helping our clients optimize financial performance. We are domain experts that help organizations meet real-world challenges. Highest Gartner rated. Use across service lines. Services: Consulting, software, analytics.	Our approach: You Know Your Business Like No One Else. At Chartis, we work alongside our clients, learning the nuances of each situation, objectives, and challenges and building relationships that go beyond the surface. We bring informed perspectives to the table so that, together, we can develop solutions to your problems in truly powerful and material ways.	ECG is a strategic consulting firm that is leading healthcare forward, using the knowledge and expertise built over the course of more than four decades to help clients see clearly where healthcare is going and to navigate toward success. With deep expertise in strategy, finance, operations, and technology, ECG builds multidisciplinary teams to meet the unique needs of every client—from discrete operational issues to bigger-picture strategic and financial challenges.
Structure	Partnership with partial ownership by third-party private equity firm Madison Dearborn Capital Partners	Partnership with partial ownership by third-party private equity firm Audax Private Equity	Majority interest of the partnership owned by Siemens Healthineers
Scope of practice	Companies are made up of people. And when those people have the right tools, they can turn business dreams into reality. In an ever-evolving landscape, society's foundational institutions need a partner to help them fulfill their missions. We are practitioners and domain experts who help organizations meet real-world challenges, transform, and succeed in dynamic industries. Healthcare, higher education, financial institutions. Axiom software for integrated financial planning and decision support. Issue research reports and white papers.	Comprehensive advisory and analytics services firm dedicated to the healthcare industry. With an unparalleled depth of expertise in strategic planning, performance excellence, informatics and technology, and health analytics, we help leading academic medical centers, integrated delivery networks, children's hospitals, and healthcare service organizations achieve transformative results.	ECG partners with providers to create the strategies and solutions that are transforming healthcare delivery. Addressing the critical challenges facing the healthcare industry is what we do. Simply put: We're problem-solvers. Through more than four decades of experience, we've learned that successful problem-solving requires deep industry knowledge and expertise, rigorous data and analytics, strategic foresight, political and organizational savvy, and most important of all— practical solutions that get implemented.

(continued)

Exhibit 10.2: Comparison of Medium General Healthcare Consulting Firms (*continued*)

Variable	KaufmanHall	The Chartis Group	ECG Management Consultants
Services	Integrated strategy; mergers, acquisitions, and partnerships; performance improvement; treasury and capital management	Strategy, performance, informatics and technology, revenue cycle	Strategy, finance, operations, technology
Size	Unavailable	Unavailable	Unavailable
Contact information	10 S. Wacker, Suite 3375 Chicago, IL 60606 847-441-8780 www.kaufmanhall.com	220 W. Kinzie, Third Floor Chicago, IL 60654 877-667-4700 www.chartis.com	Multiple offices with no corporate office given 800-729-7635 www.ecgmc.com
Glassdoor comments	3.3 rating, 58 reviews, 55% recommend, 100% approve of CEO	4.1 rating, 34 interviews, 83% recommend, 94% approve of CEO	4.1 rating, 72 reviews, 78% recommend, 89% approve of CEO
Other considerations	Founded in 1985 by Mark Hall, Ken Kaufman, and Terri Wareham. Thought leadership through *Insights* newsletter (subscription). 150 Great Places to Work in Healthcare, *Becker's Hospital Review*, 2017	Thought leadership through the Chartis Forum (subscription)	Founded in Seattle in 1973 with a focus on faculty practice plans. ECG's Thought Leadership (subscription)

Sources: Adapted from publicly available information accessed October 1, 2019: KaufmanHall (www.kaufmanhall.com); Chartis (www.chartis.com); and ECG (www.ecgmc.com).

Exhibit 10.3: Comparison of Global Consulting Firms with Healthcare Practices

Variable	Deloitte	PwC	Navigant
History	Consulting assists clients by providing services in the areas of enterprise applications, technology integration, strategy and operations, human capital, and short-term outsourcing. By 2011, Deloitte ranked number one by revenue in all areas of healthcare consulting—life sciences, payer, provider, and government health.	In 2002, PwC sold its entire consultancy to IBM. It has since reconstituted its consulting practice through acquisition of many other firms, including Paragon, Bearing Point, and Booz & Company, to name a few.	The company was formed in 1983 by Richard Metzler as The Metzler Group Inc.; it provided management consultancy to businesses in the energy and other regulated industries. The company has grown through many acquisitions, including Quorum Consulting in 2017. Publicly traded (NYSE: NCI).
Structure	A private company in the United Kingdom that functions as a network of professional services companies, each legally incorporated in the countries in which they operate.	PwC is a private professional services network.	
Mission/ values	If you're ready to innovate and transform your business, Deloitte can help you imagine, deliver, and run your future, wherever you compete, using the latest technologies, from strategy development through implementation. Because impact isn't created alone. Together we can make history. Our vision and strategy, developed in collaboration with leadership and member firm partners from around the world, focuses on working together as one across geographic, functional, and business borders to deliver excellence in all of the services provided by the member firms.	Our values and behaviors define the expectations we have for working together and with clients. Although we come from different backgrounds and cultures across the firm, they are what we all have in common. They capture our shared aspirations and expectations, and guide how we make decisions and treat others. As PwC professionals, we align our actions with the values and behaviors of PwC. We think about the values as a full set—all are equally critical to our success.	We enable our clients to shape the world by tackling today's most critical issues and tomorrow's most important challenges.

(continued)

Exhibit 10.3: Comparison of Global Consulting Firms with Healthcare Practices (*continued*)

Variable	Deloitte	PwC	Navigant
Scope of practice	Audit, financial advisory, consulting, risk advisory, tax and legal, GovLab (internal think tank). *Human capital* leverages research, analytics, and industry insights to help design and execute critical programs from business-driven human resources to innovative talent, leadership, and change programs; *strategy and operations* works with senior executives to help them solve their toughest and most complex problems by bringing an approach to executable strategy that combines deep industry knowledge, rigorous analysis, and insight to enable confident action; and *technology* delivers solutions that help drive transformation, improve productivity, and streamline business operations. Our practical, innovative solutions are linked to measurable goals to help our clients achieve competitive advantage.	Partial list: Aerospace and defense; asset and wealth management; banking and capital markets; capital projects and infrastructure; consumer markets; energy, utilities, and mining; engineering and construction; financial services; health industries; health services; hospitality and leisure; pharmaceutical and life sciences; real estate; and technology, media, and communications.	Navigant Consulting, Inc. is a specialized, global professional services firm that helps clients take control of their future. Navigant's professionals apply deep industry knowledge, substantive technical expertise, and an enterprising approach to help clients build, manage, and/or protect their business interests. Major industries served include energy, financial services, government, healthcare, and life sciences.
Services	Technology-enabled transformation, healthcare regulatory solutions, strategy and M&A, talent optimization, sustainable margin, value-based care, physician enterprise and ambulatory services	Consulting: Benchmarking, data analytics, finance, global advisory, operations, risk and regulatory, strategy consulting, sustainability services, and technology	Business process outsourcing, data and analytics, enterprise operations consulting, revenue cycle, risk and compliance, strategy consulting, sustainability solutions, transformation solutions

Size	$935 million in provider-based revenues, 39% of $2.3519 billion in total healthcare related fees. In 2018, consulting grew by 15.7%.	236,000 people, $13.78 billion through its advisory practice in 2018	5,001 to 10,000 employees; founded 1996; revenue $500 million to $1 billion (USD) per year
Contact information	Online sign-up at www.deloitte.com	Online sign-up at www.pwc.com	Online sign-up at www.navigant.com
Glassdoor comments	3.8 rating, 33,000 reviews, 79% recommend	3.8 rating, 26,000 interviews, 79% recommend, 93% approve of CEO	3.2 rating, 694 reviews, 74% recommend, 69% approve of CEO
Other considerations	Largest healthcare consulting firm (revenues) across all healthcare entities. Tied with Bain as 2018 most recommended consulting firm in the United States.	As of 2018, 28% of the workforce located in Asia, 28% in North America and the Caribbean, and 30% in Western Europe. The company's global revenues were $41.3 billion in FY 2018, of which $17.06 billion was generated by its practice and $10.45 billion by its tax practice. PWC provides services to 420 *Fortune* 500 companies.	Since our founding, Navigant has evolved through acquisition, organic growth, and strategic investments in people, processes, and technology. Each step in our rich history has been carefully planned to ensure we anticipate, meet, and exceed our clients' needs. As a result, our business portfolio is diverse and deep, enabling us to serve clients with capabilities that span consulting, technology-based solutions, and disputes and forensics.

Sources: Adapted from publicly available information accessed October 1, 2019: Deloitte (www.deloitte.com); PWC (www.pwc.com); and Navigant (www.navigant.com).

The global firms tend to be enormous, employing many people across many countries, serving many industries. Comparing them is a real challenge. More than anything, such a comparison can come down to people and locations. Industry focus varies, with some more focused on life sciences in healthcare rather than provider-based clients. Global firms are more eclectic as compared to the smaller and medium-sized specialty firms that tend to be focused only on the healthcare industry. Global firms tend to have strong cultures built around internal training and education centers. Their engagements tend to be large, across different industries. Many of their projects are multidisciplinary and broad in scope. Information on these very large firms seems very similar and is, perhaps, of limited value in differentiating one from the other. Interviews are critical in trying to compare these larger firms at a more granular level.

CHAPTER 11

Joining the Right Firm

I HAD AN INTERESTING EXPERIENCE when interviewing someone to join our firm. The candidate happened to be related to someone I cared a great deal about, someone who had a big influence early in my career. The experience brought some things into focus for me. This highly intelligent and energized person was about to graduate from a great MBA program with a concentration in healthcare.

The candidate had an internship that was more focused in life sciences, and seemed to really like the research angle. Although I was quite impressed with this person, I simply did not feel that provider-based consulting was the right fit. However, I would never presume to make such a recommendation, as that is a decision best reserved to the individual. What I tried to do instead was to offer my perspective on consulting versus other pursuits. I'm not sure how much influence this discussion had, but this person chose not to go into consulting.

Knowing whether or not consulting is right for you is only *part* of the battle. Joining the right firm is the other part. Since this is truly a personal decision that can be based on many factors that are important to you, our hope is to give you some food for thought by sharing some criteria for you to consider and some sources that you might find useful.

In this book, we take a somewhat unconventional approach to the process of selecting a consulting firm. It was Maya Angelou who famously said, "I've learned that people will forget what you said, people will forget what you did, but people will never forget how you made them feel." While we review different criteria, in the end, the right decision for you will be determined by where you *feel most comfortable* based on the *experience* that you have had in meeting with several different firms.

THE RIGHT FIT REQUIRES THE RIGHT CULTURE

I was reminded about the importance of culture recently when I read an article in *The Wall Street Journal* headlined, "Considering a New Job? Beware a Culture Misfit" (Lublin 2020). The author defined corporate culture as consisting of "prevailing beliefs and behaviors that guide workplace interactions." She goes on to present an intriguing set of data that underscored the pitfalls. "About 30 percent of executives taking new jobs fail to figure out the company's culture correctly and end up leaving relatively soon," suggests Peter Crist, chairman of executive recruitment firm Crist/Kolder Associates. Exhibit 11.1 shows data from a recent survey asking job seekers what matters most to them.

Clearly, cultural fit is not a secret, as job seekers ranked it second only to salary and bonus. It is not the purpose of this section to provide precise tools for evaluating culture, but there are some insights that should be useful.

In doing a word search, we've mentioned *culture* numerous times throughout this book. It is time to clarify what we really mean by culture. Daniel K. Zismer, PhD, who has spent a career studying different cultures, described it as follows during an interview with me: "Culture is the foundation of intrinsic beliefs that bind and inspire people to pursue a mission and vision with unity and purpose."

Exhibit 11.1: What Matters Most to Job Seekers

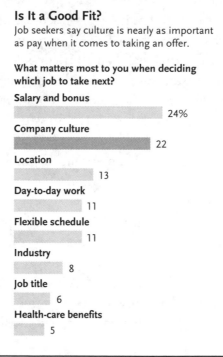

Is It a Good Fit?
Job seekers say culture is nearly as important as pay when it comes to taking an offer.

What matters most to you when deciding which job to take next?

Salary and bonus — 24%
Company culture — 22
Location — 13
Day-to-day work — 11
Flexible schedule — 11
Industry — 8
Job title — 6
Health-care benefits — 5

Source: Lublin (2020). Used with permission.

I had the advantage of having started my own firm early in my career. Doing so gave me insight into just how much effort is required to develop and support a corporate culture. While it can be argued the culture will evolve on its own if you let it, serious people want corporate culture to develop intentionally and would choose not to leave it to chance. Indeed, I invested considerable time and effort into developing a tangible and supportive culture for the firm. These values were in writing and included as part of our standard proposals. Culture is dynamic and not static, so there were internal discussions about values and expectations, with case presentations where we discussed situations that arose where these values played out. I believe we mostly succeeded, although I learned that it takes work and commitment of the entire team. Many founders have learned the hard way that conceptualizing culture in your head is insufficient to get others to contribute. Occasionally, it was necessary to counsel people out of the firm if they were not able to support this culture.

Developing corporate culture goes hand in hand with the personal brand(s) of the founder(s) and with the experience that they hope to develop as part of that brand. Clients who hire a firm are seeking good experiences. To be clear, a good experience does not imply that all such experiences are easy or go according to plan. And while good experiences can occur due to chance, the more sophisticated firms work hard to make such experiences intentional. There is no disputing that the greatest asset of a consulting firm is its people. When a private equity firm considers investing in a consulting firm, it focuses first on the people and evolves from there. So, it stands to reason that the best firms are those that really pay attention to their culture and its impact on their business. I believe this starts with how effective the leadership is in fostering a culture that positively affects their people and directs them toward producing ("staging") consistently positive outcomes for their clients.

It is challenging to gauge corporate culture in a disciplined way. Like the general concept of brand and how it can influence customer choice, culture must ultimately resonate with employees (and clients). What elements of their mission and vision are getting through versus those that are mere words? Paying attention to conventual wisdom in the firm is always important. How does the firm view the world, the industry, their clients? Is there a consensus view or do views vary widely? There may be no correct answer to these questions, but they can serve as a baseline for you to assess the firm's compatibility with the views that you hold.

Often culture is reinforced through stories, and COVID-19 has presented some opportunities for new stories. Any firm can do well when things are good; it is more challenging when things are tough. One firm that I am familiar with took a key question to their employees regarding how to handle the pandemic. The choices were to have widespread furloughs and layoffs or for everyone to take a pay cut. They voted to take the pay cut. This defining event is now actively cited in the firm's recruiting efforts.

In this book, we refer to Glassdoor as a key source of employee feedback. The comments people make about firms and how they take care of their people rank high. Exhibit 11.2 outlines what was said in 2019 about the cultures of the three global firms we previously reviewed in chapter 9.

Notice anything interesting? The subjects of the comments don't really differentiate the companies from each other. These common themes just reinforce the generic pros and cons of consulting. Do these comments help you decide which companies might be a good fit for you? It is clearly open to debate. In the end, such comments may reflect "comfort" with people as much as anything else.

While interviewing with a firm, you will have opportunities to ask what it is like to work there. After a few interviews you will likely hear some common themes. You might also get a sense of what is not being said or addressed. Again, consulting is an *experience*. How do people feel about working there? What do they like about it? What one thing might they change if they could? How do they see their firm as different from others that do the same kind of work?

Exhibit 11.2: Comparisons from Firm Survey, 2019

Firm	Pros	Cons
Deloitte Consulting	• "Great work–life balance at Deloitte" (in 1,917 reviews) • "Employee friendly, good work culture" (in 1,234 reviews) • "The work environment is amazing" (in 1,202 reviews) • "Working alongside some great people" (in 994 reviews) • "Great place for technical people" (in 974 reviews)	• "You won't really have a perfect work–life balance if you wish to succeed here in Deloitte" (in 4,806 reviews) • "Long working hours are expected" (in 3,135 reviews) • "Long working hours but sometimes" (in 1,381 reviews) • "No work–life balance during busy seasons" (in 1,044 reviews) • "Sometimes long hours during busy season" (in 770 reviews)
PwC	• "Great work environment in the company" (in 937 reviews) • "Great people, good mentorship culture" (in 925 reviews) • "Management emphasizes work–life balance" (in 922 reviews) • "This is a great place to start your career" (in 807 reviews) • "Great flexible working policy and hence work–life balance" (in 509 reviews)	• "They have very long working hours" (in 3,508 reviews) • "Little focus on work–life balance" (in 3,346 reviews) • "Long working hours with sometimes tight deadlines" (in 1,215 reviews) • "Long hours especially during busy season" (in 1,135 reviews) • "Absolutely no work–life balance" (in 700 reviews)

(continued)

Firm	Pros	Cons
Navigant	• "The work–life balance is very reasonable" (in 73 reviews) • "Great life sciences team, work from home benefits, laidback work environment" (in 35 reviews) • "Work with a lot of smart people" (in 34 reviews) • "Great people and interesting work" (in 29 reviews) • "Flexible work culture, many employee engagement activities" (in 24 reviews)	• "Work–life balance and work load" (in 43 reviews) • "When the business activity is low you could still work long hours on proposals" (in 37 reviews) • "The senior management actually sits behind locked doors that nobody is allowed to go in" (in 21 reviews) • "Unorganized upper management and high turnover" (in 20 reviews) • "Managing Directors can get away with some pretty appalling behavior if they're bringing enough business" (in 12 reviews)

Source: Selective information from Glassdoor (www.glassdoor.com), November 2019.

WHICH FIRM IS BEST FOR YOU?

Obviously, the best firm for you can depend on several different factors. Is reputation the most important thing to you? Look at firm ratings. Does the firm take corporate culture seriously? Look at survey feedback from employees. Sometimes, finding the right fit just means finding the firm with the best fit *for you at this time*. With this as your focus, it seems more likely that you will enjoy the work, the people, the culture. This is not a time to ignore your feelings. Rather, be in touch with your feelings. What feels best, why? Does this represent something tangible (i.e., not trivial) or did you just enjoy lunch better than elsewhere (you get the idea). You will learn better and feel able to put this to good use regardless of what might be the next step. Also, recognize that this best fit now might not be the best fit in the future when other considerations also come into play, as discussed below.

When considering different firms, do not overlook the track record of the global firms that attract the best and brightest graduates. They will have the best reputations and the strongest recruiting programs and will be easily the best-known firms in consulting, though this might not be true for all industries, such as healthcare. The massive size of global firms should not be overlooked. This larger size can also be a disadvantage—it all depends on your outlook.

Choosing the first consulting firm to join is mostly about risk and reward. In order to manage risk, you have to know what your personal risk profile is. Do you have a high-risk profile? Are you able and willing to take a flier? If so, you might want to go with that firm that is a little more edgy and less traditional than others, where you can envision yourself staying for a while but not for the long run. If you do not like taking risks and feel more inclined to go for stability, then it is hard to top the global firms. However, while they have a lot of attributes in common, they are not all the same.

TIP FROM THE TRENCHES

While considering which firm might be the best fit for you now, look at whether you are in it for the short term versus as a career. Truth be known, while some consultants find their firm right out of the box, others begin with a large or global firm and then join another firm or form their own firm after a few years, if they are focused on a consulting career. Many new recruits might not yet know if this is a short-term career for them until they experience consulting firsthand. That is a perfectly reasonable approach. Another key consideration is recognizing that what is important to you now could change along the way. Does a 25-year-old unmarried person want the same things as a 40-year-old married parent? Probably not.

There are a number of reasons why the global firms usually score high among recruits in surveys. Larger firms have longevity. In the consulting business, the more sustainable the business, the better. Consulting is a volatile industry, with many firms coming and going. The market is the ultimate judge. A firm cannot survive for long unless it does things consistently well. In consulting, there are at least two tracks to doing things well—external and internal.

In the external track, a solid client base is determinative. It reflects how the market is responding to the services offered and delivered by the firm. This is a relatively simple concept, because firms are hired and rehired by the best health-care organizations. Does the client list include some of the best known and best performing healthcare organizations? Repeat business is so important to consulting that those firms with a lot of repeat business tend to brag about it (e.g., "40 percent of our work is repeat business for existing clients").

The other track is internal, which is more complicated and quite different from external. Internal considerations involve such things as culture and how a firm treats its people, and how the firm operates in terms of processes and priorities. We cover these internal factors in the remainder of this chapter.

EMPLOYEE RETENTION

All firms care about their people, but some do it better than others. Reputations of companies tend to rise or fall on this single variable. But how far does caring about their people go? How do they invest in their people? Do they provide learning opportunities and send them to external seminars? Most firms do at least some of this. How well a firm treats its people ultimately adds up to employee retention— are people happy and remain with the firm?

Employee retention is also related to how people are treated when they leave the firm. While I founded my first firm as a solo practice, it quickly evolved into a small firm with a few people and then up to four to five partners with 17 people overall. Anytime someone left our small firm, it tended to have a big impact on the rest of us. But I always tried to honor and respect those who decided to leave and was outwardly grateful that they had elected to spend part of their professional life working with us. Most people, especially those who were partners, worked to make the firm their own. Not everyone left on good terms; some people were counseled out. For those I counseled out, I tried to give them time to find their next job. I think I mostly succeeded in managing this with dignity. It helped that I genuinely liked most of the people and stayed in touch with many of them. Some even became stringers and helped with various assignments after leaving the firm. Things are different for a larger firm with extensive HR capabilities. How much attention do they pay to the exit process?

I had the good fortune to have my first consulting experience with Booz Allen—one of the best-known global firms. Remember, there was pure luck or divine providence involved in my being hired there. What has never been lost on me is the reaction I get when I list this firm on my resume. The firm has been around for more than 100 years (founded in 1914). Edwin Booz, the founder, said it well: "Start with character . . . and fear not the future" (Kleiner 2004). People are universally impressed. I think the solid reputation of Booz Allen over its many years as one of the best consulting firms is highly correlated with what they did for me after I left, and not just while I was in the firm.

If a firm really cares about you, they recognize that they are making a huge investment in you. They don't take this lightly. The global firms make a remarkable investment in their new recruits, who go through extensive training. Global firms pay more than most, and this cost is covered during down times where they are not billable. They work hard to keep you busy and interested. It is logical to assume that they care about what you do next. You have the potential to become a a future client. After you leave you have the opportunity to become an ambassador for the firm, or a detractor. Major firms spend significant resources keeping their alumni informed of their ongoing activities and research. They feed their network of professionals.

WHAT HAPPENS WHEN A CONSULTANT LEAVES?

It is relatively straightforward to gauge the people who stay on in a firm by meeting them and talking to them, and by reviewing what they have accomplished. Interview a few of the clients of the firm if this is possible. Customer loyalty is something firms work hard to achieve and retain.

A less obvious approach is to understand how firms treat the people who leave. Every organization experiences turnover, but organizations can differ substantially in how they deal with this turnover. The smaller firms, as noted before, operate like a family business or perhaps a partnership; everything is personal in these smaller firms. These smaller companies tend to revolve around the founding partners and their personalities. Founders of small firms can take turnover rather personally. The larger, global firms with so many more people are able to be more disciplined (some might translate this as "rigid"). What happens when someone leaves is more a true test of how they treat their people than almost anything else you could consider. Allow me to make the case.

I am part of the Booz Allen alumni network. They have stayed in touch with me. They have followed my career, and I like that. But it is my impression that this is the exception. A consulting acquaintance shared their experience with me about Deloitte Consulting. This person was with the firm for several years as a new careerist. A particular person they knew announced that they were leaving, and Deloitte *celebrated* this announcement. While my acquaintance did not know whether the person was leaving by choice or was counseled out, the company tried not to make the distinction. As described to me, it seemed like a fully scripted process. This occurred more than once when my acquaintance was with the firm. They suggested that this process is part of their culture. Imagine what that does for self-esteem and the ability of someone to maintain personal relations with the people with whom they worked.

In contrast, I have experienced firms where, if the grapevine was not active, it was possible that you would not even realize when someone had left. It is buried. No statement is issued. The person is discouraged from saying goodbye, and simply leaves. This is a very uncomfortable experience for both the person and the firm. What impression does this leave with everyone? It leads to many questions. We simply don't know. I am not talking about gossip here. Rather, I am talking about caring for the individual. That person spent some time with the firm and was part of various consulting teams; they made friends. Does the firm not appreciate the contributions they made? Shouldn't the firm say so? Where is the person going? What about any forwarding information? Is the firm embarrassed? What does all this say about the culture of the firm?

I could certainly be wrong, but it is my impression that burying the news of a departure is more common among consulting firms than the celebration. Of course, there can be extenuating circumstances. Like many other people, I was once the victim of a private equity takeover, in which I was not in the favored group who kept their jobs. I know what it feels like to be ignored by the new owner and then shown the door. It's not a good feeling.

It can be made even worse when you are treated like a common criminal and escorted out or asked to sign a separation agreement with a "nondisparagement" clause. You are asked to turn over your computer and your key card, and you are shown the door without so much as a thank you or the professional courtesy of finishing your current engagements with your existing clients. This last point really sticks in my craw. When a firm espouses a "client first" culture but doesn't allow people to complete their existing work before they leave, how is this consistent? The consultant suffers the indignity of being removed from an ongoing assignment, and the client suffers the inconvenience of the disruption involved. In my view, separations that are managed in this fashion are unprofessional.

That is not to ignore that firms often have some legal exposure to deal with. Don't get me wrong, I am not naive to the damage that a disaffected employee can do. But there are processes to sort things out in a mutually agreeable way, without so much collateral damage.

For obvious reasons, I strongly favor the firm that is able to maintain relations with consultants who have left the firm. In researching a firm, it can be helpful if you can find someone who is no longer with the firm. How were they treated? Why did they leave? What do they have to say about their experience? If everyone who has left the firm has mostly negative comments, it does not speak well of the firm and raises some issues of sustainability.

My experience is that this can be a subtle issue. Beware the feedback in which people seem reluctant to discuss the experience they had with the firm. As noted previously, this can sometimes involve a separation agreement. Other times, it is simply too painful to recall these memories and people have moved on.

The notion of continuous improvement comes to mind. The best consulting firms are constantly working to reinforce their values and tweaking how they approach their people in an effort to improve their processes. Having a positive culture is something every consulting firm works hard at. Exit interviews are one of the most important forms of feedback on how the culture and values are resonating. The opportunity to capture impressions from people as they leave should not be lost. Some of the best firms not only do exit interviews, but they use a third party to conduct the interviews in order to ensure that the impression is a lasting one, demonstrating that they are truly interested in meaningful feedback. Why? They want the unvarnished truth.

It is not an exercise to simply check the box as every person exits the firm. They sincerely want to know what impressions were made while people were there. How are they feeling as they leave? Why are they leaving? Were they encouraged to seek the next opportunity? Were they discouraged from considering other opportunities? Did they feel the firm supported what was best for them personally? They say people don't leave firms, rather they leave their supervisors. How was their supervisor? How did their supervisor respond to the news of their leaving? Was this a surprise? Was there anything that happened or did not happen that pushed the person to leave? Is the person leaving with a positive impression of the firm? If not, is there something the firm could or should do that would make things right (*service recovery* in retail speak)?

Having counseled a number of people out of firms, I am impressed with some companies' ability to leave a lasting impression on someone through one last act as the person goes out the door. Exit interviews are never fun discussions, but they are utterly necessary. What should be involved? Perhaps an offer to smooth things over with someone, to make an extra effort to reach out to a client to explain why the person is leaving, or perhaps an unpaid bonus they are leaving on the table. It is best to tie up loose ends whenever possible. It can be something small and simple, yet to the person leaving, it could feel very important. I confess that I did not always succeed in this effort.

A recent variation on the exit interview is the *stay interview*. Citing the book *The Power of Stay Interviews for Engagement and Retention* by Richard P. Finnegan (2012), Bill Conerly (2019) suggests the following:

> Stay interviews are like exit interviews, but for employees who remain with the company. Exit interviews are like talking to cows who walked out of the barn when the door was left open. Stay interviews are like walking into the barn and asking the cows what they like about the barn, and if they have ever thought about leaving.

THE BOOMERANG PHENOMENON

So let's add another question to the exit interview: Would you consider coming back to the firm at some point? This reflects on the so-called *boomerang phenomenon*. Such a phenomenon was unheard of when I first got involved in consulting but seems to be a bit more common today. It clearly says something positive about the firm for a consultant to leave and then decide to return. Relations were positive to the point that the consultant was willing to consider coming back. The firm thought enough of that person to stay in touch and approach the consultant later on.

Perhaps there was a life event when a person's circumstances changed and they left. In the past, firms did a rather poor job of retaining women who left the workforce temporarily during pregnancy. Fast forward to today, and we now see many firms that have advanced light-years with progressive family-leave policies.

The boomerang situations that I have witnessed probably involved a consultant leaving at one level in the firm, gaining some highly valuable experience, and then re-entering the firm at a higher level. Sometimes global firms offer what are essentially sabbaticals, during which the person can do a number of things such as gain a graduate degree, start a family, complete a job with another firm, and then returns to the firm they left. Some of the more progressive firms actually have career tracks that include financing graduate education with an obligation to pay back the grant with a few years of service later.

I find the boomerang phenomenon intriguing in that much of the guesswork about corporate culture and other challenges related to onboarding are effectively eliminated because the consultant previously spent quality time with that firm.

THE PARTNERSHIP

As stated before, most small to medium firms tend to operate like a family business or a partnership, whether or not they are legally structured as such. The essence of this organizational form is that there is a small group of individuals who operate interdependently in both running and growing the firm. These people are financially at risk together, just as they share in the rewards. They are bound by some agreement, such as a partnership agreement, that specifically spells out how the proceeds are divided and what people can expect from their performance. The smaller the firm, the more intimate and personal these relationships tend to be. In larger firms, these partnerships can get quite complicated and relationships can vary greatly.

Depending on the experience that you bring to the firm and the level at which you might be entering the firm, this might or might not be important to you. If becoming a partner is important to you, certain essential questions arise. How did this group form? If they have added members, how did new members qualify? There is likely to be a buy-in provision. What is the buy-in amount and how is it calculated? How has the firm performed over the years and how have the partners been rewarded? Have there been equity calls?[1]

TIP FROM THE TRENCHES

If the possibility of becoming a partner at this firm is something that is important to you, I strongly advise you to agree on/understand the criteria for membership in this partners group **before** you join the firm. Making such a commitment on the basis of a verbal wing and a prayer should never occur. Well-established groups will already have these criteria carefully documented. There tends to be little flexibility. This is not going to be important for the new careerist but may come into play later in your career.

Groups tend to bond together over time. They operate in the trenches together. They go through economic ups and downs. There is no substitute for these shared experiences. After a time, these groups have developed bonds that are hard to replicate, and legacies are established. These shared experiences can make it hard to bring in new members and bond with them. Interactions can feel different, and can be different. Legacy groups over time can become effectively "closed," where they are unable or unwilling to open up their membership in meaningful ways.

Another possibility is where partners are equal, a rare but ideal situation. In my own firm, I owned the vast majority of a firm (it was not a partnership technically, but I tried to operate as one). This meant that it did not always operate like a partnership. That is to say, some partners are more equal than others. Part of the value of partnership is that people are rowing the boat together. They all have a stake in the outcome. If one or two partners have a significantly larger stake, it is natural that there will be times when the other partners feel like they are working for the majority partners (e.g., managing partners). While there are certainly examples when this has worked, it is my experience that unequal partnerships can also have unintended consequences.

Private equity firms have come to understand that new partners buying into a firm where majority partners are trying to retire will affect the business's valuation materially. Not all partners are rainmakers with the same networking abilities as the founding partners.

Synergies can also be important. Two partners can work together to offer a new line of innovative services. Not all partnership groups generate such synergies.

---

1. An equity call occurs when the firm needs capital and elects to tax the partners instead of going to the debt market or pursuing other funding options.

How important is this to the portfolio of services offered by the firm? Is the firm just selling the same thing over and over or are new services being developed? No question that there are commodity consulting services (e.g., fair market value analyses, revenue cycle, space planning), but a diversified portfolio will also involve some new services designed to help healthcare organizations move in a new direction, like community-based ambulatory care or service line strategies.

Regardless of these cautions, it is worth noting that financial success can overcome a multitude of such barriers. What does the new partner bring to the party? To the extent that they contribute significantly to the growth of the firm, nothing else might seem that important. Ultimately, the worth of an individual partner is calculated on the basis of what the persons brings to the firm. Some partners are better at selling. Others have talent in thought leadership. Still others excel at interpersonal relations. At the end of all these considerations, does the group work well to sustain valuable clients, to resolve issues, and grow the business?

THOUGHT LEADERSHIP AND REVENUE GROWTH

One of my favorite articles is titled "Polarity Management" (Burns 1999). In it, the writer makes the compelling argument that we tend to be fixed in our view that everything is binary: up *or* down, black *or* white, and so on. The reality is that this polarity limits us in countless ways. To foster more productive dialogue, one has to reject this view by substituting *and* for *or*. Strategically, this translates into shifting fundamental analyses away from considering options A *or* B, to consider implementing options A *and* B. This opens up myriad new possibilities. I can't tell you how often I have been able to put this new orientation into play in my own strategy practice.

Thought leadership usually requires some investment of time and resources to develop new approaches. Much has been written lately on establishing *cultures of innovation* (Watson 2019). Time put into thought leadership is not time that can be charged to clients. When times are tough, what wins? When external owners (i.e., investors) are involved, how do they look at thought leadership? What sacrifices are made? When an engagement does not fully meet the needs of the client, how does the firm respond? Will the firm go the extra mile to make sure that the client is fully satisfied, despite the fact that it means writing off some time because you go over budget? Or are they more concerned that they stay strictly within budget limits and prevent any negative financial performance? How does the firm deal with service recovery? These are the kinds of considerations that separate the best from the rest. Anyone can print a statement of mission and related values. But what do key people in the firm say about this when interviewed? Is there some consistency or are the responses varied? What is the firm willing to enforce in the way of values? How does the firm communicate with new staff? How does this translate into client relations? These are among the key considerations in looking at different consulting firms and how they practice their craft.

While thought leadership and revenue growth can viewed as an either/or proposition, I think they tend to be more related to each other. To use Burns's idea, it is about thought leadership *and* revenue growth, at least conceptually. However, I must say that in my experience, they rarely coexist, especially among small- to medium-sized consulting firms. I have had the privilege of working for a number of firms, including my own, and then visiting many other firms during collaborative efforts that involved working together on specific client engagements. This has afforded me the opportunity to witness different cultures. Culture is usually most evident in terms of what people talk about and where they focus their time. What are their values? What do they try to reinforce? What themes are evident in the words they use and values they share with others? Words matter. Perhaps most important, culture is evident in what is rewarded or recognized.

My observation is that firms that spend most of their time thinking about client challenges and looking for new ways to solve problems are more oriented toward cutting-edge thought leadership—the craft of consulting. Firms that spend most of their time talking about selling their existing services and revenue generation orient more toward growth—*wealth creation*. Does that mean that the latter isn't interested in thought leadership? No, it does not have to mean that. While it may not be a binary world, there are trade-offs. The more time that is spent on one, the less time is available for the other. We are talking about balance.

Balance is hard to achieve when viewing these two areas. Clearly, any firm is compelled to do some of both. After all, consultants must be able to multitask. But doing either thing really well is very time-consuming. Firms that are the best at thought leadership seem almost obsessed with this pursuit. It demands significant attention and resources. What if we approach issue A like this instead of the conventional way? How have others attempted this? What has worked? What has not? Are there different ways of looking at this? What does the literature say? Who can I talk to who might shed some new light on the issue? As noted earlier, the process of thought leadership can be involved and very time-consuming. Yet, the absence of such inquiry can lead to shoddy work. At issue here is how evidence-based the consulting practice is. Best practices are defined by results. The role of consulting as a knowledge transfer vehicle applies here. Take what is working and sell it to others. It is no secret that creating new knowledge is an essential part of what separates McKinsey Consulting, Boston Consulting Group, and Bain Consulting from the pack.

Firms focused more on revenue generation pose a different set of questions. *Grow or die* is a common business tenet. What is my pipeline? How can I grow it? How often do I need to attend to it? What are the most effective ways of connecting with each prospect? Are there others I can talk to about new prospects? How should I spend marketing dollars? What emphasis should I put on staying in touch with old clients? How often should I contact them and for what purpose? Should I publish? What conferences should I attend? Like thought leadership, to perform revenue growth correctly can be very time-consuming. I admit this comes more naturally to some people than to others.

Clearly thought leadership, done well, can lead to revenue growth. Everyone brings different gifts to their profession. Some people are thinkers, others are doers. Some like to speak and write, others like the certainty of numbers and analysis. The benefit of a diverse leadership in this regard could not be clearer. Finding ways to incentivize people to both sell what you have and devote time to developing new services by anticipating future needs creates vibrancy and excitement in the best consulting firms. So, while thought leadership and revenue growth are not opposing forces, in my experience it is rare that firms excel at both. Those that do are truly among the elites.

STANDARDIZATION AND QUALITY CONTROL

It is perhaps standard operating procedure for most small firms with multiple offices to vest responsibility for growth and quality to the lead person in each office. Specialized services are offered in each office (e.g., facilities planning), depending on which consultants work in each office. Leadership is responsible for overall performance of the firm. It is a common structure in the smaller firms that office leaders are fully responsible and accountable for office performance. Some offices will do better than others. But the real challenge in such smaller firms is consistency. Will a strategic plan completed by one office look anything like the same type of study done at another office by another team with the same firm? Probably not. As these firms grow, there is pressure to standardize and exercise quality control to ensure that consistent service is being provided to all clients, regardless of the location of the office (i.e., across all offices). This is when the office-based model (where each office provides oversight and quality control for a standard list of services) shifts more to the specialty-based model (where practices are organized by a lead person who manages the practice across all offices). Under the specialty model, practice leaders become responsible for the quality and consistency of specific service offerings.

Standardization can be considered a stop along the thought-leadership continuum. To me, thought leadership consists not only of new ways of thinking, but also determining and verifying what is consistent about existing best practices. Most consulting firms are made up of multiple leaders, where a shared viewpoint exists on a number of key issues and where each leader may have an area of focus or specialty interest with a unique point of view or level of expertise. When enough engagements are completed for different clients in similar practices (e.g., planning), they can develop a *corporate point of view*. How do we approach operational turnarounds? What are the important steps to a revenue cycle engagement and in what sequence? What are the essential design features of a freestanding ambulatory care center? What are the essential features required to effectively source a search process for a hospital CEO position? Perhaps this process is better characterized as oversight.

I believe oversight is truly one of the most important differentiators a consulting firm can have. Done right, oversight naturally leads to thought leadership. Where a firm takes the time to examine its existing work and standardize it around best practices, this is likely to result in greater consistency. Such standardization enables oversight. This is similar to the development of clinical guidelines and protocols in the quality improvement world of healthcare. But anyone who has spent some time in these pursuits recognizes that, with such standardization, comes a genuine encouragement to innovate. Finding best practices involves seeking variation from the standard in order to find novel ways to achieve a better result. When I had my own firm, I would encourage engagement leaders to come up with at least one innovation for a standard study that they were completing for a new client and to share it with the group.

Standardization involves establishing similar attributes for a given type of study. It becomes the way that the firm completes certain engagements—a similar look and feel. Peer-to-peer evaluation is a powerful tool. In a culture that encourages innovation, people are eager to show off their work. It can involve a competitive "show-and-tell" environment—"Look what I just did for a client related to best practices in managing clinical service lines," for example. Standardization also lends itself to training. Standardizing key studies allows firms to train people on how they want them completed.

Again, standardization can be one of the most important differentiators in comparing one firm to another. Some firms hold a formal review process before a report is issued to a client. This adds time that must be worked into the process of getting a report out of review and into the hands of the client on a timely basis. Such a process can help to achieve a standard "look and feel" to a report from that firm. While a poor analogy perhaps, McDonald's serves a hamburger exactly the same whether in Portland or Miami. This does not happen by chance. The training occurs at Hamburger University in Chicago, and its operating manual reportedly includes some eight pages devoted solely to the preparation of French fries. You get the idea. I know at least two consulting firms that have an internal report review process for all reports issued by the firm, a significant investment in standardization.

While not all firms have an internal real-time review process, some perform a review after an engagement is completed. Some firms do both. Unfortunately, many firms don't do any of this, but rather delegate all reviews to a lead person or rely on each partner to check their own work. The argument against such review processes is that, done right, they are time-consuming and expensive. While review time is usually taken into consideration when billing rates are calculated and proposals are written, some of the review might not be billable time. It can fall to the leader of the practice, where it is added on top of the billable targets. Or some of the review work might fall on the shoulders of editors or full-time people who are considered overhead.

Hourly billing rates must cover both the direct costs of the consultant (salary and benefits) and overhead, including product review and profit. Firms with more resources can devote more time to standardizing, providing oversight, and investing in new knowledge (i.e., thought leadership). These larger firms can not only produce a far more consistent product—reducing risk to the client of producing an inferior result—but also to allocate some resources to new breakthrough thinking.

Standardization was really brought home to me when the American Association of Healthcare Consultants (AAHC) existed. We offered a credential to both individuals and firms. (See appendix A for a review of AAHC processes.) Firms could be credentialed for different types of work, such as strategic planning, facility planning, and search, based on evidence that they would provide. Firms were allowed to self-report a list of services they offered. But to be credentialed (i.e., certified) for that service required the rigor of peer review to confirm the necessary expertise. It was essentially a *Good Housekeeping* seal of approval.

In order to review this work with some discipline, it was necessary to reach consensus regarding what basic elements each key study should have. It is here that the joke of how many consultants does it take to change a light bulb comes to mind.[2] Remarkably, we found a lot of consensus. For example, a strategic plan should have at least mission, vision, values, strategies, goals, and objectives, and it should be tied to finance. Lest you think this was a futile exercise, I was part of a group of reviewers that rejected, on two separate occasions, submissions by a prominent consulting firm to qualify for credentialed status for strategic planning

---

2. There are many answers used in telling this joke. I like the one that says, "We don't know because we never got beyond the feasibility study phase."

studies. When I think back, it was really quite remarkable that firms would allow peers to review their work for this credential.

REFERENCES

Burns, L. R. 1999. "Polarity Management: The Key Challenge for Integrated Health Systems." *Journal of Healthcare Management* 44 (1): 14–31.

Conerly, B. 2019. "Hiring to Improve Employee Retention: Learning from Stay Interviews." *Forbes*. Published October 3. www.forbes.com/sites/billconerly/2019/10/03/hiring-to-improve-employee-retention-learning-from-stay-interviews/.

Finnegan, R. P. 2012. *The Power of Stay Interviews for Engagement and Retention*. Alexandria, VA: Society for Human Resource Management.

Kleiner, A. 2004. *Booz Allen Hamilton: Helping Clients Envision the Future*. Old Saybrook, CT: Greenwich Publishing Group.

Lublin, J. S. 2020. "Considering a New Job? Beware a Culture Misfit." *Wall Street Journal*. Updated January 15. www.wsj.com/articles/considering-a-new-job-beware-a-culture-misfit-11579084201.

Watson, M. D. M. 2019. *Enabling Innovation: Building a Creative Culture in 45 Minutes*. Meridian, ID: 9m Consulting.

PART III

Exceptional Consulting

THIS FINAL PART OF THE BOOK is where we separate the extraordinary from the ordinary. The truly exceptional consultants with whom I have worked and seen work are those who, from the start of an engagement, seek to provide a unique and authentic experience for their client—to be extraordinary. It is in their DNA. *Just getting by* is a foreign language to them. They set out to impress, to stand out from others (i.e., provide a "Wow" experience) in all that they do.

A case study appears below that tracks the real experience of two new careerists who went into consulting at about the same time. It highlights how an understanding of what to expect coupled with a focus on the right things (some of which are quite subtle) can greatly influence the consulting experience. It also points out that there are always a number of things that are simply beyond your control—consulting is an adventure, after all. Before reading the case study, I invoke Reinhold Niebuhr's "Serenity Prayer," which really captures the essence of the case study:

> God, grant me the serenity to accept the things I cannot change,
> Courage to change the things I can,
> And wisdom to know the difference.

CASE STUDY

Two consultants graduated from the same top 50 college one year apart. Each had a similar major and was socially active. They both listed a ten-week paid consulting internship on their resume. They both participated in a campus recruiting process in which a number of prominent global and local consulting firms visited the campus and conducted interviews among several hundred students. Both consultants accepted offers from a global consulting firm. The campus recruiting process was highly competitive with fewer than 10 percent of those who were interviewed receiving employment offers. Both candidates stood out from the crowd.

In the first few years, Consultant A had an excellent experience, working primarily for one client for the first two years. The primary client was a short plane ride away, where the consultant would be on site for three to four days per week. They completed several engagements for this same client with slightly different team members under the same partner-in-charge. There were several opportunities for Consultant A to volunteer for non-billable activities during these first two years, including participating in a few successful proposals for new work with that same client. Working for different project managers, Consultant A was awarded several recognition awards and was introduced to a number of leaders of the firm because of these voluntary activities and the awards. Promotions were received on schedule, and the consultant was at the top of the compensation range based on tenure. The consultant got to know key people at the client company, and even was involved in scheduling some joint social outings. The client was pleased with the work to the point where members of the client team asked the firm to have the consultant assigned to future engagements. When asked about their experience, Consultant A indicated, "Living the dream."

Consultant B had a different experience over the first several years. While rewarding in some ways, the first two long-term projects were with difficult clients that involved a similar amount of travel as Consultant A had. These challenging clients made the work less enjoyable, which was at least partially offset later by a positive experience of working with a third, more positive client. Promotions came on schedule with average bonuses paid along the way. Because of some of the challenges of the engagements, Consultant B was not able to get close to key people in either of the two first clients. Consultant B left the firm after three years to work with a regional consulting firm, which involved less time on the road. The experience with this firm was mixed.

Did we mention that both consultants worked in the same office for the same firm? Even though these people had similar attributes and overlapped at the same time with the same firm, they had very different experiences. Clearly, clients can greatly affect how a consultant feels about the experience. So how much does the culture of the firm matter? Does the experience really depend on the clients involved, which is typically beyond the control of the new recruit? Or is the experience more reflective of who is on the consulting team? Is it just a roll of the dice?

Consultant A did a better job of connecting with the internal consulting teams on engagements. Consultant A made friends with several people on each of the teams, and earned individual recognition through several service-related awards. The clients were certainly different for the two consultants and had a big impact on how the experience felt to each. Consultant A clearly had a superior client experience in comparison to Consultant B, notably including recognition by the client with positive feedback. Yet, Consultant B did not have a failed experience.

Consultant B realized they felt somewhat disconnected from the teams and did not enjoy the travel. In contrast, the travel for Consultant A was inconsequential. In fact, Consultant A established elite travel status with both airlines and hotels, and took several free trips using points during the first two years. Consultant A openly characterized a far more favorable experience than Consultant B.

The simple observation is that Consultant A was more invested in the teams and got closer to other team members. Consultant A made more of an impression internally, which led team members and leadership to help Consultant A advance in the firm. Consultant A was on an accelerated promotion track after only two years, and was requested for future work by the client.

We believe that Consultant A had a better experience than Consultant B at all levels. We do not believe that this better experience happened entirely by chance. Yes, the client experience made a difference, but there is reason to believe that Consultant A would have reacted more positively to the situation even if the roles were reversed. The difference between the experiences might have less to do with the clients and more with the expectations and lens that each consultant applied to the situation, and how each consultant reacted to these different client experiences. We think the more favorable client experience of Consultant A was largely due to several things, including a superior outlook, more focus on team dynamics, and other skills covered in this last section on exceptional consulting. It really matters how professionals approach their craft!

CHAPTER 12

Defining Exceptionalism

Do you remember a time when you observed someone who was really exceptional at their craft? It could have been a server or a flight attendant. It could have been a janitor or someone working in retail, an actor, a teacher, or a professional athlete. What stood out that caused you to notice? It could have been several things. The person was totally focused and obviously took pride in the work. The person knew what to do, and did it better than others. They showed great energy. What might stand out that would make a consultant exceptional? That is what this chapter is about.

THE ODDS OF BEING EXCEPTIONAL

I remember distinctly, when I entered consulting as a "grinder," that I was confronted by the odds of getting to the next level ("minder"), and then the level after that ("finder"). (See chapter 9 for discussion on Grinders, Minders, and Finders.) The odds were not good. Mind you, I already had a heightened awareness of the odds against me when I was hired by one of the leading consulting firms in the world, getting chosen from among the hundreds of applicants. This experience was not lost on me. To this day, I don't know if stating the low odds of advancing was a way for leaders to tear down our oversized egos at the time (à la military boot camp protocol), or to prepare us for what lay ahead. What I do know is that, looking around me over time and seeing what happened with others, the low odds played out.

About three out of every four consultants will wash out in the first year or two before they are considered for a manager position (minder), and less than one in ten managers will ultimately reach partner (finder). I imagine the odds are similar in most professional organizations, such as accounting, law, and engineering.

One of the more common things I hear consultants say among themselves, especially after they have been in the business for a few years, is "I enjoy what I do." It is my belief that those who do it exceptionally well enjoy it even more. As strange as it might sound, this does not mean that every engagement is joyful or every outcome exceeds a client's expectations. It does mean that the feedback you receive over time remains consistently good, if not even improving over time. The market is a keen barometer of success. Pavlov's dogs come to mind, because being rewarded is a great motivator. Those who do something well get rewarded and tend to stick around. So, what is it that contributes to this longevity?

As I mentioned before, to me there is nothing more gratifying than seeing someone who is exceptional at what they do. If they have a passion for it and take pride in it, this feeling can be infectious. This is one of the things I most enjoy about consulting. It seems like I have always been surrounded by high-energy, motivated people striving to do their best in all that they do. To do this work well takes passion and skill. As in many other trades, consultants feel a certain devotion to service and to pleasing others. Make no mistake, I have been blessed to have many clients with key executives who displayed a similar devotion to their work.

To be exceptional at anything takes more than occasional success. The greats are also able to bring a certain consistency to their craft. They are their own toughest critics. Some of my favorite interactions with people are when they have met my expectations, but they did not satisfy their own high standards. So, they correct the situation. I recall the contractor who renovated the floor of our house, only to show up a day later, indicating that he was not satisfied with the way one corner was completed and wanted to do it over again. Or the tailor who was not satisfied with the fit of a suit after alterations were made, even though it seemed fine to me at the time.

DO EXCEPTIONAL FIRMS ATTRACT EXCEPTIONAL CONSULTANTS?

Yes. Exceptional firms have learned over the years to look for the right attributes among candidates, and they successfully compete for the best and brightest. But it is not just candidates' intellectual powers that count in the job. Other factors are even more important. "Recruit for character, train for skill," as the saying goes. As with a good athlete, there is coaching involved.

I believe the best firms start early with key candidates. They attract them out of the best schools with or without relevant experience. The good firms know how to mold raw talent into solid consultants. Their leaders model such behavior. Like the old apprentice system of the crafts, these firms provide hands-on experience and training so that those so inclined have every chance to succeed.

EXCEPTIONAL CONSULTANTS ARE AUTHENTIC

There is no exceptionalism without authenticity, and a number of points can be made about authenticity, especially given recent world events.

Although perhaps elusive, authenticity has become even more important today as a result of an unregulated internet and the recent coronavirus pandemic.

We live in unique times. The internet, for all its benefits as a technology, has also become the repository of much false information. Such things as "fake news" and questionable remedies have become ubiquitous. "Buyer beware," as the lawyers tell us. As a result, all of us are challenged to determine what is real and what is hyperbole or just plain false.

Perhaps this is best illustrated with the recent pandemic. People constantly invoke "the science" in their discussions. But even the science has changed. First masks are helpful, then not, then mandated in some places. Even the science, which is code for facts, is changing. When something as consequential as a pandemic involves findings that are less than clear, we have an authenticity problem. Politicians don't study epidemiology, but even the epidemiologists have to admit that they have changed their minds on some critical elements of the virus and this has created some confusion. While authentic, even the epidemiologists have been occasionally wrong.

Authenticity is usually associated with art and fashion, but in a negative way because something is inauthentic or fake.

Defining authenticity is like the quote from Potter Stewart, associate justice of the US Supreme Court. While attempting to characterize pornography, Potter said, "I know it when I see it" (*Jacobellis v. Ohio*, 1964). Authenticity might best be understood by focusing on its opposite. The concept of authenticity comes first from the art world, where works of famous painters, composers, and sculptors are carefully examined, which has led to new ways of testing to find copies or fakes. We also think of something authentic from the world of jewelry (real diamonds) or fashion design (it is a genuine Calvin Klein).

So, authenticity applies to art and fashion, but how is it connected to consulting?

Consulting has an image problem; some people are anti-consultant.

On a few occasions, I have tried to understand why certain people have become anti-consultant. There has invariably been a bad experience in their past, or a larger agenda. I remember once being confronted by the leader of a large health system. The engagement involved seeking an appropriate partner in the region. A joint meeting was held involving my client and the potential partner organization. The intent of this first meeting was to do a little "show and tell" about our respective hopes and aspirations for such a partnership. The leader of the other organization proceeded to spend the first 15 minutes of his presentation demeaning the use of consultants in such a collaborative undertaking, stressing, "We don't use consultants."[1]

I am persuaded that the negative image of consulting has its origins in two key elements—lack of training and qualifications, and lack of execution.

In our advertising and sales, we want to put our best foot forward. But such efforts can and do go overboard, and result in false claims. I once subcontracted on a project for a firm that had T-shirts made up for all their consultants that read "We can do that." Well, they couldn't do everything. The firm, a small firm, went out of business some months later (and I never got paid). In retrospect, they lacked training and were clearly unqualified to do certain things, which is one of the reasons that they asked me to help.

Given the lack of barriers to using the term *consultant*, the potential for deception is high. But even some consultants who have some relevant experience might lack formal training. I believe that trained consultants can be easily distinguished from those who are not. This has been a major motivation for writing this book. It is a critical problem that there are too many people in the business who lack relevant training and produce suboptimal work.

It gets more complicated than that. We all have bad days, including failure to execute. When consultants have bad days, it can result in a bad experience for their clients. This has many consequences, including a hit to your reputation (i.e., your brand). Too many hits can put you out of business. Clients that have poor experiences with consultants make it harder on the rest of us.

---

1. Later I noted that not only did they use consultants, they were using one at that time for this purpose. My guess is that the other firm had advised them to try to undercut any advice that we might be offering our client. It turned out to be wise advice because the process then became more difficult to navigate.

Authenticity in consulting produces exceptional client experiences.

Paying closer attention to authenticity can raise performance; there are tools and approaches to help demonstrate authenticity to clients (these are addressed in the following pages). Being qualified and trained is only part of authenticity; another part has to do with sincerity and integrity. Like Justice Stewart, people can tell when someone is sincere. Just as customers really own the brand of a company (they assign the real value of the brand by virtue of their loyalty to it; e.g., some like Coca-Cola, others like Pepsi), they also determine if it is real based on their preferences. Authenticity is in the mind of the client. The willingness of a client to hire a consultant and recommend them for future work is the ultimate reflection of authenticity.

At the outset, we said this book speaks to the consulting experience. Authenticity and experience are inextricably linked. Throughout the book, we have explored some of the nuances of authenticity and some techniques that can be used to both establish and sustain it with a client. The consultant who brings authenticity to an engagement will produce exceptional client experiences more consistently.

GENERAL CONSIDERATIONS

While some attributes of exceptionalism can be quite subtle, others can be rather mundane. Firms look for certain attributes in their candidates, related to certain factors that play out over time. These factors might appear somewhat trivial, at least on the surface.

Traveling Well

To those who are road warriors, there is something to traveling well, but some people simply do not. Can this be learned? Yes. But for those for whom fear of isolation is real and are uncomfortable when not in control, travel might never be easy. Since most consultants require face time with clients (even after we recover from the pandemic), travel is inevitable. Far better to steer away from consulting if travel does not suite you. The seasoned consultant views travel the same way anyone views a simple commute to work, even though one trip alone might involve planes, trains, and automobiles.

Seeking Work–Life Balance

In consulting, multitasking is required, and some people just like to be busy. Clearly, you can stay busy without being a consultant; however, the opposite is probably not true. You cannot be a consultant without enjoying the feeling of always having something to do. It follows that being organized is a must. There are simply too many details to consulting for someone who is disorganized.

The real challenge of consulting is seeking that elusive work–life balance. There are critics of this view, including Jeff Bezos of Amazon, who dismisses this as "a debilitating phrase" (Bernard 2019). Bezos believes that attempting to achieve balance between professional and personal lives implies a strict trade-off. He sees a more holistic relationship between work and life outside the office. There is nothing wrong with seeking a balanced life. The critics seem more focused on where work ends and life begins. Fair enough. However, if work is not enjoyable, then life becomes a chore. "Do something you like" applies, for sure. What about "Do something you are good at?" Not everyone will make a good consultant. It takes passion, energy, and skill to do consulting well. Lacking any one of these will severely limit anyone's success as a consultant.

Some firms have done some innovative things to address this. At National Health Advisors, the firm I founded in 1981, we implemented a credit system where hours in excess of a certain amount each week were tracked and people were encouraged to spend this additional time out of the office when work permitted.

What Matters to You?

At an early age, one of my children remarked that they did not like group activities in school. This raised red flags, of course. The reason was that our child felt the others weren't doing any of the work. Effectively, it would have been fun except for the people. Oops. Do you enjoy being around people or working more on your own? Are you comfortable performing with people looking over your shoulder or more by yourself? Are you energized by working with others who push you? Do you like visiting new cities and meeting new people, or are you more driven to be around close friends you have known for many years? These could well be a few of the more important questions that will ultimately determine your success as a consultant.

What Matters to Your Clients?

Consulting is at its best when the interests of the client coincide with those of the consultant. This is not always the case. And, yes, style matters. As explained in an earlier chapter, shoot-outs between firms are sometimes called "beauty contests." This terminology might sound insulting, but there is an element of truth to it. How a client feels when they are around you matters, just as much as it matters for you. When there is a match, all parties are comfortable and approach their work with confidence, at least initially. It can truly be difficult to function well where there is not a match.

The exceptional consultants seek out the opportunities that fit them best. They might prefer large complex jobs over small engagements. They might prefer working mostly for a CEO versus executive teams or middle management. Some might even prefer not to work with physicians, although this is hard to completely get away from in healthcare. Over time, consulting directs people to areas in which they tend to excel. Like bugs are attracted to light, people migrate to the areas where their efforts are appreciated and where they achieve success. Some people are better with numbers; others are better with people. Most consultants need to be good with both.

Early in my career, I worked with a number of religious leaders, including nuns, in a variety of assignments, such as merger facilitation and strategic planning engagements. With very few exceptions, these women were very accomplished and served as strong role models. Their skills, especially at what they called "discernment," were always impressive to me. (I was warned early on to never play poker with them.) I was at ease working with them in a variety of settings, including some difficult personnel decisions. However, I became uncomfortable when their requests related to what I thought about a certain key executive. I did not feel it was my proper role to have an opinion, nor did I have sufficient information with which to offer a formal opinion.

This is not an uncommon request of a strategy consultant, but it can still be uncomfortable. Such discussions can be consequential; people's careers can even be at stake. Many of the faith-based hospitals that I worked with were built in the 1940s and 1950s, and most were Catholic. By the time a good sister was asking for my opinion on a personnel matter, she typically already had an idea that the hospital might need to make a change.

Over time, what I became comfortable with was sharing the strengths I thought each person had, as well as observations about some areas in which they might benefit from additional training. I never made a recommendation directly to terminate someone, nor was I asked to. The other thing I tried to do was offer my observations about what the good sister seemed to be saying about the person. Had they made up their mind? Could the person be rehabbed, or was it too late?

CRITICAL SUCCESS FACTORS

Critical success factors (CSFs) are to strategic planning as a combination is to a lock. If you understand and successfully implement CSFs, you will unlock the key to success. For many years, Americans accused the Japanese of copying what we did instead of being innovative. Copying the business approach of a successful industry is not necessarily a bad idea. If someone wanted to jumpstart a business, they attempted to determine what was important and then replicated it. Seems simple enough.

What are those things that make one consultant better than another? It would be disingenuous to suggest it is something simple; rather, it takes a lot of little things. For sure, one of them is to be comfortable in your own skin—*be authentic*. People who have to force themselves to behave in a way that does not come naturally will likely struggle. Those who are most comfortable with being constantly on stage and are attracted to the rigors of consulting will likely enjoy more success. The CSFs for consultants to become exceptional include the following:

- Proficiency
- Staying relevant
- Peer-to-peer networking
- Superior team dynamics
- Avoiding occupational hazards
- Exhibiting passion and empathy
- Achieving self-actualization

Proficiency

There is no question that some consultants take too much time to do routine things that others are able to knock out more quickly and with better quality. Some consultants take advantage of automation and have the ability to use tools and technologies. Others seem unwilling to use new technologies or are or unfamiliar with the tools that are available to them.

In one bizarre situation, I hired a senior person I had known tangentially for several years, but was met by a big surprise. As it turned out, their productivity was a serious issue because they had never learned to type. This was something they conveniently left out of the interview process. It wasn't just that they never learned to type; they were unwilling to learn to type. This ultimately affected our professional relationship because I considered the omission a violation of trust. While the fix seemed simple to me, they assumed that someone else would be willing to convert their work. Our relationship did not end well.

Time management is a particularly important proficiency as a consultant enters the "minder" or "finder" levels where they work on multiple assignments at once. It was common in my career to be managing four to six assignments simultaneously. This was on top of the discipline required to maintain a high level of networking to seek out that next client. Anyone who thinks this is easy has not been a consultant for long.

Gaining proficiency early on at basic consulting skills (see chapter 5) plays a big part in your success or failure. Whether it is analytics or writing, I found that mastering these was essential to my productivity. What seemed more like "work" during my early years, when I was trying to gain these competencies, became more enjoyable after I had mastered the basics and adopted more of a clear routine in attacking the work. Over time, I noticed the improved efficiency with which I was able to assess a situation, identify possible solutions and their implications, and make a sound set of recommendations to the client.

The more efficient I got at understanding the context of a given situation (i.e., providing a situational assessment), the more time I was able to spend pondering the fun stuff—alternative scenarios and their implications. Taking care of the basics frees you up to think outside of the box and be innovative: "Have you considered this?" "Thought about doing it this way?" "What have others done under similar situations, maybe from other industries?" I learned to plan such engagements with more purpose and intent. Less time spent in the office with the computer translated into more time testing key conclusions and recommendations directly with the rest of the team and the client. The transformation allowed me to spend more time on higher pursuits, something that did not occur by chance. Mastering the art of preparation is also important in order to both anticipate and respond to questions.

Being able to anticipate how a client will react to certain information stems from preparation that occurs as one becomes more experienced and/or gets to know a client better. Efficiency at analysis and preparation is also important as your individual billing rate increases. As you advance up the ladder, you will be required to come to conclusions in less time, and rely on others more junior to turn out some key work to help make the case. This is the essence of the team consulting business model. Granted, in a solo practice, one is often doing all of these tasks. But even in solo practice, I always preferred working with a consulting team (involving other stringers or collaborating firms[2]), each of whom offered different perspectives. Of course, interacting directly with the client often provides a similar level of input to the process. It can be useful to "rehearse" such discussions ahead of time with the consulting team.

---

2. It should be noted that working with other firms usually meant working from different locations, thus requiring scheduled time on conference calls or video calls to complete this task. Some of the most productive meetings I had involved multiple meetings of the consulting team working out the challenges of a particular engagement.

Staying Relevant

Lifelong learning is a recognized requirement of our fast-changing economy. This coincides with the prediction that millennials will have five or six jobs in their careers, and not the longevity with one employer that was more common among older generations. Millennials are tagged with frequent job changes as a lack of loyalty on their part. But this is not fair. Many jobs will undergo change in the coming years as new technologies are developed. Artificial intelligence, or AI, will clearly affect many professions. Some recent estimates have claimed that as many as 40 percent of jobs will be eliminated or changed dramatically by new technologies.

Dr. Nido R. Qubein is the charismatic leader of High Point University in North Carolina. The school is known for teaching that focuses on experiential learning, and High Point has trademarked its approach *The Premier Life Skills University®*. One of the foundations of the approach is to focus not on how the world is now, but how *it will be*. Dr. Qubein refers to this as relevance, which is what bridges the present with the future. Current practices might survive the future in some form, but they might have to be adjusted or new approaches could be needed to remain relevant.

Another way of referring to relevance is staying fresh, which, of course, is the opposite of getting stale. In professional services, getting stale translates into a couple of things. One is loss of interest. Repetitive work over many years tends to lose its luster. One thing about consulting is that you are working for different clients all the time. The result is constant change, and therefore you need to tailor your craft to the different personalities of each team. New situations can bring excitement, and much of consulting involves helping people understand and deal in different ways with issues that have become quite familiar. There is no question that all consultants spend some time with their clients in the role of teacher.

A second concern is that the consultant gets set in their ways and not open to new approaches. I think the market helps to influence this factor somewhat. The truth is, if your approach or delivery is getting stale, people will point it out to you one way or the other. Most consultants fear the phrase "That information is dated." If clients don't confront you directly, they will do so indirectly by not giving you a good reference or not hiring you again.

At issue is how to stay fresh. It is my impression that, like first responders who run toward danger, consultants are attracted to a challenge. Organizations are complex on many levels. Trying to motivate people to achieve greater gains is never easy. Healthcare is clearly among the more challenging areas in which to operate. Even physicians, some of whom deal with relatively few ailments,[3] find solace in working with different people and finding ways to better connect. The actual work might be similar, but every patient represents a new challenge. How can I improve their health, help them better understand what is happening to their bodies, and help them adopt better lifestyle habits? Likewise, the consultant, faced with a new set of circumstances, takes pride in diagnosing what the problem is and attempting to forge solutions that stand a good chance of being implemented by each client. Some solutions might be tried and true from past engagements. But you also search for the unique in each client engagement that might demand a slightly different approach. As I learned many years ago, clients can suffer a similar problem, but they can also have a different set of skills with which to address it. Not every client is able to implement the same solution efficiently or effectively. If the client fails to implement a recommendation, then the problem is not solved and the engagement is a failure. The best consultants recognize the back end of the client challenge—not only must a solution be found, but the client must be prepared, able, and willing to implement it.

Peer-to-Peer Networking

For the career consultant, it is not possible to excel in consulting without confronting the competitive nature of the business. You might be very good at what you do as a consultant, but others might be better at selling it and/or completing the work. There is an art to respecting the competition and not viewing it as a threat. Some people who are by nature not comfortable with competing should stay clear of consulting. Some firms make a point of finding examples of competitive athletics in the resumes of preferred recruits.

I don't know if getting a sportsmanship award was all that meaningful in high school (I would have preferred most valuable player), but there is one way that it might have foreshadowed good things in my future as a consultant. I have been disappointed in how some people have reacted to competition in the consulting industry. While it is not unique in consulting to disparage a competitor or competing firm, I find it very unattractive. More important though, clients react negatively to this. Sportsmanship for me translates into respecting your competitor and always expecting them to play their best against you. While in college, I found that Duke University rarely got a poor effort from our competitors in basketball, because they thrive on playing the best. Competition pushes teams to perform better and avoid letting down their guard.

---

3. It has been suggested that pediatricians can spend their careers seeing only a limited number of health problems over thousands of visits.

Early in my career, something I really enjoyed was being involved in an association devoted to consulting, which offered the ability to relate peer-to-peer. It quickly became clear to me who the most respected consultants were. They were not just the ones who provided the best services to their clients. This was important, to be sure, but not sufficient. The most respected ones also had a great ability to share their expertise and their craft, and were highly respected by their peers. It is one thing to be respected by your clients, something else to be respected by your peers, who tend to set an even higher bar. It is a great compliment to be referred to as "a consultant's consultant." There is no substitute for peer-to-peer networking and approval.

I took great pride in occasionally taking client referrals from other consultants. Perhaps they had a conflict that prevented them from working with a particular organization, or they felt that my unique skill set could benefit an existing client of theirs in an area in which they were not proficient. Whatever the reason, there was always an added incentive to do good work, and the best way to return the favor was a job well done. I proved to them that the confidence they showed in referring me was paid back whenever their client received a superior outcome by meeting, if not exceeding, expectations.

Superior Team Dynamics

In the case study that we offered about the two new careerist consultants in the introduction to Part III, one of the more subtle dynamics was about teamwork. In the early parts of this book, we talked about brand. We referred to several dynamic speakers who had well-established brands. To be exceptional in consulting, it is necessary to develop and manage your personal brand. For the early careerist, that means defining what you want to be known for. How will you distinguish yourself? You might recall that the more successful consultant in the case study volunteered for various tasks early on. They became a "go-to" person for proposals and other assignments. Eager to gain more experience, this consultant clearly made an impression on other members of the team.

Forgive the sports analogy, but it is important here. A football team is made up of players with different body types, skills, and attitudes. A defensive cornerback lacks the bulk and strength to play on the offensive line. The right tackle of the offensive line would not make a good safety, who has to run fast and be able to cover significant ground. Further, there are techniques that offensive and defensive linemen use that the "skill players" (e.g., those who run, catch, and throw) don't have. You get the idea. Likewise, the consulting team is made up of different people with different skills and attitudes. Only through the application of the collection of skills does the team ultimately succeed. What develops

Avoiding Occupational Hazards

Remember the tired story of the doctor who is visiting with a patient that goes something like this? The doctor asks the patient to press on a knee. "Does that hurt?" To which the patient replies, "Yes."

"Then stop doing it," says the doctor.

Consulting is not for the shy and retiring personality, but it can also cripple a strong person over time. It is hard to be constantly on stage and process the frequent feedback and criticism. It wears on you after a while. For people who might not be that proficient at consulting, it can quickly become painful. This is a difficult topic to address, but it is one that must be more openly acknowledged.

I take no joy in sharing the observation that I have seen consulting destroy people. The destruction can become evident through excessive drinking, drug abuse, and other high-risk behavior. Constant absence from home can make personal life difficult. Over the years this can take its toll. Those of us who have been lucky enough to derive the benefits of a consulting career seem to always have the backing of an understanding spouse and family.

Rather than focus on the time away from the family, I would focus on what can be accomplished in the time you have together. Recognize that time at home is special and should not be squandered. Just as time with a client can be special as well, but in different ways.

I know too many consultants who have reverted to self-medication as part of their routine to get through the day or a stressful situation. Beware the signs of burnout. When too much is expected of you, or what used to be rewarding is no longer gratifying, take those signs seriously and examine other opportunities to which you might be better suited. There is no shame in taking on a different professional role if you no longer derive the satisfaction that feeds the passion required to be a good consultant.

Exhibiting Passion and Empathy

As noted earlier, if only one word was allowed to determine exceptionalism in consulting, I would pick *authentic*. After that, I would pick *passion*, but passion can be a runaway train if not tempered by empathy. I have seen a number of consultants over the years who just ran over people, they were so passionate. Their over-the-top passion made people uncomfortable. When controlled and used for motivation, passion comes through in a positive way to clients.

Passion, as part of authenticity, cannot be faked. The fakes don't last. Passion helps make the mundane meaningful. It allows you to look at each situation with new insights, regardless of how similar it might appear to others you have seen. Passion involves a sense of adventure. Each new client is an opportunity to discover something new about your client . . . and yourself. It is an opportunity to contribute something that the client was unable or unwilling to do for themselves. This is a high calling that must be respected.

Empathy is also required. I once worked with a senior consultant who was passionate and very knowledgeable. We were doing a board retreat and the senior consultant gave one of the final presentations. There was an intensity to this retreat because the client was dealing with some dire issues and things were building toward a conclusion. The consultant became so engrossed in their presentation that they effectively began talking to themself; they completely lost touch with the audience. People got restless. Yet, the consultant kept presenting. Eventually, I had to walk up to the front of the room and assume control of the discussion.

That is a severe example to be sure, but this consultant's extreme focus had overtaken the situation to the exclusion of the client.

By losing connection to the group, the consultant lost any ability to influence the client. Passion overtook empathy. Empathy would have had them monitoring the group and making continuous eye contact to get real-time feedback on how they were (or were not) connecting. In the proper balance, passion and empathy can take a consultant from average to exceptional.

Achieving Self-Actualization

Maslow's well-known hierarchy of needs starts at the bottom level with meeting simple needs and ends at the highest level with self-actualization. This is when you have arrived. When you reach this exalted level, some people suggest, "You have met your calling." This is what you were meant to do. There is no greater feeling as a consultant than to receive praise from a client who needed your help. Don't get too comfortable, because achieving success with one client might be followed by a difficult engagement just around the corner.

No one hits a home run every time at bat. The really talented consultants are able to read a situation and modify their approach to fit each client need. This is truly rarified air. Having a diversity of clients and different types of projects helps to develop these recognition skills, and to add refinements to your consulting style. Emotional intelligence (EQ) is a major part of achieving this status. Recognizing key attributes, learning how to read a group, and adjusting your style to meet each client where they are at that moment is a highly advanced skill that can only be developed through experience. This highly evolved skill will be reflected in your brand.

So again, what do you want your brand to be? The things that stand out in the brands of high-performing consultants or trusted advisors seem very clear:

- Willingness to try new things, take risks
- Ability to master tasks quickly and effectively
- Consistently positive outlook and can-do attitude, even when things get tough
- Willingness to volunteer and devote extra time to various efforts
- Takes pride in their work and requires relatively little oversight
- A caring attitude, not only about the work but also about other team members
- Ability to play different roles as required by the team
- Ability to adjust their approach according to the unique needs of each client

In the competitive world of consulting, it would be hard to overlook the consultant who exhibits these traits.

FUTURE CONSULTING TOOLS

Like many people, I suspect, I am excited about the potential represented by artificial intelligence. AI is already in use in challenging training programs (e.g., surgery) and is starting to be used in decision support. IBM's Watson is being aggressively introduced—with promising results—into population health clinical diagnoses and other multivariate situations. Pairing up data analysis with decision-making processes is nothing new. What is new is the number of variables that can be supported in such an effort, and the ability to increasingly rely on larger and larger datasets to help make decisions.

For many years, consultants have attempted to supplement their tools by developing software that provides analytic efficiency. The whole field of *predictive analytics* holds great promise across many platforms. *Population health* is built around predictive analytics, as is *personalized or precision medicine*.

Clearly, there are many dramatic innovations in medicine expected in the future, and many of these have implications for consultants. While there is some fear of automation and the resulting loss of jobs—especially for repetitive work—I do not think this will be the case in the creative work that is increasingly demanded of consultants. Time will tell.

REFERENCE

Bernard, Z. 2019. "Jeff Bezos' Advice to Amazon Employees Is to Stop Aiming for Work–Life 'Balance'—Here's What You Should Strive for Instead." *Business Insider*. Published January 9. www.businessinsider.com/jeff-bezo-advice-to-amazon-employees-dont-aim-for-work-life-balance-its-a-circle-2018-4.

CHAPTER 13

Achieving Trusted Advisor Status

MANY OF THE TOPICS OF THIS CHAPTER have been noted before in this book. However, the intent here is to describe what *going the extra mile* looks like to achieve the desired impact on the client. Some of this involves merely placing the emphasis in the right areas during the consulting process, which is not as easy as it sounds. It is helping the client to distinguish what is more important than something else (the 80/20 rule)—avoiding rabbit holes, for example. Remember, overall success is defined by at least meeting, if not exceeding, client expectations on time and on budget. Doing this creates trust. It creates a client reference that can be used to generate future work. Here are some small but meaningful things that have worked for me over the years.

SCOPE OF WORK

Being exceptional starts with buttoning up the scope of work (SOW). The transition from most proposals to a final engagement almost always involves some interpretation and negotiation. Recognizing this up front in an engagement is invaluable. Many consultants skip this step and rely, instead, solely on the proposal language. While understandable on one level, over time I came to the conclusion that it represents a lost opportunity. This is your chance to raise some ideas with the client that they might not have thought of since the proposal was written, so why not share any additional thoughts you might have? It can involve considering other options, understanding better what the goal is, and being innovative in how this might be approached. Yes, there were preliminary answers in doing this proposal, but the consultant is more knowledgeable now about what is being sought, and some modifications might be in order.

Nothing gets in the way of an enduring client relationship (covered more later) more than a misunderstanding. That is why I will reiterate here: Get the SOW finalized before proceeding on any engagement.

The SOW often becomes the final contracting vehicle, so I advise you to have legal counsel look it over for any final adjustments. An addendum can be added to the contract and will supersede the original. It is helpful to avoid being overly legalistic while still accomplishing the clear understanding that must exist before beginning the assignment. It is worth taking additional time as necessary to make sure both parties are totally comfortable with the scope and deliverables. Avoid the dreaded "scope creep," where the client asks for more and more that exceeds the initial scope of work.

DISPUTE RESOLUTION

Most firms approach dispute resolution through arbitration, simply because any client will want the legal venue to be its state. Politics often comes into play. If your business is not located in that state, you start off at a disadvantage. It is always helpful to have outside counsel review your standard documents periodically to keep dispute resolution tight and clear. Securing this contractually up front can save trouble later. Obviously, both you and your client hope that any misunderstanding can be cleared up through direct communications.

COMMUNICATION

There is no substitute for staying in close contact with the client during an engagement. In fact, lack of communication is one of the most frequent complaints of clients. Although communication can be delegated, it is important that the lead consultant stay in touch with the client's main contact on a regular basis. Nothing less than weekly contact should occur, and an appropriate amount of face time should be scheduled depending on the nature of the engagement. A study focused on process issues should probably involve more face time than a heavy analytics study.

Communication is so important to the success of an engagement that I recommend scheduling all meetings, video calls, and phone calls for the entire engagement at the very outset. This sets expectations and assures the client that they will stay engaged.

DISCLOSURE

Never assume when it comes to disclosure. Make sure that any potential conflict is raised with the client at the outset. For example, you might get a request from a nearby organization to do a similar study. Before going any further, make sure to give your current client an opportunity to consider this from their perspective. If the new prospect is a clear competitor and the issue is strategic in nature, your current client might very well be concerned. If the work is more operational in nature, competition will be less of an issue. The important thing is that you gave your client an opportunity to weigh in before going any further with the other prospect. Their trust in you was paramount in your selection. Maintaining the trust of the existing client is an obligation that comes before adding any new business. I recommend that you share your notes regarding any discussion about disclosure with the client to ensure documentation.

ENGAGEMENT INTERVIEW PROCESS

It will come as no surprise, given the in-depth discussion surrounding the interview process in this book, that I believe that one of the most important distinctions between the pros and the amateurs relates to interviews. *The best consultants simply learn more from interviews.* They engage the client better, and they find out information in a nonthreatening way that others would not likely get. These better outcomes result from connecting with the client. Make them comfortable and earn their trust. I have found that giving up something helps to gain something. Making yourself vulnerable (e.g., "Truth be known, that is is not my strong suit") can help them loosen up and want to share more with you.

One example is conducting competitor interviews, something we generally do as part of a strategic planning process. Our clients have been astounded by what their competitors are willing to reveal in an interview with an independent third party. Often, competitors like to brag. My observation is that people who are comfortable with the concept of competition are less concerned with secrets and more concerned with execution. It is like the old Notre Dame football story, where Notre Dame lets the opposing team know that they will be running the same play on offense every time (e.g., off right tackle). Notre Dame is essentially announcing that they have so much confidence in their ability to execute this play that they take the mystery out of the offense. Your competition no longer has to guess what play you are going to run. You are daring the other team to execute better.

REPORTS AND DELIVERABLES

The look and feel of deliverables count. Part of managing the little things is to take the time to make the final product perfect. Booz Allen had their reports professionally bound in expensive covers. The reports were not only well written but also looked good. As we have moved away from written reports over time, other presentation media like PowerPoint provide tight, well-organized reports that look good and accomplish their purpose. A final report should communicate clearly and simply what is required with minimal extraneous material. Details can be contained in worksheets and other pieces not part of the core presentation. Exceptional consultants have well-organized work papers in their files. Deliverables are always presented to the client on time, with no surprises. This point is critical; the last thing a client wants is a surprise.

FIRST IMPRESSIONS

When you first get started in consulting, you meet a lot of people and it can be overwhelming. You meet people both in the firm and with the client. At a firm, you get to know your peers over time, but I've found that traveling can make this difficult. It has always been amusing to me that Monday through Thursday, many consulting offices are empty except for administrative staff. This makes internal monthly meetings and retreats very important, because, other than while you're working together during client engagements, they represent the few times that you can really get to know the people with whom you work. It gets even more challenging when multiple offices are involved, because much of the time you spend together is in conference or video calls.

Clients are a different story. Most client engagements are rather short in duration. While you are at the client site, you are *a guest in their house*. Of course, you as the consultant will schedule regular meetings with specific client representatives. But do not forget that the client is the one who ultimately dictates where you can go and how long you can stay. Remember, you are their guest. You learn to size up people quickly because you know that your time with them is limited to the engagement.

During my career, the typical engagement lasted only three to four months. First impressions, therefore, are even more important to a consultant than in other professions. There is a saying, "You never get a second chance to make a first impression."

In the case of some people you meet at the client site, first impressions might be your only impression. You will see them only once, perhaps for an interview. Others you will interact with extensively, depending on the assignment.

No one is more important at the client site than support staff. They not only keep the client organized, but they are often the face of the organization to anyone visiting the client. They will play a large role in your site visits, so take the time to get to know them. It will pay off. They, as a rule, are some of the nicest people you could ever hope to meet. Really smart organizations thoroughly train their support staff because they know that this group has a significant impact on corporate culture and is an important extension of the brand. In fact, many CEOs treat their assistants as peers. Some even take them with them to their next job. I had an assistant for many years who was so important to me that when I moved to a new company I insisted on a package deal in which they took both of us.

Critical analysis is something that is deeply imbedded in my psyche, even going back as far as my childhood. Perhaps it is a character flaw. It took observing some of my colleagues and how they approached new situations to improve my own approach toward meeting new people. Simply stated, I learned from my peers to always look for the good in people.

This may not be immediately obvious to some. The simple reality is that not everyone is going to respond positively to you at first. Sometimes the way someone relates to you might actually have nothing to do with you but rather relates to a bad consulting experience that they had previously. Sometimes you have to work harder to earn their trust. It just comes with the territory. Occasionally, animosity can develop, and rectifying this situation is not always possible. When it can be addressed, there is a simple technique that I developed over time.

Whenever I sensed that I was not connecting well with someone, during a break I would approach them privately and ask if I had offended them in some way, or if there was something that I could do to gain their participation. Sometimes a person would simply acknowledge that they were distracted and that I should not be concerned about it because it was unrelated to the discussion. When this method worked, confronting that person truly created a breakthrough, and they appreciated that I made myself vulnerable out of respect and had tried to make things better.

Sometimes, elements of a client situation just are not made clear to you in your role as consultant. This took many years of experience for me to understand. The reality is that certain team members might not get along and other circumstances may be affecting the situation. I like to share with new clients that "You will always understand your circumstances better than we do, but our hope is to bring a fresh eye to your situation that will allow us all to look at things in a new way."

I was never good at remembering names. This is a liability in consulting, especially with regard to networking. It makes a better first impression if you can quickly remember everyone's name. A few small things can make this much easier. Ask to have participants' names provided to you prior to every client meeting. Also, I liked to map out the seating arrangement at all meetings. First meetings with a group usually involve introductions by everyone sitting around the table. Take a minute to record their names on a seating chart as they go around the room. This is an easy way to create some muscle memory with that client. The consulting team should discuss everyone who will be at a meeting beforehand to reinforce names and share impressions about where everyone stands with the engagement.

MUSCLE MEMORY

As a pretty good athlete, I was always intrigued with the concept of muscle memory. I majored in neuroscience in college, so I learned early about the reptilian brain versus the more advanced cerebral cortex. I think of the reptilian brain as being similar to *instinct* exhibited by the rest of the animal kingdom, defined by Merriam-Webster as "a largely inheritable and unalterable tendency of an organism to make a complex and specific response to environmental stimuli **without involving reason**" (emphasis added). When a practice becomes a habit or part of your routine without consciously thinking about it, this is muscle memory. Adopting good work habits from the start will last your whole career. Small things like a seating chart can make the process of orientating to a new client much easier and more fun.

I have also found an interesting thing about muscle memory: It can become somewhat fluid over time. Let me give you an example. One of the training exercises that I particularly enjoyed as a new consultant was related to public speaking. I don't care how experienced you are at public speaking; little things can creep into your delivery, like using a word too often, such as "OK," or swaying while you speak. These little quirks become distracting to the audience. The reason many speakers try a little humor in the beginning is that they want the audience to know that you are comfortable speaking to them. You need to put them at ease so they can give you their full attention. Distractions will divert their attention, which means they might miss some of your important messages. I am convinced that such distractions in public speaking often reflect a situation in which the speaker has become too much at ease—too casual. Public speaking, by definition, means that you are onstage. You are performing. To do this well, you must maintain an edge.

Throughout your consulting career, you will find that many things become part of your routine, become muscle memory, and work well. Occasionally, however, things come up that involve changes you would like to make. I used to play a lot of golf. Like many people, it did not come naturally to me. I developed some bad habits in the game when I was young. One time, during lessons, I was trying to make a specific swing change. The teaching pro asked, "How does it feel?"

It was a trap, and I fell right into it, replying, "Great."

Oops. He quickly responded, "Then you are doing it wrong!"

His point was that if I was really trying to change something, it would never feel great. Change is hard, and never easy. It is uncomfortable, awkward. It takes time for the change to feel good as it becomes more natural and part of your muscle memory. Consulting, at its core, is about change. The more consultants have experience with and understand change, the better consultants they will be. I advised many clients over the years on mergers, and yet it was not until my own merger with another firm that I was able to experience the many emotions that accompany such a radical change.

FALL ON YOUR SWORD

There are times when things can get truly messy. I found this was more often the case during merger discussions than any other type of engagement. People become fearful of losing their jobs. The reason for this is simple: In a merger of two hospitals there will be people in duplicate positions. The surviving organization, as it is called, only requires one of certain key positions. Thus, winners and losers are created. The politics of vying to survive a merger can get very complex. Sometimes the threat can be so great that people sabotage the discussions in a desperate effort to save their jobs. Such was the case in one situation.

My client was a hospital that was looking for a partner, and the sooner the better because the future was looking quite negative. Negotiations had proceeded after a protracted and difficult search, and we ended up selecting from among three potential partners. By coincidence, the one that was selected happened to have a CEO with whom I was well acquainted, but my client did not know that.

During a particularly stressful part of the discussion, my client told me that the CEO of the potential partner organization had challenged my credibility to continue in my role as facilitator. When I heard this I knew immediately that it was a ruse, because my client was not aware of the relationship I had with this person. I immediately offered to contact the CEO to correct the situation. Essentially, I called my client's bluff. My client instinctively realized he had made a serious mistake and asked me not to do that. So, what to do?

In this moment, it was important to step back and remember who my client was. If I disclosed that my client was making a false accusation, showing a lack of integrity, it would have created a compromising position at a critical time. I knew that this merger was very important, and I did not want anything to get in the way. My client was trying to push me out of the discussions so he could control them himself, or perhaps to get the credit. Regardless, it became clear that he felt threatened. I had a decision to make.

I interpreted this incident as a sign that it had somehow become important for my client CEO to move forward with the negotiations without my help. We had essentially taken this client as far as we could go in this process, under these circumstances. While I might have had an alternative route to the board to help address the issue, there was no real appetite or ability at that level of the organization to step in. We had already shared our recommendations for the merger and how it should be structured. Any surprises or disturbance at this critical juncture would likely spook the partner.

So, I fell on my sword.

TIP FROM THE TRENCHES

Exceptional consultants understand where and when their egos might get in the way. This involves recognizing the needs of the client and the client leader, who are not always the same. It also requires the ability to be in the moment, to see forward and enable the intended outcome by removing yourself from the picture when necessary. It is trusting that you have injected sufficient guardrails into the process that its ultimate success is assured without your further involvement. Occasionally, it requires swallowing some pride and losing some recognition for yourself.

THE ENDURING CLIENT RELATIONSHIP

Managing the client relationship represents the core of the consulting process. Any consultant with experience knows that the single best opportunity for the growth of any practice is to do more for existing clients—to become their trusted advisor. This can involve add-on work related to current assignments, or cross-selling other services that the firm offers outside of the existing assignment. Taking care of existing clients requires a far lower cost of marketing than attempting to attract new clients.

Nothing is more fundamental to the success of any business than identifying your real customer and understanding the essential requirement to meet their needs. There can be no more profound concept in business. While this might sound simple, in healthcare it is also probably seldom successfully accomplished. In most healthcare organizations there are usually multiple stakeholders, and they might very well want different things.

Different customer segments have different requirements, and resolving the inherent conflicts can become the key challenge to a consultant. Mass customization applies to healthcare as much as it does any other industry.

The holy grail of consulting is clearly the *enduring client relationship*. This happens when a relationship has become well established, and causes the client to think of using this consultant in all future related work. These kinds of relationships never occur by chance. Rather, they result from a calculated investment of time and effort by both the consultant and the client in which value is clearly derived. In my experience, this involves a complementary relationship between the competencies of the client and those of the consultant—synergy. Value derives from providing different perspectives on important issues for the client.

While the view of the client is ultimately determinative (i.e., it is the client that is hiring the consultant), I often find that the consultant can gain considerably from the experience as well. What do I mean by this?

Clearly, for the relationship to be enduring, the client must want to hire the consultant again. At a minimum, that requires that prior engagements went well. Rarely, however, is this enough. A certain level of trust must have been established, and this might have developed separately from the engagement itself. It might relate more to the style of communication, or because of a sidebar issue that arose during an engagement that the client shared with the consultant. It also involves a certain level of vulnerability, and that vulnerability can go both ways. In one dramatic case, a client pointed out that a member of our team rubbed some members of the client team the wrong way. I had to remove the consultant from the engagement and take a large write-down because the consultant was perceived very poorly by the client, and I was required to back out any charges for his time.

Being open to feedback from the client creates vulnerability for the consultant, but it can also help establish trust with the client, if managed properly. When the issue is effectively addressed, better interactions follow. This example shows that there are an infinite number of ways that trust can be established during an engagement. The key is to have this translate into a relationship in which both parties are comfortable sounding out the other. A certain level of candor is part of this relationship. Of course, while this will be surprising to some clients, not every consultant wants to work again for every client. Where things really click, consultants are usually willing to work hard to be worthy of future work.

A variety of things bring value to the client, including sharing key information on a timely basis (e.g., market trends), occasional entertainment (dinner or a sporting event), or simply exhibiting a willingness to be a sounding board when the client is confronted with challenging issues. In my experience, these can become very personal relationships that can be rewarding on many levels. While it is always a bit daunting to have a professional-level relationship cross the threshold to personal (after which objectivity is no longer really possible), I have certainly benefited greatly from these relationships.

I have been honored in my career with six to ten enduring client relationships—trusting relationships in which all strategy work was effectively funneled my way for at least a few years, if not decades. Most of these clients had an in-house strategy and marketing team. We learned to work well together to formulate options and make sound recommendations. It helped, of course, that recommended actions succeeded over time. Positive results reinforced the relationship.

These were among the most satisfying clients because there was a level of trust that bound us close together. Both the client and I were each invested in the success of their organization. We shared confidences and we were successful in what we did together. Most of these relations were through the CEO, but not all. In some cases, I helped a senior executive who helped the CEO succeed in their capacity.

None of these situations came easily. In fact, to achieve this elevated status required navigating some challenging circumstances. Facing key challenges with a client and succeeding sets the table for more meaningful work. Sometimes such bonds are formed in challenging "foxhole" situations.

In my experience as a strategy consultant, the vehicle for such enduring relations tended to evolve out of one of two things: regularly updating a strategic planning process or continued involvement in implementing a specific strategy (e.g., in mergers and acquisitions, or a clinical service line strategy) that helped grow and integrate a health system. I can give you examples of both.

Working with one client involved a serious turnaround situation that became the foundation of an initial strategic plan. These were not easy times, especially given that the client initially had a very different understanding of their strategic position than the reality that faced them. No one likes bad news. The strategic planning process became somewhat dramatic in that it placed the brutal facts before the client, and we succeeded in transitioning the organization from disbelief to resolve.

While the full turnaround took years, it was eventually successful, largely because of a unifying vision that allowed for other strategies to be more fully embraced. A trust grew, and participation by all stakeholders in an open process ultimately succeeded in creating momentum for this client that allowed the hospital to break out from the pack. This was one of three community organizations serving overlapping markets with a similar mix of services.

The key to creating this enduring relationship was participation by the consultant in the strategic planning process. This became the basis for additional work over the years to bring these strategies to fruition.

In one merger process, we had an opportunity to create a new regional health system involving a community hospital and an academic medical center. As new merger opportunities arose, the trust created during the initial engagement resulted in additional requests to facilitate these discussions. In one situation, two competing hospitals asked to have an *exclusive* discussion with the system that we had created earlier (i.e., my client would have to choose between the two potential partner organizations). We were able to suggest that joint discussions occur with all three parties. There were some antitrust issues that had to be managed, but we were commissioned to conduct such a process, which subsequently had a successful outcome. The beneficiaries of this approach were clearly the communities that would eventually experience significant improvements in local healthcare delivery. This success led to additional merger discussions for many years thereafter.

Having these enduring client relations over many years was very gratifying. It is rare that a consultant is able to see the results of their work evolve over such a long period of time. It made me smarter as lessons were learned, and these clients clearly helped grow my practice.

CHAPTER 14

Lessons from the Road

PURSUIT OF LIFELONG LEARNING has allowed me to see firsthand what makes certain consultants exceptional in an overcrowded field. While I'm not sure I ever fully cracked the code, this chapter includes some observations from the road worth sharing. As before, some are success stories, others are not. Many of the mistakes you'll read about are my own, and I offer them here to help you avoid repeating them. As always, I have tried to shield clients in confidentiality.

The vast majority of stories I could tell were successes, to be sure. The ones I present here are those I feel are the most consequential and have left a lasting impression. The case studies might appear a bit skewed to the negative, but these tend to be best to illustrate opportunities for learning.

Realistically, every client engagement offers something new. I have learned some lessons that were tough to accept, which I characterized as "learning lessons I did not need to know." But the best consultants must guard against getting too fixed in their views or too quick to come to conclusions. They must remain open to new learning throughout their careers. This is part of the fun of consulting, because just when you think you have seen it all. . . .

LESSON 1: THE THREE MOST IMPORTANT PEOPLE

The success of a project hinges on the consultant's relationship with the client team. One person in the client organization often holds the key to any particular engagement. Rarely is it more than three people. The challenge is to figure out who these important people are, how to position the issue in such a way that it appeals to their self-interest, and to time the intervention appropriately so that the desired change is implemented. What is often most important is not what the consultant does during a given engagement, but what they leave behind. Bolstering a leader or a team by helping them to deal effectively with a given issue can embolden them for future good deeds. It's also not bad for future business!

In one dicey engagement, a power struggle developed among a few board members of a regional health system. It did not help that this was playing out on the front pages of the local newspaper. It became an issue when the same board terminated the system's CEO and created a vacuum. It was not a pretty picture. Mind you, these were highly engaged board members who brought a great deal of experience to the organization—but not necessarily from healthcare. There were multiple dimensions to the power struggle, including among the interim executives who were appointed to temporarily hold the fort while things got worked out. In a situation like this, how do you figure out who the really important people are?

One lesson that I have never forgotten was that the people who had the most to say (i.e., made the most noise) were not necessarily the people who ended up being important in reaching a new equilibrium. In fact, some of the most important people did not say much in the open meetings, but worked more behind the scenes (informal leaders) and had established strong credibility within the group. This only came to light through extensive interviews.

I have put this observation to work in many different situations over the years. A consultant has to be careful not to come to conclusions too early in an engagement. The people who seem most in charge at the outset might not be. A healthy skepticism should exist; there is more than meets the eye in many such engagements. ("If it were easy, they would have already solved it themselves.") The key question to ask yourself is, Why did this situation develop to the point of needing intervention by an outside group, versus something that could be resolved internally? There has to be a good reason.

In my experience, finding and making active use of the opinions of the true leaders can be very important. You could also become an active participant in a succession plan that was years in the making, even though this might not have been part of your original agreement with the client. Figure out the relevant context and correctly determine who to listen to about what is going on and what options exist to resolve the issue.

LESSON 2: CAPTURE THE KEY EXCHANGE

I believe that one key exchange always stands out from each engagement. When you're starting out, that exchange might become apparent only in hindsight. Over time, however, you should try to learn to capture it as it occurs. This is a great skill to develop, one that can improve efficiency and will influence the rest of the engagement. The point is to learn from experience, to recognize and exploit it. This key exchange or breakthrough concept can be leveraged considerably, especially if it comes out of a group exchange in such a way that the group takes ownership in its development. "As we realized at the meeting on Tuesday . . . " Even if the consultant actually came up with it, give ownership to the group, and you will dramatically improve your potential for buy-in and implementation.

In one situation, I was facilitating the completion of a strategic planning process for a large community hospital. It was perhaps the third iteration of their strategic plan that I was facilitating, each one having a time horizon of three years. When I returned approximately two years after completing the last iteration, I was shocked to find that less than 50 percent of the annual initiatives had been successfully implemented. This was quite different from the performance results of the prior two iterations. Something was very wrong.

As it turned out, although some consensus had been developed during the last process, which had involved most of the executive team and the board, the CEO did not support the outcome or the supporting strategies. For some reason—which never became clear—the CEO chose to "sit this one out" and not participate actively during the planning process. In one key session, there was a pregnant pause and the door was wide open for the CEO to become engaged. The team was literally waiting for his comment, but it never came.

I rationalized at the time that it was merely a stylistic change the CEO was making, which was a conscious attempt to empower other members of the team. In retrospect, I came to realize that the vision of the CEO was different from what had been worked out with the team. For some reason, the CEO decided not to share this openly or to deal with it directly. I had lost control of the process as far as the CEO was concerned, and this became a dangerous situation.

It could be suggested—rightfully—that I had inadvertently failed to create a safe space and had imposed my will on the group during the last process. In doing so, I had failed to convince the CEO of this point of view, or failed to more directly solicit his vision. I had become an advocate and violated the rule of facilitation in which consensus is allowed to surface from the group. Either way, I did not read the situation correctly. Perhaps I had been impatient in getting to consensus.

The result was a poorly executed plan that did not enjoy support from the top. This turned out to be the beginning of the end of this client relationship. Several years later, the CEO was terminated by that board, and the vision of this particular plan was allowed to replace the one championed by the CEO. I had somehow missed this essential disconnect along the way.

LESSON 3: THE WORLD'S SMARTEST—HOUSTON, WE HAVE A PROBLEM!

It is inevitable, in larger engagements, that there is always at least one person who qualifies as The World's Smartest *fill-in-the-blank*. The "World's Smartest" considers this type of work to be sport; they try to test the different dimensions of the engagement and attempt to trip up the consultant with a visible "gotcha." This type of person is insecure and/or has a history of trying to show to the group just who has the most insight or smarts for particular issues. Sometimes their motivation may be that they feel threatened since they have line responsibility for the area in question and they resent having an outside consultant involved.

This contrasts greatly with the confident executive who is only too pleased to have a consultant help fix a problem. Unfortunately, sometimes it is the consultant who brings on the fight. It is important not to come across as a know-it-all. I have seen more than one consultant, often young and inexperienced, fall into the trap of coming across as arrogant in a meeting with a client, like the marketing executive who was perceived as condescending when addressing a foundation board. This was a board made up of highly engaged, experienced, and wealthy donors, and at one point it just became too much and one board member commented to the executive, "Excuse me, but you are not the only person in this room with marketing experience." Part of this was clearly attitude.

There are a few things that can be done when you are confronted by a situation where someone is trying to trip you up. It begins with your attitude. I believe that the client team in most engagements actually possesses the ability to find a proper solution to the challenge at hand. As a result, these engagements are more process oriented (i.e., facilitation), in which the aim is to bring this knowledge to the surface in a coherent form that is nonthreatening to the participants. One can set the stage by approaching such engagements first with questions. Start with some simple ones that give the client team members confidence that they understand the issues, and that invite their active participation in the dialogue. Asking the right questions sets up a safety zone for discussion so that it's easier for the more introverted participants to enter into the fray and not just observe. It also levels the playing field for the extroverts who might otherwise dominate such discussions. The result is that anyone who aspires to come across as the smartest in the group will not be allowed to stand out since the facilitator has succeeded in getting everyone to express themselves.

The ultimate success of such interactions is that the smarter folks do not feel cut off, but come to respect the insightful comments of others in the room. A consensus occurs with buy-in by those who were involved in creating this result. The consultant helps steer the conversation and prevents it from getting stuck by directing the dialogue in a way that is more substantive. There is no substitute for allowing the client team to own the result, and participation should result in commitment.

TIP FROM THE TRENCHES

It is easy to spend someone else's money. The challenge is to create a framework in which the decision-makers take on the mindset of the owner, with the need to have the result justify the decision. Superior consultants find ways to help people empathize, get out of their comfort zone safely, and take on new attitudes (ideally without losing passion). Sometimes this is nothing more than looking at familiar data in a different light. This can be done temporarily through such techniques as role-playing and case studies, or it can be done more permanently by changing related structures and incentives.

Yes, significant team dynamics are often at work in consulting engagements. The key for the really talented consultant is to find the right approach toward directing engagements in ways that are not threatening to the executives, who are ultimately responsible for managing their teams, and that create a safe space where title and position mean nothing—rather, all are empowered to participate fully in the discussion without threat of any kind.

Depending on the nature of the issue, there might be clear differences of opinion at the outset. It is imperative to make the point that such differences are not only to be tolerated, but encouraged. It is important that no participant be so invested in a particular point of view that being open to other thoughts and positions becomes difficult. The consultant should establish up front that the end result could take the best approaches from each option to create something that does not yet exist. When participants take firm positions and the discussion becomes adversarial, it might be necessary to do some role-playing in which those involved are asked to advocate for a position they do not support. This can break some tension and at the same time be entertaining.

LESSON 4: ABILITY TO SEE YOURSELF AS OTHERS SEE YOU

It is important to always bring your A game. Recognize from the outset that there are situations in which you might fold under pressure. Preparation helps, but it is even more important to be able to elevate yourself from the situation to see how you are connecting with your audience. Some lessons are learned along the way that have a lasting impression.

One lesson that was particularly hard to learn occurred somewhat early in my career. It was a full weekend retreat at the culmination of a board-driven planning process. The stakes were very high—the discussion was about rebuilding a hospital in an historic city.

The stakeholders were split: the traditionalists versus the modernists. The traditionalists were dominating. They wanted to keep the hospital located in the middle of the city. This spot was rather restricted in size; thus there had been no growth for the past 50 years. The modernists wanted to move outside the city boundaries into what was projected to become one of the fastest-growing counties in the country. (And the projections proved true!) The dialogue involved some 30 people, including an older, rather dignified ex-military gentleman who seemingly represented the traditionalists. He did not speak often, but when he did, all listened carefully.

We spent the first day reviewing data and providing information to the group that would set up the ultimate discussion about possibly moving and rebuilding the hospital. As I recall, up until this point, the option of possibly moving the hospital had not been openly discussed, only rebuilding it.

I spent a somewhat sleepless night at the end of the first day knowing that I would need to make the case for such a move. I came in the next morning energized to meet the challenge. I spent about 45 minutes with solid slides and had nice interaction with most of the group. I asked some probing questions to get everyone engaged. After my final statement, we took a break. I felt good about where we were until . . .

The dignified gentleman walked up to me, handed me a handwritten note, and walked away. The note looked like this:

I stared at it for a moment in shock. The person I needed most to hear the key arguments had not heard a word I said for the entire presentation. I had distracted him by saying "OK" exactly 39 times. I went from king of the mountain to roadkill in less than ten seconds. It took me the rest of the day to restate the case and gain his engagement. While others were convinced, this key leader was distracted, in part because he was hearing certain arguments for the first time (since he missed my earlier presentation). How you present matters as much as the content of the presentation.

LESSON 5: HELPING PEOPLE SEE THEMSELVES IN THE VISION

Vision is sometimes referred to as *grand strategy*. Too often, vision is in the mind of the CEO but is otherwise not shared by the group. At the next level, vision might be committed to writing, but people are unable to connect with it.

There is a tool in consulting called *learning maps*. Much of what I know about this came from many collaborative client engagements with a firm now called Root. Root was founded by Jim Haudan[1] and his managing partner, Randy Root. Their unique approach is based on the central premise that "strategy execution" has the greatest impact on a company's success. As Haudan (2008) explains in his book *The Art of Engagement*, their group went on to develop learning maps and other tools that provide a means for engaging people across a firm in strategy execution. Simply stated, through application of this process, participants are able to envision themselves in scenes that represent the future.

A good example of Root using these tools in healthcare comes from Dr. James Merlino. He described how my friend, Arden Brion of Root, took the Cleveland Clinic through a service-enhancement visioning project. At the time, Dr. Merlino was the chief experience officer for the Clinic and was faced with the daunting task of addressing a key challenge (Merlino 2015). They had just gotten the results of their HCAHPS[2] scores. As he put it:

> How could a hospital ranked as one of America's best by *U.S. News & World Report* be among the lowest performers with regard to the patient experience?

Applying learning maps at the Cleveland Clinic allowed nearly every member of the team to become immersed in the vision and thereby determine how best

---

1. Read Haudan (2008) to learn more about Root.

2. HCAHPS stands for Hospital Consumer Assessment of Healthcare Providers and Systems, provided by the Centers for Medicare & Medicaid Services based on a sample of patient surveys.

to fit into that vision. The result was a level of commitment that could not be otherwise achieved.

Visioning is a term that is used to mean many things. One variation that I subscribe to comes from the sports world. For example, a golfer tries to "envision" a shot before they attempt it. With a professional golfer one can often hear the caddy's last piece of advice, "Now commit to the shot," which means see it before you attempt it. There is power in vision if correctly directed. I believe artificial intelligence will ultimately find ways to leverage this as well. A vision-driven strategic plan that provides a detailed description of the desired future state is many times more powerful than another plan where the future state, or vision, is less clear.

TIP FROM THE TRENCHES

Diagnostics are about recognizing patterns. There are a limited number of patterns, yet the variations can be unlimited. Good diagnosticians learn to recognize what they have seen before and then contrast that with things that might not be similar. Everyone has a need to feel unique. Skilled consultants learn to "mention the unmentionable in a mentionable way." They learn techniques that allow each participant to see things through their own lens, and then come out in support of the ultimate decision. Note: It is rare that consultants can do this by simply sharing their vision. Rather, you must create a process that allows each participant to do it for themselves. The engagement is of no value if the findings, conclusions, and recommendations are sound but do not get implemented. They only have value if implemented effectively, which means that the participants have found a way to insert themselves into the process and own the results.

I have participated in many strategic planning processes with healthcare organizations and associations, and I have observed that each one has a slightly different view of what this entails. I subscribe to Joel Barker's view of vision,[3] where there are four key elements:

1. Leader-initiated
2. Shared and supported by all
3. Comprehensive and detailed
4. Positive and inspiring

---

3. In 1986, Joel Barker published his first video, *The Business of Paradigms*, which by 1988 became the most popular business video of all time. It was followed in 1990 by his second video, *The Power of Vision.*

In my experience, gaining consensus around a well-defined and measurable vision through an immersion process is a powerful tool for strategic planning.

One dramatic engagement with a large health system client took place at an annual leadership retreat. In attendance were 150 board members (from the different boards of this diversified regional health system), physician leaders, and executives. We had them construct the Golden Gate Bridge from a large model, then walk across it, symbolizing "Bridging to the Future." Of course, this walk was surrounded with all kinds of discussion that helped everyone understand the future vision and feel motivated to make it a reality.[4]

LESSON 6: FAIRNESS AND GETTING FIRED

There is a saying in retail that "the customer is always right." Personally, I don't believe this applies in a consulting practice, but there is no denying that a client has the never-ending right to fire the consultant.

Unfortunately, I have had a number of experiences that reinforce that adage. On one particular case, I had just finished conducting three days of intense interviews with board members, physician leaders, and executives to start a new client engagement. Shortly thereafter, I was informed by the partner in charge that I was no longer welcome on the campus of this hospital.

I had become persona non grata, so the firm provided other consultants to complete the work. Of course, I was reeling from the shock of having been informed of this in this fashion (it had never happened before or since), so I started to ask questions. The first was logically, "What had gone wrong?" Even though I never got a very good answer to this, it was notable that the client contact was a CEO who was not only brand-new to this position, but also was brand-new to being a CEO. Regardless of the circumstances, my usually reliable antennae had failed to read the situation correctly. I had screwed up.

By far my biggest disappointment was that the client felt unable to confront me directly. Clearly, that is on me; I had failed to establish trust with this individual. I was embarrassed and disappointed. On reflection I also came to understand that I was at a distinct disadvantage in trying to diagnose what had transpired. I had not been involved in the selling process of this engagement. In fact, I only met the client upon arriving to conduct the initial interviews. While not uncommon to consulting overall, it was rare in my experience that I held a lead position with clients in which I had had no role in selling the engagement. As I've mentioned

---

4. This engagement was completed in collaboration with Gary Adamson and his team from Starizon Studio.

before, one of the things unique to consulting is that it is common for those who sell the work to also do the work, but that is not always the case.

I offer this case study to emphasize that some vetting occurs between the client and the potential consultant during the selling process. Indeed, the sales process is designed primarily to do just that. It didn't happen this time, and clearly I have nothing to brag about from this experience. Did I feel that I was treated unfairly? For sure. Did that seem to matter to the client? Not at all. There are times when fairness does not enter into the equation.

LESSON 7: EMBRACING DIFFERENT PERSPECTIVES

When orienting myself to the strategies and culture of a new client, I explore key strategic decisions that were made in the past. As I have delved into the context of these decisions, my favorite question has been "Compared to what?" (This is similar to the "So what?" question asked when formulating conclusions, as reviewed in chapter 5.) In other words, you decided to do A, but what other options did you consider? Usually, I get a blank stare and then a bit of stuttering. More often than not, I have found that an idea quickly coalesced and a consensus formed around it. What was lacking was consideration of other options, and this client has not been very strategic in their decision-making. I would like to tell you that this is rare, but that is not the case in my experience with healthcare organizations.

I have thought long and hard on this issue and here is what I have come up with: Control is fleeting within nonprofit organizations. The presence of an independent medical staff in the past reinforced this view, as does having a volunteer board of trustees versus a paid board, where incentives are created. The title of CEO, which used to be enough to carry a lot of weight, has given way to the power of persuasion. How? Loyalty might be old-school from a stylistic point of view, but it can still be present regardless. Unfortunately, loyalty can easily supersede merit, stifling innovation and snuffing out alternative points of view.

An organization, when facing a key decision, often places too much emphasis on achieving consensus quickly. This can result in missing out on the richness of examining different options. Over time, identifying and discussing alternatives has a proven track record of fostering better decisions. As challenges are confronted and opportunities pursued, the best leaders surround themselves with competent people who are encouraged to offer different points of view. Beware the "consensus culture," one that stifles different perspectives. Consensus should be the result of examining alternative approaches, not something that limits their consideration.

To be successful, healthcare must embrace the transformation to "disruptive innovation" that is taking place. The value in this approach is that it empowers examples from outside healthcare to go beyond a hospital-centric world into new ways of delivering care. This approach is obviously very appealing to the creative consultant who is not invested in the status quo.

LESSON 8: WHEN CLIENTS NO LONGER LISTEN

It is not uncommon for consultants to have their advice questioned by the client. Indeed, many consultants welcome this process and are prepared to make their case. Healthcare involves passions. It encompasses the overall health of a patient and a community. It becomes a cause. When emotions become part of the mix, things can easily go awry. Make allowances for these passions while at the same time being able to calm a situation so that a rational decision can be made. Being dispassionate is critical. But it is also important to recognize when the work is done and the client no longer needs to rely on the advice of the consultant.

In one engagement, I was brought in to help with a difficult merger discussion. My client needed to find a partner. The client was fortunate to have an active board of trustees, a number of whose members took personal interest in securing a better future for the organization. The merger situation had become severe, which required aggressive intervention. Management was being challenged, and the board needed some assurances that progress was being made and that a partner could be secured.

In the ensuing months, we went through the normal procedures for establishing the story and then seeking appropriate partners based on interests and capabilities. That was the challenge. Some of the potential partners might be interested, but lacked the requisite skills and/or resources that would be required to turn this situation around. Vetting these parties and then determining both their interest and level of competency was a tall order.

While a mergers and acquisitions process can get hung up on a variety of issues, getting stalled during due diligence was an unexpected setback. That, however, is what happened in this case. The structure of the deal was in a Letter of Intent, and it was announced to the public (a rare approach). But the deal tanked on due diligence. There is no sugar-coating this. The client was looking for a partner to help bail it out of its precarious situation. Anything short of that would be a failure. It is hard to recover your credibility after such a failure, yet this kind of a setback can occur in virtually every consulting engagement. The consequences can range from minor to horrific. In this case, it was horrific.

An attempt was made to keep the process going, but credibility had been lost. It was at this point that we had to consider the merits of continuing the current engagement with a different potential partner, and, given the past interactions, there was an intense aversion to this idea. The options were clearly limited. This was tough medicine to be sure, and some board members balked, unwilling to embrace the only remaining viable option: merge with the other hospital in town.

The previous process had taken the better part of one year. To give up at this stage was a big step back for all concerned. But it became clear that the client was no longer willing to follow the advice of the consultant. Emotions ran high, but there was no denying that our work here was done. Tragically, the client eventually filed for bankruptcy several years later.

LESSON 9: STAYING ABOVE THE FRAY—PALACE INTRIGUE

This is a difficult story to tell, but an important one. We were processing a potential merger with a large healthcare organization. At the time, the leader who was at the helm of one of the two organizations involved, and who was close to retirement, was required to be absent during several key internal meetings. We were surprised how the team acted when the leader was not present; the group behaved completely differently, with an informal hierarchy displacing the existing structure.

During one such meeting, one of the younger members of the team essentially took over the conversation and pointed it in a different direction. This person clearly had an agenda, which was odd in that the more senior executives in the room (most of the C-suite) seemed content to let the consulting process go forward to see what came of it. Not so this junior person, who was clearly challenging the consulting process and advocating a personal position, competing with the consultant for the attention of the group.

It was a power play. It became a sensitive issue because we felt the ensuing discussions were sending us a mixed message from the team. One version occurred when the leader was present, the other when the leader was not. Sorting this out was a challenge. The junior person was effectively competing to facilitate the group discussion, setting up an us-versus-them scenario.

While the challenge was not that direct, it proved to be quite consequential. In the end, the political landscape with the client got simply too complex and disturbing for us to think that we could effectively participate. Sometimes this is the case; the consultant ends up being marginalized.

It was in effect a coup orchestrated by this junior staff member, who succeeded because the rest of the group offered no resistance. We made our case for continuing the initial joint merger discussions, but the die was cast. The dysfunction of this client group at this critical time in the merger process became something that we were required to bring to the attention of the other party. There were simply forces present that we were powerless to fight, and so we were done.

TIP FROM THE TRENCHES

The politics of healthcare cannot be ignored. Healthcare has almost become a "third rail," as they say in politics. Everyone has an opinion. This can also extend into the C-suite of a healthcare organization. I once had a senior executive say to me, "I wish I worked for a faith-based organization." The executive felt constrained by the "conservative approach" taken by management at the hospital. I admit that I am not entirely sure what they meant, but my guess is that it reflected the schizophrenia of operating in an industry that embraces two opposing business models: nonprofit charitable services (think utility) and competitive business services (think retail).

The consultant value chain that was reviewed earlier in chapter 2 includes some discussion about staying above the fray. This can be exceedingly difficult at times. Some of the truly extraordinary consultants have thrived on these opportunities, but this is a rare skill. The simple reality is that politics is hard to manage even when you are fully immersed in it. The engagements that involve complex politics can easily overwhelm what might otherwise be routine. This goes back to the famous phrase from Donald Rumsfeld, "There will always be unknown unknowns." The consultant is always at a disadvantage relative to the politics of these complex situations. Some of the feuds can date back decades. Memories die hard, especially for those who feel they were dealt with unfairly. My advice is to steer clear of such engagements whenever possible.

REFERENCES

Covey, S. R. 2015. *The 7 Habits of Highly Effective People: Powerful Lessons in Personal Change*. Miami, FL: Mango Publishing.

Fisher, R., and W. Ury. 1981. *Getting to Yes: Negotiating Agreement Without Giving In*. London, UK: Orion Hardbacks.

Haudan, J. 2008. *The Art of Engagement: Bridging the Gap Between People and Possibilities*. New York: McGraw-Hill.

Merlino, J. 2015. *Service Fanatics: How to Build Superior Patient Experience the Cleveland Clinic Way*. New York: McGraw-Hill.

CHAPTER 15

Consulting to the Healthcare Industry

To be exceptional as a healthcare consultant, you must have not only exceptional consulting skills but also a clear understanding of the healthcare industry. For the consultant who is not familiar with healthcare, a lack of relevant experience becomes painfully obvious very early into an engagement. Every consultant interviewed for this book began with the observation that doing well in healthcare consulting begins with understanding the clinical care process. More specifically, this includes the interaction by physicians, nurses, and other caregivers with patients and their families. Healthcare delivery is not just a concept; it is an *experience*.

One thing on which most experts agree: US healthcare is too expensive and many people can't afford it. While most of the comparisons to other developed countries are bogus (i.e., not apples to apples), the simple fact remains that it costs more than it should. With incentives that are more properly aligned, there is a solid case to be made for dramatically improving the healthcare experience, including access, quality, and costs. In other words, the healthcare industry is a target-rich environment for management consultants.

Management consultants are working with nearly all segments of society, so what is it about healthcare that is so enticing? Part of it must be the realization that sooner or later everyone comes into contact with healthcare. This chapter discusses what makes the healthcare industry intriguing to the well-motivated consultant.

COMPLEXITY OF HEALTHCARE IN THE UNITED STATES

There can be little doubt that part of the unnecessary cost of healthcare relates to its complexity. The well-known management guru, Peter Drucker, wrote that hospitals were the most complex organizations ever created, describing them as a "two-headed monster," referring to the medical and nonmedical aspects of healthcare (Drucker Institute 2020). Additionally—and try to wrap your mind around this—he suggests that some organizations can develop complexity to the point where they no longer have value.

I have long believed that part of the responsibility of those who consult to healthcare organizations is to make things simpler, to take the complex and make it understandable. I liken it to taking something like organic chemistry and reducing it to a few simple tenets that can be understood by all. (As far as I know, this remains a fleeting goal.)

There is no doubt that healthcare is too complex. It starts with the extraordinary nature of the human body, and human beings add complexity to a grand design that defies full understanding. No less than Voltaire suggested, "The art of medicine consists of amusing the patient while nature cures the disease." Customizing what is known to what is required for every individual patient is hard to fully contemplate. Clearly every patient is different. Add to that the challenge of managing people and technology, and you begin to recognize the true nature of the healthcare industry.

The legendary news anchor Walter Cronkite once said, "America's healthcare system is neither healthy, caring, nor a system." I don't think it was meant as a compliment. Perhaps the clearest conclusion about complexity in healthcare is that it represents a problem that needs to be solved. Medical illiteracy is merely one related symptom of this complexity. Healthcare is clearly a rich environment in which consultants can practice their craft.

THREE THINGS ABOUT HEALTHCARE

Besides complexity, healthcare has three characteristics that stand out:

1. *Healthcare is counterintuitive.* As consumers, we want more of the things we like. Healthcare services are not among these. Typically, the more healthcare services we consume, the less healthy we are. A new mission is replacing the older one in the healthcare industry. Historically, healthcare's intent was to give everyone access to healthcare services, cover the costs, and provide an acceptable level of quality. The new mission is to reduce the cost for the most effective care. Quality and access are assumed, but healthcare in the United States simply costs too much. Much of the excess cost is due to where and how certain care is delivered. It can be delivered just as well or better at less costly sites (i.e., nonhospital) that are more convenient (e.g., located in a retail zone), by less expensive staff (advanced placement providers such as physicians' assistants and nurse practitioners), and at far lower cost (think retail).

2. *Healthcare is a study in contrasts.* I have long been an advocate of healthcare being one word instead of two (health care); the more you have of one, the less you need of the other. The vast medical-industrial complex is focused mostly on care, not health. Care is what is needed as health subsides, and much of care deals with symptoms, such as headaches, not diseases like diabetes. While insurance in healthcare complicates things even more, the simple truth is that it deals almost exclusively with care, not health. Most of the people who have insurance can afford it and don't need it. Most of those who don't have insurance do need it but can't afford it. Contrasts. The whole concept of health insurance has been displaced by expensive *bill-paying*. Invoking the concept of insurance generally speaks to a pooling of resources from many to cover the "unexpected events" of a few (think car insurance or homeowner's insurance). This does not correlate well with what healthcare insurance plans cover, which is the predictable events of many. Said differently, much of what insurance pays for falls outside the boundaries of a risk-related event. What insurance covers today would be expenses borne directly by the consumer, were a purer insurance model being followed. Indeed, we are headed in this direction under the new banner of "value-based care," as more financial risk is pushed off on the consumer under copays and deductibles. Deductibles and copayments did not exist in the United States before 2000 (Hoffman 2006). In a relatively few short years, every insurance policy on the market, including Medicare and Medicaid, has significant deductibles and copayments. The highly controversial Affordable Care Act (ACA) of 2010 was, for all its good intent, an ill-conceived attempt to apply a wealth-creation vehicle (health savings accounts or HSAs) to poor people. It turned out to be less about healthcare and more about income redistribution. The concept of HSAs has inherent appeal because it is targeted toward moderate- or high-income consumers during younger, healthier years to save for later. On average, elderly patients consume four times the amount of health services as younger patients. The people who have tax-deferred HSAs accumulate wealth that is then used to pay for services later in life. This allows them to opt for the less expensive "high deductible" policies, and thus save significant money along the way. Applying this concept to lower income Medicaid patients never made sense because they cannot afford to set aside "savings" to an HSA. Those who qualify for a federal subsidy are able to reduce the cost of premiums. However, part of the ACA added significant cost to these premiums in numerous ways, not least of which was including the ten "essential benefits." The result is that even though subsidies made premiums

more affordable, deductibles and copayments made healthcare less affordable than before ACA. (It's worth noting that the cost of premiums increased because of additional requirements, some of which were never considered part of healthcare insurance, such as birth control.) The result has been a disaster. Many plans today include deductibles and copays that are simply unaffordable.

3. *Eventually, everyone needs healthcare—some far more than others.* What makes healthcare so intriguing is that, by definition, it involves people. Everyone is exposed to healthcare at one time or another, and especially as we get older and closer to dying, we need and use more healthcare. According to a seminal study of healthcare costs, 1 percent of consumers account for 23 percent of total costs, and the top 5 percent account for 50 percent of total costs (Claxton, Rae, and Levitt 2019). The difference between resources used by an average consumer and those used by a sick consumer can be dramatic. A patient today with end-stage renal disease requires regular dialysis that costs an estimated $90,000 per year, for a national total of $28 billion in 2016 (University of California San Francisco 2020). This is one of the rare identified diseases covered by Medicare, so the burden of this is buried in government reimbursement. Heart disease costs an estimated $200 billion per year (Centers for Disease Control and Prevention 2019) and is the leading cause of death in the United States for men and women, responsible for one in four deaths each year. The National Cancer Institute (2011) estimates there will be 18.1 million cancer survivors by 2020, 30 percent more than in 2010. The national annual cost of cancer care is estimated at $157 billion (in 2010 dollars). Cancer is correlated with age, among other factors. The aging of the US population is the primary cause of the increased incidence of cancer. It is perhaps ironic that as medical practice helps extend life, people are more likely to develop a cancer. Clearly, for the healthy person, the costs of healthcare are less of a concern. But for the sick, such costs often involve a threat that extends beyond the disease itself and becomes a financial burden as well.

THE ECONOMICS OF HEALTHCARE

At the core of the healthcare debate is whether healthcare is a basic right. Those who say it is point to the language in the Declaration of Independence that all are "endowed . . . with certain unalienable rights . . . among these are life, liberty, and the pursuit of happiness." I won't try to litigate that here except to say that, regardless of one's point of view, what is the true conundrum of healthcare relates to economic considerations. The adage that I reference on this topic comes from the late Uwe Reinhardt, the noted Princeton University professor of political economics, who suggested that there are three keys to the American healthcare system: cost, quality, and access. He went on to say that we cannot afford all three, so which two do we want? Therein lies the rub.

The third-party payment system remains unique to healthcare. The insurance component is injected between the healthcare provider and the consumer. While this is beginning to change, the vast majority in the United States do not pay for healthcare services, but rather rely on government programs such as Medicare and Medicaid, or a private insurer, like Blue Cross or Humana, to handle a substantial part of their bills, net of copayments and deductibles.

Does this third-party payment system add value or, as the critics would say does it simply add cost? Third-party payment has expanded way beyond any semblance of an insurance product to more of an expensive bill-paying service. Is healthcare a commodity, in which case a single-payer system (e.g., government) might work best? Or does it deserve status as a service that can and should be customized (*personalized care*), assuming people can pay for it? It is not clear how or when this debate will be resolved.

I facilitate leadership retreats for healthcare organizations in which people devote a day or two away from their shop to discuss key trends and their implications. It is one of my favorite activities because it brings the leadership of these complex healthcare organizations together for a real bonding experience. There is no better place to have an impact on the future directions of a healthcare organization.

I tell this story at most retreats:

Imagine that you are an investor, and you are presented with a business that is both capital and labor intensive. It has one very large customer that consumes over 50 percent of the services offered—the government. The government also determines what can be charged for these services. Technology is a key driver of this business, with new discoveries occurring over time that require sophisticated equipment to deliver. In many states, the ability to acquire such technology is controlled by a quasi-governmental entity related to a Certificate of Need policy. This business provides services customized to the needs of individuals in complex settings that are strategically located. Sometimes the wants of consumers overtake actual needs, but customers both seek and pay for these services through a combination of insurance and out-of-pocket dollars. In most cases, payment for such service lags 45–90 days after they are provided, and the consumer rarely has any idea what a procedure will cost before it is performed. It is a highly regulated business at many levels, requiring licenses to operate with close monitoring of activities that can carry penalties if certain quality thresholds are not met. Regulation of this business continues to change dramatically. Clinical outcomes can vary as much as 100 percent for certain procedures. There is significant competition for the mind of the consumer and about the method of delivering such services.

I go on to ask, "Is this a business that you would invest in?" Invariably, the answer is a resounding "No!"

In effect, there are competing business models that operate simultaneously in the healthcare industry that add to the confusion. At the macro level, one model can be labeled *public utility*, in which prices are fixed and regulated like any other utility (e.g., water, electricity, gas). In a true utility model, there would be limited competition if any, and a single-payer model would therefore be appropriate.

The other model can be labeled as *competitive*, in which one has the ability to set prices and offer services in a variety of settings that might be tiered according to price points. Competition, when unfettered in other industries, has proven to positively affect both quality and prices. Its application to healthcare remains somewhat unclear, with a few noted exceptions such as dentistry and LASIK eye surgery. Where the normal economic principal of supply and demand applies (notably to commodity-type services), there is probably no need for insurance (i.e., the patient can/should pay for this out of pocket), and there is real competition that will, over time, improve quality and lower price.

The challenge is that the current payment environment represents a curious mix of utility-type regulation and competition. These different business models are often at variance with each other. It is not a binary opposition, but one in which elements of both models apply. Government beneficiaries covered by programs such as Medicare and Medicaid pay less than cost for most of the services they receive. In other words, most hospitals lose money providing services to most government beneficiaries. This startling reality, which is not well understood, helps explain the current problem in healthcare. Now that government is the majority user of healthcare services, and this share is growing even greater as the population ages, the gap between cost and payments is increasing. This is occurring at the same time that commercial payers and self-pay patients are doing more shopping based on price. Ttraditional *cost-shifting*, which allowed hospitals to make up the gap between revenues received from government payers and costs incurred to care for their beneficiaries, is becoming less possible.

Most inpatient (hospital) services are experiencing this growing payment gap, but it is also happening in ambulatory services, as regulations are being changed there as well.[1] With ambulatory services, government payments are closer to costs, prices are more flexible, and payment is often in cash. Ambulatory services are generally lower in cost and represent the fastest-growing segment of the industry. Not only that, they are leading in innovative technology (e.g., virtual medicine and remote monitoring) that is making it easier to provide services in alternative settings (e.g., in-home and at urgent care centers). These are the kinds of actions that characterize health *reform* that will ultimately bend the cost curve.

Timing is of the essence. Over the years, as profitable services were giving way to lower payments, notably from government (e.g., *site-neutral payments*), healthcare systems have been challenged to make up the difference elsewhere. Commercial payments are being ratcheted down through aggressive managed care, including a number of performance-based programs, such as bundled payments for major procedures and per-member/per-month plans. Higher copays and deductibles are being assumed by patients, and there are fewer places to find marginal gains to cover these losses.

This has created a perfect storm, as people like to say. Reducing costs can only go so far before a hospital organization must drop certain services from its portfolio. To say the least, the status quo is simply unsustainable, and ways must be found to offer services at less cost, while keeping revenues and costs more closely aligned.

QUADRUPLE AIM

If the different business models are often in conflict, what will bring them together over time? That is not clear. In the meantime, the industry is experiencing significant reform, as noted below. In place of policy, reform is happening regardless of regulation or legislation. It is change that occurs naturally as an industry evolves. This reform can be organic or it can be disruptive. One organic reform that has come to represent an important vision for healthcare in the future is the "Triple Aim," which has now morphed into a "Quadruple Aim," as shown in exhibit 15.1.

The familiar refrain in politics is "It's the economy, stupid!" Well, in healthcare, "It's the experience, stupid!" The patient's experience is an essential feature of the transformation that is occurring. Not only do people need to take more responsibility for their health (something that seemed to get lost with third-party

---

1. These services were traditionally called "outpatient services" and were provided in hospitals (e.g., lab, imaging) but increasingly are being displaced into more appropriate freestanding settings located in retail zones, providing such services more conveniently and inexpensively.

Exhibit 15.1: The Quadruple Aim

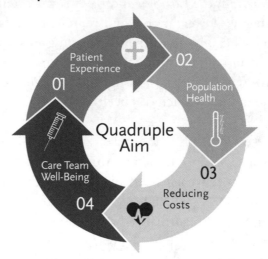

Source: Kinetix Group (2020). Used with permission.

payment systems), but the healthcare experience must improve. It must become more like retail in at least two ways. First, there must be more transparency, including price transparency, and some price flexibility. Second, there must be more information available that allows for shopping services among alternative providers. Granted, trauma or emergency services do not lend themselves to comparison shopping because urgency is at a premium. For most other services, consumers must have an opportunity to compare among competing providers. This is what advocates for change consider the core of the transformation that is taking place.

If healthcare is to behave more like a retail business, the first change that must occur is greater transparency of pricing before a particular procedure takes place. This allows the consumer to shop to get the best quality service at the best price.

GOVERNANCE

Stakeholders abound in healthcare organizations. No discussion of healthcare can do justice without a brief discussion on the unique element of governance. The vast majority of hospitals and healthcare systems in the United States are tax-exempt organizations. Sometimes referred to using the unfortunate label of *nonprofit*, such organizations do not have individual investors and are required to pursue a charitable purpose, which means any excess revenues over expenses (profit) are put back into the business. I say unfortunate because the connotation of "nonprofit" is that the organization is not required to generate a profit. This is, of course, not true. No organization can sustain itself over time if revenues are not greater than expenses. An organization that is unable to invest in its future has no future.

It is governance where healthcare is truly unique. Governance is dominated by people who volunteer their time to help guide an organization. Providing advice at the governance level also represents a huge opportunity for consultants to have an impact on the future of a healthcare organization.

The boards of these organizations, most of which started as relatively small community enterprises, have evolved over time into multi-billion-dollar health systems with broad geographic networks. Some of the largest regional health systems span many states and dozens of hospitals and related facilities. They are branded and can be labeled as big enterprise under any reasonable definition.

I feel quite sure that the originators of section 501(c)(3) of the US tax code, the one that pertains to charitable organizations, did not contemplate this scale of operation (I'm not sure they contemplated the Red Cross or some of the other huge global operations, either). As healthcare has evolved and scaled new heights, governance has had to keep up with the level of sophistication that is required. The truth is that large health systems compete with other corporations for board members, but with one key difference—most health systems do not compensate their board members.[2] Compare this with corporate boards that not only compensate board members but also often provide stock and other inducements to gain their attention.

As charitable organizations, hospitals and health systems have board members who volunteer their time, much like attorneys who offer pro bono work to organizations. As they have increased in scale, it is not uncommon that a hospital or health system CEO would be better compensated than the vast majority of board members (through their own businesses). As you might imagine, this can make for some fascinating dynamics. I have personally seen a board member be tempted to become the CEO of a healthcare organization once they realize the compensation involved. Since the board's most important responsibility is the appointment of the CEO, the potential for conflict is rather striking.

One of the most enjoyable clients I had honored me with the opportunity to be the facilitator for their annual board retreat for more than a decade. This not only afforded me the opportunity to work closely with a highly progressive CEO and their management team, but also to get to know and influence the culture of

---

2. There is no legal prohibition against paying reasonable compensation to such board members. For more information, read Jeremy Barlow, "Board of Director Compensation: What to Pay, or Not to Pay," Board Effect, February 8, 2017.

an innovative health system from its early beginnings. It was indeed gratifying to see the culture of this organization evolve over time, and to help spawn the evolution of an integrated regional health network. I was also able to influence the retaining of other notable consultants who I thought would be of benefit to the organization. Watching how they brought members along from being on committees to becoming full board members is something that has stayed with me over the years. Board retreats remain one of the most impactful opportunities any organization has to change a culture and/or launch a new vision for the future. As a strategy consultant, I cannot imagine a more target-rich environment in which to spawn a strategic dialogue.

MEDICAL STAFF

As if governance did not create enough complexity, what about the independent medical staff? When I first entered the industry in the 1970s, most physicians at most hospitals were independent contractors with privileges to use hospital facilities for their patients. They were credentialed based on state licensure and experience-based criteria to perform certain procedures and/or treat their patients within these facilities. The key term here is *independent*.

Those of us who have toiled in the trenches for decades can recount many a tale of mystery and intrigue in dealing with physicians who are part of independent medical staffs. It used to be that attendance was mandatory at monthly medical staff meetings to maintain such privileges. These were often quite raucous affairs, in which debates of all nature occurred, from managed care (suggested by one physician, who was quite serious, as a "communist plot") to advanced placement providers, and the need for a new category of providers (advanced practice registered nurses and others).

CONSUMERISM AS A GREEN SHOOT

Finally, no discussion of stakeholders in healthcare would be complete without recognizing consumers and the communities in which they live, work, and shop. This last item might surprise you. Healthcare, hospital care in particular, has a tradition of being located in isolation from other goods and services. Historically, this occurred so as to isolate the general population from being exposed to infectious diseases. As medicine has conquered most infectious diseases, healthcare has tried desperately to become more integrated into the community.

Now, consumers want healthcare to become more convenient, like other retail businesses located in strip malls, covered malls, and high-traffic retail zones. Focusing more on a consumer who has choices is recognition of the competitive nature that is an important component of the current healthcare landscape. While some in healthcare seem to fear the implications of consumerism and the call for transparency, I view consumerism as an economic boost, as it can lead to improved clinical and financial outcomes. But it has not been an easy change to make.

A recent article does a very nice job of describing consumer-driven care as an elusive concept in healthcare and characterizes the consumer movement in healthcare as "largely failing," and questions "whether it's worth saving" (Kacik 2019). More specifically, the article notes that people have long waiting times for appointments, quality data remains scarce and obscure, and overall transparency is lacking. The article suggests that the consumerism effort has been characterized as trying to "catch up" by borrowing the best from industries that are further along in their improved consumer orientation, as noted in exhibit 15.2.

While some ideas have worked out, many have not. The increased use of online portals, remote monitoring, virtual consultations (telemedicine), and better-integrated tools for scheduling and billing represent some improvements. Yet there is a long way to go, and greater price transparency could very easily be co-opted into a public utility model with standardized pricing, versus a competitive model that supports true variable pricing. Hope springs eternal, as new rules from the Centers for Medicare & Medicaid Services (CMS) require greater transparency. According to CMS Administrator Seema Verma, "Price transparency puts patients in control and forces competition on the basis of cost and quality, which can rein in the high cost of care. CMS' action represents perhaps the most consequential healthcare reform in the last several decades" (US Department of Health and Human Services 2020b).

Exhibit 15.2: Catching Up: Borrowing the Best from Those Who Are Further Along

INDUSTRY	IDEA BORROWED
Airlines ➡	Check-in kiosks
Hospitality ➡	Luxury waiting/patient rooms, meditation gardens
Technology ➡	Automation/AI, open co-working spaces
Transportation ➡	Using Uber/Lyft
Banking ➡	Online processing/mobile transactions
Retail ➡	Convenient locations, extended hours

Source: Kacik (2019). Used with permission.

SOCIAL DETERMINANTS OF HEALTH

Poor health has been proven to be related to low income, as well as rural locations. More than just access to healthcare services, improving health involves so-called social determinants of health (SDHs). These include housing, food, education, and crime. Without addressing these areas, the healthcare system is relegated to the far more expensive mission of treating the results of poor health, rather than affecting positive health, which would delay or avoid the downstream expense of being unhealthy.

Healthy People 2020 presents a goal to "create social and physical environments that promote good health for all" (US Department of Health and Human Services 2020a). Recognizing that SDHs exist is an acknowledgment that a variety of factors beyond the current scope of most organizations can greatly influence the health of an individual or a community. Five specific factors are recognized, as shown in exhibit 15.3. (The University of Wisconsin Population Health Institute notes fully 40 percent of health determinants involve socioeconomic factors, and only 20 percent are due to the health system.)

Exhibit 15.3: Social Determinants of Health

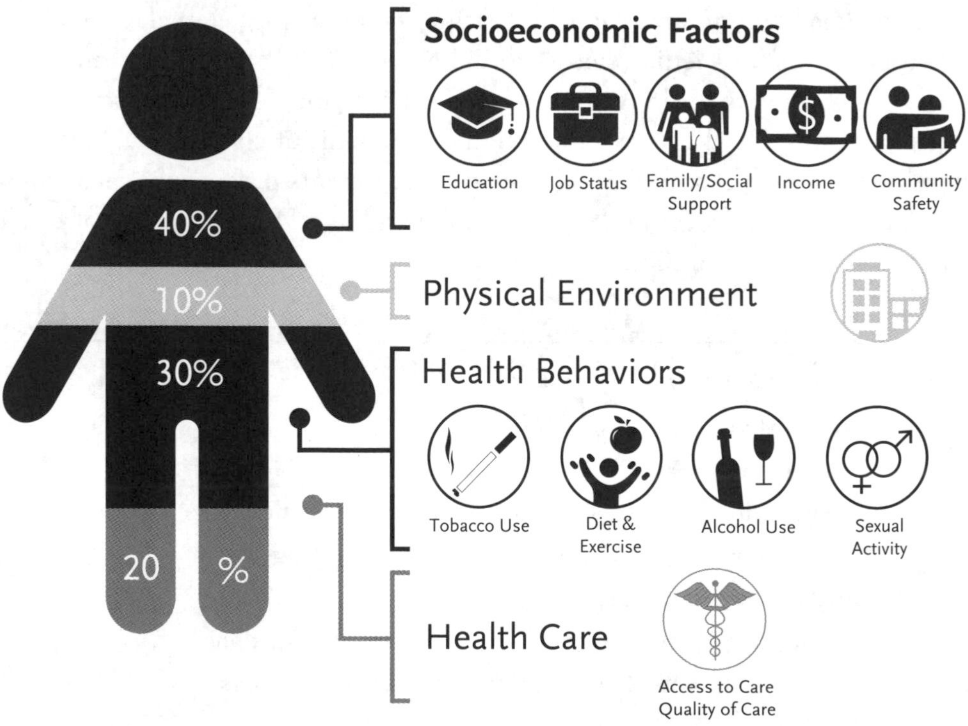

Source: ProMedica (2020). Used with permission.

What we have come to learn is that a community's overall health (i.e., population health) is determined as much, if not more, by certain SDHs than by all the resources amassed by the medical industrial complex. Truth be known, the health system as constituted today has more to do with illness care than with health.

One of the positive things to come out of the ACA is the requirement to complete community needs assessments. After participating in a few of these for clients, I have come to recognize that strategic plans for most hospitals and health systems traditionally only scratched the surface of what is required in such plans. Additionally, I have come to understand that there is a specific deficiency in the US healthcare system in comparison to other industrialized countries—we have simply underinvested in our community social infrastructure, including many elements of what people refer to as the public health sector. It is suggested that any future strategies for hospitals and health systems must factor in how to collaborate better to enhance the capabilities and reach of these resources. They need to be directed toward improving these SDHs.

REFERENCES

Centers for Disease Control and Prevention. 2019. "Heart Disease." Accessed October 13. www.cdc.gov/heartdisease/heart_failure.htm.

Claxton, G., M. Rae, and L. Levitt. 2019. "A Look at People Who Have Persistently High Spending on Health Care." *Health System Tracker.* Published July 22. www.healthsystemtracker.org/brief/a-look-at-people-who-have-persistently-high-spending-on-health-care/.

Drucker Institute. 2020. "About." Accessed January 15. www.drucker.institute/perspective/about-peter-drucker/.

Hoffman, B. 2006. "Restraining the Health Care Consumer: The History of Deductibles and Co-payments in US Health Insurance." *Social Science History* 30 (4): 501–28.

Kacik, A. 2019. "Fractured Use Experience Fuels Consumerism Criticism." *Modern Healthcare.* Published November 16. www.modernhealthcare.com/providers/fractured-user-experience-fuels-consumerism-criticism.

Kinetix Group. 2020. "The Era of the Quadruple Aim." Accessed September 22. https://thekinetixgroup.com/the-era-of-the-quadruple-aim/.

National Cancer Institute. 2011. "Cancer Prevalence and Cost of Care Projections." Published January. https://costprojections.cancer.gov/.

ProMedica. 2020. "Social Determinants of Health." Accessed September 22. www.promedica.org/socialdeterminants/pages/default.aspx.

University of California San Francisco. 2020. "The Kidney Project." Accessed January 20. https://pharm.ucsf.edu/kidney.

US Department of Health and Human Services. 2020a. "Healthy People 2020." Office of Disease Prevention and Health Promotion. Accessed February 12. https://health. gov/our-work/healthy-people.

———. 2020b. "Trump Administration Finalizes Rule Requiring Health Insurers to Disclose Price and Cost-Sharing Information." Published October 29. www.hhs. gov/about/news/2020/10/29/trump-administration-finalizes-rule-requiring-health-insurers-disclose-price-and-cost-sharing.html.

CHAPTER 16

The Evolving Healthcare Consulting Profession

CONSULTING IN THE HEALTHCARE INDUSTRY has been a truly exciting pursuit since I first entered it in the 1970s. No doubt, being near the ground floor of modern medicine has greatly contributed to this experience. But as I reflect on this journey, I stand in awe of the people who came before. For them, healthcare was very undefined and entrepreneurial. It was hard to wrap your arms around where to focus your consulting practice. The needs were so great and the resources fairly limited. I believe that consulting to healthcare organizations has gone through a number of eras corresponding to industry trends, as described in exhibit 16.1.

These consultant pioneers tried all kinds of approaches to get their foot in the door of growing healthcare organizations. Once their services were introduced and refined, they became a mainstay in C-suites. Administrators would find it difficult to address any major issues without significant help from independent consultants. During this "golden age" of healthcare consulting, the number of hospitals was expanding rapidly thanks to funds from the Hill-Burton Act of 1946.[1] Following World War II, veterans found access to healthcare to be quite limited, especially outside urban areas and in rural locations. Between 1946 and 1963, when the Hill-Burton hospital construction program ended, some 5,000 hospitals were built. By 1968, it had helped to finance 9,200 new medical facilities, with a total of 416,000 new beds (McBride 2018).

---

1. The Hill-Burton Act was "intended to improve the supply, distribution, and quality of general hospital beds across the United States." It was signed by President Truman in 1946 and its target was to increase the supply of hospital beds to 4.5 per 1,000 population. The intent was to have at least one hospital in every county in the country.

Exhibit 16.1: Consulting Eras Track Industry Trends

Age of Growth and Expansion (1960s and 1970s)

Cost + reimbursement, Medicare + Medicaid, Boomer expansion, robust economy, medicine highly respected, independent practice dominated, diversified services

Age of Consolidation (1980s to 2015)

All components consolidate, focus on best practices, single large payer (government), challenging economic conditions, medical practice more demanding/less satisfying, integration among components and across components, little transparency

Age of Contraction (2015 to 2020)

Less payment than the year before, elimination of cost shifting, tax-exempt status truncated, feels like utility/single payer, more transparency

Age of Value (2020 to ?)

The primacy of an office visit is replaced by a monthly retainer that provides unfettered access to services that are conveniently located and covered by the monthly fee. Handoffs between acute care and post-acute care are seamless, and the medical record is both ubiquitous and accurate, owned by the consumer. Providers are paid less by procedure and more out of the monthly fee.

THE AMERICAN ASSOCIATION OF HEALTHCARE CONSULTANTS

What distinguishes a qualified healthcare consultant from one who is not? This question has existed from the beginning, and as hospitals were being built in communities all across the country, the question became even more important. It is helpful to review some of this history because it gives insight into gaining confidence in those who profess to be consultants in this unregulated consulting industry. As philosopher George Santayana (1905) said, "Those who cannot remember the past are condemned to repeat it."

In 1984, Frank Briggs looked back on the American Association of Healthcare Consultants (AAHC), established in 1948, and wrote a brief history of the origins of healthcare consulting (see appendix A). George Bugbee, who was the leader of the American Hospital Association beginning in 1943, played a big role in the development of healthcare consulting during the time of Hill-Burton funding. Bugbee was beset with requests for recommendations of consultants who could help with hospital building projects. As the leader of a trade association, he felt conflicted about handing out such advice when individuals were competing for this business. He recognized the need for some way to identify qualified people for such work. As he wrote in an editorial in 1947 in *Hospitals* (emphasis added):

> *Hospital administrators and boards of trustees need a means of judging the qualifications of persons who call themselves consultants. A number of*

firms and individuals have been at work a long time and can stand on their records. A number of newcomers are ex-administrators, widely and favorably known. . . . But there are other newcomers. Some have skills and knowledge that are needed, but no reputation, while others appear to have little to offer. Reports are current of low-grade service, which hospitals cannot accept without complaint.[2]

THE CALL FOR DISRUPTION

Yogi Berra, the Baseball Hall of Fame catcher known for his malapropisms, once famously said, "The future ain't what it used to be." Truer words were never spoken when it comes to consulting to healthcare organizations. There are essentially two kinds of change: organic and disruptive. Change these days seems to be increasingly disruptive (Christensen 1997), a concept that was later brought to the healthcare industry (Christensen, Grossman, and Hwang 2008).

Some interesting statistics speak to the disruption that is required in healthcare. According to a nationwide survey conducted by the Centers for Disease Control and Prevention (CDC), as published in *JAMA Internal Medicine*, the number of working-age adults who reported being unable to see a physician due to cost increased from 11.4 percent in 1998 to 15.7 percent in 2017 (Twachtman 2020). For individuals earning $50,000 to $75,000 per year, costs went from an average 6.9 percent of income in 1998 to 12.4 percent in 2017. Nearly one out of five individuals with any chronic condition in 2017 said they were unable to see a physician because of their inability to pay for services. The lead on the study was Dr. Laura Hawks, a research fellow at the Massachusetts-based health system Cambridge Health Alliance. She notes, "The quality of private health insurance is getting worse, and the cost of healthcare is rising significantly. We know that private health insurance plans increasingly rely on high premiums, high deductibles, high co-pays, and other forms of cost-sharing. This suggests that insurance generally is not doing what it is supposed to do—ensure that people have access to healthcare when they need it" (Johnson 2020).

Trying to make major changes in any industry is challenging, and I believe it is even more challenging in healthcare. A classic finding from the quality literature in healthcare some 20 years ago noted that it took an average of 17 years for proven new clinical protocols to be adopted in healthcare (Christensen, Grossman, and Hwang 2008). While some reform has developed organically, there is no question that much of the impetus for change today is coming from outside

---

2. The effort really culminated in 1964 with the publication of the first "Statement on Selection of a Hospital Consultant," which dealt with when to retain a consultant, how to select a consultant, the consultant's role, and how to use a consultant.

the industry. Convenient care centers in CVS Health, Walmart, and Walgreens; urgent care with Wall Street and private equity funding; freestanding ambulatory surgery; these are all examples of innovation that is coming to healthcare from outside the industry. The new mandate to shift toward value is a green light for innovation to lower the cost and increase access to services.

THE GAP BETWEEN PUBLIC HEALTH AND HEALTHCARE MANAGEMENT

Graduate school programs focused on healthcare generally reside in the departments or schools of public health, business, or public administration. Rarely are they part of a medical school. The journey in academia has not been smooth in some respects. I would observe that the linkage between public health and healthcare management, while intuitively related, has fallen well short of its potential. This became particularly evident during the COVID-19 pandemic, as public health officials have sent many mixed signals. This was perhaps predicable in reviewing some of the mistakes of the past. Allow me to cite a dramatic example.

The disconnect between public health and hospital management was clearly in evidence during the Ebola crisis of 2014. At the time, Dr. Tom Frieden, director of the CDC, said, "Essentially any hospital in the country can safely take care of Ebola. You don't need a special hospital to do it" (Cohen 2014). No doubt some lessons had been learned previously with respect to the AIDS virus, but the fear of the Ebola virus was that it might spread outside of West Africa, where it killed nearly 5,000 people in the worst outbreak on record (Lansford 2017). The story unfolded when Thomas Eric Duncan, a 42-year-old Liberian, died at a community hospital in Texas after having flown to Brussels, then Washington, DC, then Dallas, where he fell sick because he had been exposed to the virus earlier in Liberia (Vidal 2015).

One of the saddest things about this story—effectively unknown by the general population—is that the expense and turmoil almost permanently closed an excellent community hospital related to this one case. Texas Health Resources is an enormous regional health system of some 27 hospitals, and trying to take care of this patient had a devastating effect on the staff and the community at Texas Health Presbyterian Hospital Dallas. Mind you, this was no average community hospital; it had 875 beds and around 1,200 physicians on its medical staff. The idea that any community hospital could have handled such an event was simply delusional.

The United States is not alone in these viral challenges. Canada tracked their experience with SARS very closely in 2003 and found that 75 percent of those who became infected had contracted it in the hospital (McCaughey 2020). Clearly, we have a long way to go to better manage infectious diseases.

When it comes to healthcare delivery, there remains a gap in perception by public health offices versus the reality of our health delivery system. Iatric disease continues to haunt the industry, though to be sure gains are occurring. While we can applaud the disease research that is conducted through public health efforts, the collective ignorance of such professionals regarding patient care delivery and the capacities of infrastructure is alarming. If we are to effectively build a future vision around population health, we need to do a better job to connect this great divide with more accurate knowledge and innovation coming from academia.

The simple point is that healthcare management remains complex and will continue to be controversial in terms of where it should reside within academia. Continued focus on this is warranted, and I expect academics to play an integral role in bringing predictive analytics into play as part of the healthcare landscape, including in consulting. As Dan Zismer once shared with me in conversation:

> The best consulting should stem from a growing base of practical research, that is, ongoing analyses of what works and what doesn't, converted to probability scenarios for leadership understanding and consideration.

WHAT MAKES HEALTHCARE CONSULTING DIFFERENT?

How do these nuances of the healthcare industry impact consulting? Exhibit 16.2 sums it up.

Certain engagements with healthcare organizations are more focused on asking the right questions, and then working with a talented client team to figure out the answers. However, solutions that have worked elsewhere might not be right for them. In these situations, it doesn't matter who comes up with the answers, as long as there is a collective dialogue that reinforces the participative process of discovery. Following the guidelines of such an open process consistently allows the correct answer to surface, and gives it a higher probability to be successfully executed.

Everything that is happening to and within these complex healthcare organizations makes for an interesting mix from a consulting perspective. As noted, certain trends are clear, but that does not make it much easier to provide high-value consulting services. Understanding the cultures that dominate these organizations is critical. The reasons why providers are exacting and the politics are oppressive should be understood, and these reasons will often show themselves in interactions with these teams. Because policymakers continue to search for the holy grail of legislation and regulations designed to make healthcare better

Exhibit 16.2: What Makes Healthcare Consulting Different?

Issue	Implication
Serves an industry that is widely regarded as too costly	There is both an urgency and a mandate for change, and consulting services must produce a tangible return on investment and be able to achieve short-term results
Has the highest percentage of highly educated professionals	Dominance of scientists demands evidence; avoid the "know-it-all" syndrome
Is a complex industry that is difficult to service	With many professionals espousing a "higher calling," it can be both challenging and uncompromising
Is dominated by small, solo professionals with no real barriers to entry	There will always be opportunities for the niche player, but perhaps less so in the future
Is highly relational and political	Competition can be oppressive, but it's great when you are preferred
Characterized by significant consolidation of all components	Beware what can be lost with consolidation
Continues to attract capital	Will long remain both labor and capital intensive
Government is a market maker (similar to a utility)	Be careful what you wish for

and more affordable, it means that more tinkering is likely. There will continue to be unintended consequences and challenges in our attempts to improve the healthcare experience.

STRATEGY CONSULTING IS CONSEQUENTIAL

If consulting to healthcare organizations has some unique attributes, then it stands to reason that strategic consulting can be particularly challenging. Since *strategy* means different things to different people and is applied far too widely in common discourse, some clarification is in order. Something strategic tends to be big, important, and consequential. Strategy is about connecting the dots. While a bit hyperbolic, Yves Morieux from the Boston Consulting Group perhaps stated it best in his foreword to the book *Strategic Consulting* (Chereau and Meschi 2018):

> My dear strategy consultants, you are in the greatest job on earth. Each of you can truly make the world better . . . working every day with your clients, each

of you makes a difference in whether the coin falls in a way that makes the world better or worse.

Strategy is not something that an executive does every second of every day, but it remains something for which they will forever be accountable. Operational considerations tend to get in the way. It is a truism that strategy is sometimes the thing that busy executives never get to. This is one reason I have been hired by healthcare executives over the years as an independent strategy consultant. The biggest complaint shared universally by my executive clients is "I don't have time to think."

Consequently, I have been given the privilege of helping to frame strategic thinking for them by developing focused plans, offering alternative approaches, or identifying various opportunities that might be exploited on either a planned or an opportunistic basis. Never a dull pursuit, there have been highs and lows to be sure. Morieux notes, "As a consultant in strategy, you are really looking for trouble."

There are some additional intangibles for strategy consultants in healthcare. This observation is partially borne from the fact that nearly everyone who uses the title "consultant" in healthcare claims to do "strategic planning." However, this is not true for many of them. Even though most consultants might have a role that occasionally strays into the strategic realm, this is a far cry from doing strategic planning. That said, a consultant who spends considerable time in strategy requires three intangibles in addition to those reviewed earlier in this book: a point of view, a clear sense of the future, and market awareness. These are discussed in more detail below.

HAVE A POINT OF VIEW

Depending on the nature of the engagement, a consultant might be hired based on their point of view. It can be part of their brand. This is especially true when it comes to strategic consulting. For example, two hospitals might hire a consultant to facilitate a merger because of the person's experience, and because the consultant has published their point of view about what needs to happen for a merger to be successful. Where a point of view is seen as an asset, it also stands to reason that this should translate into a clear sense of the future.

To illustrate how this has played out in my practice over the past decade, here are some fundamental tenets of my key strategies for healthcare organizations:

- **Regional health systems become clinically integrated networks.** The number of independent hospitals has dramatically decreased as consolidation continues in the healthcare industry. The ability of hospitals to remain independent is under constant challenge. Some hospitals want help in maintaining their independence, while others want help determining how to merge. The more challenging issue is how to integrate disparate components. This involves the development of clinically integrated networks (Yale et al. 2015). It is worth noting the mantra that "all healthcare is local" is being replaced by a more realistic reorganization with a regional bent. Regional systems can be expected eventually to exercise more control over what services are offered, as well as how and when they are offered, by all of their facilities, thus eliminating unnecessary duplication.

- **Integrating the financial/insurance component.** There is no simple answer to the problem represented by a separation of healthcare delivery from the insurance component. Integration of the provider and payer components is critical, sometimes characterized as being "more Kaiser-like." While there has been a dramatic increase in provider-sponsored health plans, this has come with staggering losses and failures. More provider participation in the premium dollar has its appeal, to be sure.

- **Shifting the platform toward health and ambulatory care.** While the core business of inpatient services is shifting lower (reduced utilization), few hospital organizations have fully repositioned to capture the growth in community-based ambulatory care. Better integrating the provider component to correctly recognize the non-hospital-based and nonphysician provider has been a challenge. While many practices have been acquired, most hospital executives have done this grudgingly. Integration of the physician and hospital components continues to play out in many different ways by various consulting firms, and remains a work in progress.

- **Converting from a holding company board to an operating company board.** Many, if not most, initial hospital mergers favored a holding company approach, which from the start did not emphasize functional integration beyond the back office. As a result, these federations have achieved very little in the way of cost savings relative to the potential that exists, notably on the clinical side. Critics have rightly noted the lack of success of these new systems in reducing the cost of care or improving its quality. The lack of "systemness" continues to be a legitimate criticism of consolidation, especially among hospitals and physician groups. While the concept of systemness might not be that challenging on its face, the pace of change has clearly lagged on the execution side.

- **Think retail!** Finding a way to channel the convergence of the retail experience with healthcare has become an integral part of my consulting career. Shifting from the wholesale world of third-party reimbursement to the retail world of fixed-pricing and transparency is an essential feature of value-based care. Experience coupled with authenticity represents true breakthrough thinking for many of us who were attracted to healthcare. If we can't be passionate about providing healthcare services to people, we are truly in the wrong business.

These and related issues will be explored when a client is selecting a consultant to assist with strategic planning. Other functional consulting, such as IT services, executive and physician search, and facilities design and development, will have other issues to deal with, some of which might require a point of view.

A CLEAR SENSE OF THE FUTURE

Given the transformation facing healthcare today, the consultant's need to have a clear sense of the future might be a surprise, and could seem to conflict with the notion of objectivity. These are good points worthy of further discussion.

What does it mean to have a clear sense of the future? The devil is in the details. At the strategic level, it could mean nothing more than "more of this and less of that." The more specialized the practice (like IT), the more details required. When it comes to key shifts in the market, clients should expect that the consultants they hire have both a point of view and a sense of the future.

Transformation represents the highest level of change. This is structural change at the core, not casual change at the edges, and healthcare is undergoing a transformation. Yet, as John Kotter (2000) has explained, most transformation efforts fail. Perhaps the key takeaway from Kotter is that there must be a sense of urgency for such change, while recognizing that it won't be easy. Having a clear sense of the future does not mean that it is possible to predict how everything is going to work out. Future predictions remain more art than science.

An example of this is the shift from volume to value. This one example is anything but straightforward. It is a shift that is often mentioned as the essence of change that is required in a new value-based system. While that might be true at least at some level, it is also potentially misleading. Value is often represented as follows:

$$\text{Value} = \text{Quality} \div \text{Cost}$$

So where does volume fit? What the pundits would tell you is that volume is unimportant. This is patently false. What they mean to say is that payment for services should be somewhat independent of volume (and site). In other words, eliminate requirements like a payment for each office visit. In fact, we need a business model that does not require an office visit for a provider to get paid (e.g., virtual health visit). Clearly, the system is broken if a physician is unable to advise a patient while at church or in a social gathering, since it will not generate a payment. A central premise behind the new primary care concept of a patient-centered medical home, of which I am a big fan, is that it replaces a cost per visit with a monthly coordinating fee, as well as adding other related preventive and team health features.

The intent of value-based care is to have payment depend less on volume and more on performance. Think of healthcare like a computer service that is now sold on a subscription basis. iTunes was initially based on a pay-per-click model in which each song or album was purchased separately. Apple Music service then evolved to a monthly retainer with unlimited songs. For a simple monthly fee, you now have access to a library of music. Looking to the future, I expect a subscription approach to become the accepted standard, with the big tech firms such as Amazon (with Alexa), Apple (with Siri), and a similar Google offering (like Fitbit) leading the way. Note that a key technology breakthrough is the enabler here—voice command replaces typing.

Translated into healthcare, for a monthly fee the consumer would have access to providers, services, and more. The importance of an office visit is completely displaced in a value-based world. Done right, value-based care can eliminate the need for frequent office visits or, in some cases, stays in the hospital. For some illnesses, it might require more frequent office visits to replace what might otherwise be a visit to the emergency room or urgent care center.

The point is that a patient will not be charged for each visit, but rather pay a monthly retainer, regardless of the number of visits involved. This is not the same as saying that volume does not matter. Volume might not figure in the accounting for the payment. It does figure prominently in the planning and delivery of the service. Volume matters very much in a value-based world in terms of capacity (space and/or staffing required) and the requirements to meet the needs for access.

Volume, sometimes referred to as *piecework,* has been the historical basis for charging for most healthcare services. Under this model, the more a provider performs a service, the more the provider gets paid by adding up the number of events times the charge per event. Without a doubt, even in a more value-based world there will continue to be certain services for which a fee is charged per occurrence. Concierge services are likely to continue to have value for certain consumers, as are bundled payments, both of which involve a modified fee-for-service model.

Flexible consumption was reviewed earlier in chapter 9. This is expected to take off in any number of industries in the future. For example, you subscribe to a smartphone service, home entertainment, credible news sources, and music platforms, so why not a car? Volvo (2020) has seized on this opportunity:

> Care by Volvo is a subscription service that covers your car payment, insurance coverage for all eligible drivers, maintenance, and more for one monthly fee.
>
> For one flat monthly payment, you get everything you need:
> - Insurance coverage for your vehicle and all eligible drivers
> - Factory scheduled maintenance
> - Road hazard tire and wheel protection
> - Excess wear and use protection (we waive up to $1,000 of excess wear)
> - 15,000 annual mile allowance
>
> Choose the model that fits your lifestyle. After 12 months, you can upgrade to a new model to better fit your family's needs – and help you stay up to date with the latest technology.
>
> That's the idea behind Care by Volvo, which puts you behind the wheel for an all-inclusive flat monthly fee. And starting on August 26, 2019, Volvo's car subscription program got more appealing. What is Care by Volvo? Good question. For one monthly payment, you get: use of a car or SUV, insurance, maintenance, roadside assistance, 15,000-mile annual driving limit, ability to switch vehicles after one year.

Think back to the most recent buying experience you had for health insurance. Then consider how easy Volvo has made it to subscribe to their new service:

> Signing up is easy with our negotiation-free process. Insurance and credit eligibility can be completed online. Your Volvo Concierge will contact you within 2 weeks and help you schedule pickup at your preferred Volvo dealer.

MARKET AWARENESS

Another nuance to strategy practice is recognizing and responding to the activities of competitors. As Mike Tyson, the heavyweight champion boxer, said, "Everyone has a plan till they get punched in the mouth." Situational assessment for a strategy consultant also means that they have, or can develop quickly, an understanding of the local/regional market. This includes not only the usual demographics and related trends, but also the major strategies being actively pursued by competitors and how they might influence the options available to the client.

This level of market awareness can be quite detailed and proprietary. It involves the who, what, how, where, and when parameters. This information is not easily obtained or retained. It must be constantly questioned and updated. This is truly in the realm of the art of the strategist.

One way of describing the strategy of an organization is constructing its story. How does the organization answer the four core questions of the strategic planning process?

1. What business are we in?
2. Who are our customers?
3. What do they want?
4. How are we going to give it to them?[3]

In considering these questions, it is hard to overstate the opportunities for consultants. For the strategist, these are the questions that drive the strategic planning process. They are easy questions to ask, and difficult questions to fully answer, not to mention that the answers will no doubt change over time.

The key challenges for the consultant are translating strategy into actions and creating alignment throughout an organization. Once the direction is established through a vision or grand strategy, it is necessary to develop a manageable set of actions that are aligned and linked financially in order to act upon that vision. Ultimately, strategic planning is all about resource allocation and the performance that comes from it. But healthcare is tricky even when you have a clear view of the future. As Seema Verma, administrator of the Centers for Medicare & Medicaid Services, has noted, "The issue we have in value-based care is that many of our models unfortunately are not working the way we would like them to . . . they are not producing the types of savings [and quality results] the taxpayers deserve" (Fierce Healthcare 2020). For the foreseeable future, healthcare is likely to be a target-rich environment for the strategic consultant.

REFERENCES

Chereau, P., and P. X. Meschi. 2018. *Strategic Consulting: Tools and Methods for Successful Strategy Missions*. New York: Palgrave MacMillan.

Christensen, C. M. 1997. *The Innovator's Dilemma: When New Technologies Cause Great Firms to Fail*. Boston: Harvard Business Review Press.

---

3. This is a variation on essential managerial questions originally posed by Peter Drucker.

Christensen, C. M., J. H. Grossman, and J. Hwang. 2008. *The Innovator's Prescription: A Disruptive Solution for Health Care.* New York: McGraw-Hill.

Cohen, E. 2014. "Ebola: Five Ways the CDC Got It Wrong." CNN Health. Published October 13. www.cnn.com/2014/10/14/health/ebola-cdc/index.html.

Fierce Healthcare. 2020. "Verma Says Value-Based Care models haven't made good return on investment.'" Published October 13. www.fiercehealthcare.com/payer/verma-says-value-based-care-models-haven-t-made-good-return-investment.

Johnson, S. R. 2020. "Despite ACA Coverage Gains, More People Can't Afford Care." *Modern Healthcare.* Published January 27. www.modernhealthcare.com/insurance/despite-aca-coverage-gains-more-people-cant-afford-care.

Kotter, J. P. 2000. *Why Transformation Efforts Fail.* Boston: Harvard Business Review.

Lansford, T. 2017. *Political Handbook of the World, 2016–2017.* Washington, DC: CQ Press.

McBride, D. 2018. *Caring for Equality: A History of African American Health and Healthcare.* Lanham, MD: Rowman & Littlefield.

McCaughey, B. 2020. "US Hospitals Aren't Ready for the Coronavirus." *Wall Street Journal.* Published January 25. www.wsj.com/articles/u-s-hospitals-arent-ready-for-the-coronavirus-11579975968.

Santayana, G. 1905. *The Life of Reason.* New York: C. Scribner's Sons.

Twachtman, G. 2020. "Costs Are Keeping Americans Out of the Doctor's Office." *JAMA Internal Medicine.* Published January 29. www.mdedge.com/internalmedicine/article/216399/business-medicine/costs-are-keeping-americans-out-doctors-office.

Vidal, Y. 2015. *How to Prevent the Spread of Ebola: Pathogenesis of Ebola Virus.* St. Louis, MO: Lara Publications.

Volvo. 2020. "Care by Volvo." Accessed August 12. www.volvocars.com/us/care-by-volvo/.

Yale, K., T. Raskauskas, J. Bohn, and C. Konschak. 2015. *Clinical Integration: Population Health and Accountable Care,* 3rd ed. Virginia Beach, VA: Convurgent Publishing.

CHAPTER 17

Unfinished Business and Concluding Thoughts

Now that we have addressed the elements of exceptionalism, the nuances of consulting to healthcare organizations, and the evolution of the healthcare consulting profession, there still remains some unfinished business. As was mentioned at the beginning of this book, "It is a common affliction of consultants to feel that your work is never done with a given client; it remains unfinished business." No amount of reflection can fully prepare you for the variety of things that you will encounter as part of the consulting experience. This is worth noting, if only to point out that not all problems can be fully resolved. The tolerance for things left undone varies considerably from person to person. I am one of those with whom it does not sit well. But you must learn that sometimes you have to move on. So, I offer a few real examples in this regard.

MY FAVORITE CONSULTANT SAYING

There are many jokes about consulting, most of which have an element of truth to them. There are also a few sayings that relate to clients. I love the description of a consultant as "Occasionally wrong, but never in doubt." But perhaps my favorite is

> Give the client what they want, and they might let you give them what they really need.

On numerous occasions, this has helped me explain to my colleagues and team members why things happen a certain way. It is what I rely on when I have run out of logical explanations for a peculiar decision that a client has made, and it happens more often than you might think.

The simple reality is that even the exceptional consultant rarely, if ever, has the full picture of a situation. While this might be true of most management positions as well, it carries with it an added burden in consulting. In accepting a management position with an organization, the implicit assumption is that you will be given the opportunity to manage. There are, of course, some constraints that always come with the job. If you are a CEO, then those constraints could come from the board to whom you report. If you are in middle management, then the constraints can come from your boss. There are always constraints, and if those constraints get to be too much, or inhibit your ability to do your job effectively, then it is time to move on.

With consulting, it's a bit different. Here are a few real examples of what I have had to deal with:

- What do you do when a client signs a nondisclosure agreement with one organization and then another one with a competing organization—an ethical violation?
- What do you do when a subordinate complains to the CEO about an exchange the subordinate had with you, and the CEO, in turn, confronts you and blames you for the exchange—but the facts were misrepresented?
- What do you do when, based on everything you know, the client has selected the wrong option—one that will have dire consequences for the organization?
- What do you do when the client CEO is unwilling to follow your advice, the result of which is that the CEO will be terminated—and they are?
- What do you do when there is a misunderstanding that you would like to clear up, but the client is not interested?

The reality is that even the exceptional consultant is never really in control of a client engagement—the client is. The trust relationship between the consultant and the client makes this clear. You are a guest in their house, and there might come a time when you are no longer welcome in that house. Most of the time you leave voluntarily with a good feeling because your work is done. But leave you must. You may feel some separation anxiety accompanying this parting. Often, there can be a strong sense of unfinished business and you have to learn how to handle this.

FEELING THAT YOUR WORK IS NEVER DONE

It is unquestionably a privilege to be invited into a person's house and given the opportunity to help that person succeed. With that privilege comes certain responsibilities and accountabilities, among them, hopefully, are no surprises in the consulting engagement. But how far does this go?

For example, in any given client situation, there will always be more work to be done. Technically, beyond the agreed-upon scope of an engagement, that is not the responsibility of the consultant, but rather the responsibility of the people who hired you. So, as the consultant, how far does your responsibility go? It goes only as far as the scope of work allows, and no further.

Yet, you have some ideas about what to do next. Should you share these? How hard do you push? Obviously, this all depends on the relationship you have established with your client, and what urgency might accompany the next activity. There are often opportunities to suggest additional work. However, you must be careful not to be too pushy, or to come across as self-serving. You will need to counter the perception that suggesting more work is in the best interest of the consultant, but not necessarily the client.

Perhaps the best approach to ending a project is to get an evaluation from the client, with suggestions from the client team about what went well with the engagement and what you could do better next time. This feedback is invaluable and might include the request for a testimonial, which can be used in marketing to future potential clients. Be aware, asking for feedback makes you vulnerable, but it also allows the client to ask you for the same feedback, which might present an opportunity. The client could ask something like, "What else do you think we might want to tackle as an organization?" Some consulting firms structure feedback on their work through a third party to ensure objectivity. A variation on this theme is to build a follow-up visit or conversation 30–90 days after the project is completed. This technique can be an effective way of parting ways more gradually, and it keeps the door open for both feedback and a discussion of other opportunities.

YOU MUST BE WILLING TO CUT THE CORD

A bond often forms between a consultant and a client. This is similar to the bond between a physician and a patient. You share sometimes intimate information with each other, create some interdependency, and come to care about each other. Your relationship can easily extend beyond a professional encounter, but beware the attachment. This is a relationship, by its nature, that should not last indefinitely. The person you are dealing with at the client site might not be there for much longer. The circumstances that brought you in initially might be corrected with no need for you to remain. You must be willing to cut the cord.

This does not necessarily mean that you lose touch with each other, but you might. The simple reality is that, as an exceptional consultant, you are in demand,

and you have the next engagement to move on to. You have little time to process any lingering feelings about the last engagement because you are confronted by the challenges of the next one. I highly recommend a dinner or casual meeting at the end of every engagement to share some final thoughts. This might include the entire engagement team.

Cutting the cord takes a bit of getting used to. For some of us, it never really feels all that good. Consulting is about empathy. It feels great to improve the position of a client and leave them in a better place than where you initially found them. I find myself reflecting with pride on the continuing success of a client that I helped navigate some difficult waters. But it does not always work out that way. While it can be difficult, it is imperative to keep your feelings in check and not lose sight of the prize. The prize is to accomplish the work you set out to complete and then move on.

Yes, after spending sometimes years working with many clients in many different locations, breaking away from that involves a feeling of loss. I miss the places where I have hung my hat for a significant period of time. I miss Spokane, Anaheim, Medford, Stamford, Portland, Lancaster, Columbus, Holland, Greensburg, Morgantown, Saratoga, Jacksonville, Savannah, Houston, Boston, Annapolis, Springfield, Park Ridge, Cleveland, Milford, Cherry Hill, and Omaha. (OK, I don't miss everywhere I have traveled.) I have logged more than 5 million miles, and that has taken its toll. But time spent on the road has also exposed me to many incredible people with whom I have interacted at the board level, in management, and on the provider staff. I remain awed by caregivers and first responders who save and improve lives every day. These are people who have greatly enriched my life because they have entrusted me with their hopes and beliefs. I hope that in some small ways I have made it easier for them to do their work.

The exceptional consultant always hopes to leave something behind at the end of an engagement. It should have been a good experience for you and for the client. Even more than that, you hope it was an experience the client is willing to talk about in favorable terms. This might lead to more work in the future. Usually, but not always, you hope that the client will send you more work, should the need arise. You also hope that you will be praised for your work, praise that can translate into a referral for a future prospective client.

In many cases, you hope that you have learned something in the process and helped your client learn some things as well. Consulting is an experience. Approached the right way, the learning never stops. It is true, some of what you learn might be uncomfortable, like correcting a bad habit, but it is learning nevertheless. Most of it can help you gain valuable experience that makes your input even more valuable for your next client.

ENJOY THE RIDE!

Experience is a great teacher. Savor the opportunities. Recognize that your client has left something behind for you, just as you have done so for them. As simple as it seems, it is important to take stock of our experiences. Ideally, your consulting experiences will be overwhelmingly positive. But recognize that there is an element of risk that is always present. There are good clients and bad clients, good engagements with a client and poor engagements with a client. Over time, hopefully, these things balance out. Just don't let the bad experiences accumulate too far. If your experiences as a consultant are not overwhelmingly positive, it might be time to reconsider your career choice.

Along with the element of risk, there is another danger in consulting that must be acknowledged. As a consultant, you are constantly onstage, so there is considerable stress involved that takes a toll on your psyche, even though you might not be cognizant of it. There can be few breaks in between client engagements that allow you to fully process things. I used to insist that employees take some time off, especially upon completion of a large client engagement, to be able to process the results properly.

Perhaps the ultimate danger to the exceptional consultant is burnout. More than a few consultants who I respect have found that they needed to get out of the business, at least for a period of time. The pace was too much. They literally did not have adequate time to process everything they had been exposed to. They just needed a break.

In some cases, these consultants "boomeranged" and came back into consulting, but they took some time away from it to "get their mind straight." This is a phrase several people have used.

I have found interesting what some consultants did after they left the business. In one case early in my career, a partner who was described as intense, and even abrasive, walked away and opened a candy store in a rural community in northern California. I happened to visit him some years later with a colleague from that same firm. I barely recognized him, given his relaxed and calm demeanor. The move away from the intensity of a high-pressure consulting firm to a sleepy rural community was a lifesaver for him. Another person left and took a world tour with his family. Many other consultants with whom I worked went into operations and got off the road, at least for a while.

The people with whom I have interacted in consulting mostly enjoyed their experiences and benefited emotionally, even spiritually, from them. And, yes, they benefited financially as well. Whether you decide to pursue consulting as a career, or embrace it only for a period of time at the beginning, middle, or end of your career, it can and should be very rewarding.

Perhaps Roger Nutter, a seasoned search consultant from Cincinnati who was featured in chapter 10, said it best when I had a brief conversation with him at a recent meeting.

I commented, "Consulting is not what a lot of people think it is."

"Yeah," replied Roger, "but it sure is fun."

A Brief History of the American Association of Healthcare Consultants

THE ORIGIN OF AAHC is a rich tapestry of personalities who brought healthcare consulting into the mainstream. A few consultants began to meet around the annual conventions of the AHA until the AAHC was finally organized in 1948 around the purpose "To study and advance hospital administration and planning to improve the professional and ethical standards and services of hospital consultants." Evoking ethics in this organizing statement was no fluke. In fact, membership criteria in AAHC clearly focused on separating the pros from the rest. It started with requirements related to longevity (at least five years of experience) and separate membership categories for full-time (at least 75 percent) and part-time. Frank Briggs suggests that the prevalence of physician members who were accustomed to the rigors of professional licensure probably influenced the development of some stringent qualifying criteria. It was both a personal membership and a firm membership association with a formal credentialing process. Never easy, this process proved quite instructive to those of us who were immersed in its inner workings. At the time, the function of such an association was truly invaluable because there were virtually no barriers to individuals who wanted to represent themselves as consultants. Given the lack of entry barriers, it is not surprising that there is a wide variation of skill sets among individuals and firms.

The development of AAHC was not the only focus on consulting at the time. There is a fun story regarding the origins of healthcare consulting, which is tied to the creation of educational programs that focused on producing professional managers for hospitals and health systems. James A. Hamilton founded the first graduate program of hospital management at the University of Minnesota in 1946. It became known affectionately as the "Minnesota Mafia," and it produced many prominent executives who played a significant role in consolidating community hospitals into many of the largest regional health systems in the United States. As the story is told:[1]

> Hamilton played a prominent role in developing the Hill-Burton hospital construction program. Counties would apply for and get Hill-Burton grants to build a local hospital, and then try to figure out how to do so.[2] How large should it be? What programs should be included? What equipment is required? What are the key design components? Who can design and build such a facility? The dawn of healthcare consulting was upon us. Having advised on the original Hill-Burton legislation, Hamilton was in a unique position to play a prominent role as one of the few people who knew the answers to some of these questions. Of those questions that he did not know the answers, he would figure them out. *This legislation and the related funds clearly had a big impact on the profession of healthcare consulting.*

Hamilton founded and taught in the graduate program from 1946 to 1966. At the same time, he developed the first burgeoning healthcare consulting practice—James A. Hamilton Associates. One of the founding pillars of the graduate program was the "14-Step Method of Problem-Solving," which reads like a how-to consulting primer and has survived to this day with some refinement. (See appendix B.) It is by no means a stretch to say that Hamilton is the founding father of healthcare consulting.

As the University of Minnesota program was expanding, Hamilton was selecting some of his best and brightest students to join his consulting firm. When you think about it, Hamilton had quite a racket going. He not only was graduating staff for his new consulting firm, he was graduating future clients who would hire those consultants. One of these students was John Sweetland (1927–2007). Sweetland worked with Hamilton for many years, and then set out on his own through Sweetland Associates. He continued in the tradition of Hamilton to design and develop new hospitals and additions to hospitals around the country. He also taught in the Minnesota program, for one week each year, a capstone course of case studies from his consulting experiences. Before Sweetland broke off from James A.

---

1. As told to me by Marc Voyvodich, founder of Stroudwater Associates consulting firm in Portland, Maine, and a past Blue Cross/American Hospital Association fellow. Shared with permission.

2. The Hill-Burton Act was "intended to improve the supply, distribution and quality of general hospital beds across the United States." It was actually signed by President Truman in 1946. Its target was to increase the supply of hospital beds to 4.5 per 1,000 population. The intent was to have at least one hospital in every county in the country.

Hamilton Associates, he had married Joan, one of Hamilton's daughters. As if that was not enough intrigue, another of Hamilton's daughters, Shirley Ann, married another Minnesota graduate named Walter McNearney (1925–2005). McNearney, who earned his degree from the Minnesota graduate program in 1950, moved on in five short years to found the graduate program in healthcare management at the University of Michigan. He subsequently became the first CEO of the newly merged Blue Cross and Blue Shield organizations (Blue Cross Associations) in 1965.

Thus, these early consultants helped foster needed hospital expansion by establishing population-based metrics, sizing the facilities, designing the services, and planning for staffing and recruiting. This was the Wild West of healthcare when things got started. Before you knew it, healthcare in the United States took off with Medicare and Medicaid in 1965, and McNearney played a prominent role in their development and passage.

Within another ten years, as capital began to come into the industry, there arose a need to regulate this flow of funds and to plan a more rational system. This required that new science enter into population-based planning for new beds and the medical specialists needed in a given geography. Opportunities were arising faster than the supply of consultants to help out. Firms were formed seemingly overnight. Faculty became famous as they lent their names to new start-ups (e.g., Herman Smith Associates). Hamilton had already established a well-deserved reputation among graduate students at the University of Minnesota, where students were reportedly put through the ringer at the end of his course, presenting their projects to the group. This reputation only grew as key graduates joined his consulting firm and began to populate other new consulting firms.

It is interesting to note that virtually all of the pioneers of healthcare consulting had previous experience in administrative and clinical roles at hospitals. There were 27 charter members of AAHC when they incorporated in 1949, 18 of whom were physicians. AAHC was somewhat dominated by those from the New York/New Jersey area, where much of the hospital construction was taking place. Most of these people previously had held hospital management positions. This was true of many of the pioneers who founded the early firms:

Early Firms and Founders

- **Hamilton Associates: James A. Hamilton.** Served as administrator at Hennepin County Medical Center in Minneapolis before he founded the University of Minnesota graduate program.
- **Herman Smith Associates: Herman Smith, MD.** Was the CEO of Michael Reese Hospital for 27 years. He started his consulting firm in 1947 and was

an active partner until his death in 1977. He was honored with a Herman Smith Chair in the Graduate School of Management at Northwestern University.

- **TriBrook Consultants: Richard Johnson.** Worked at the University of Chicago Hospital in 1950–1955, and then the University of Missouri Hospital until 1963.

Early Program Directors

- **University of Michigan: Walter McNearney.** Held administrative positions at hospitals in Providence, Rhode Island, and Pittsburgh, then joined the faculty at the University of Michigan in 1955 to head the business school's program in hospital administration.
- **Ohio State University: Bernie Lackner.** Worked initially as a janitor at a hospital and ultimately led Evanston Hospital for several decades. He was singularly responsible for integrating the graduate students of Ohio State University with the Children's Hospital of Columbus as a learning lab in the program. Many future CEOs of the Children's Hospital have come out of the Ohio State program.

Some of the pioneers developed extraordinary networks that influenced many future leaders. Two who stand out to me are Fred Gibbs and Rush Jordan:

- **Fred Gibbs: George Washington University.**[3] Although not one of the first programs, GWU's had its origins in a charismatic retired Army colonel who set a unique path for hospital administration. As noted in Fred Brown's oral history,[4] "[Fred Gibbs] was a retired colonel who had run the Baylor [University] program, which was a program for the members of the United States Army. Professor Gibbs was stern, a disciplinarian, and he taught us how to be professional. We had classes in decorum that our wives were expected to attend.

---

3. Some of the information here is from an out-of-print book published by AAHC, *Fred Gibbs, Members of a Group: A History of the American Association of Hospital Consultants*, AAHC, 1984. Also, *The GW and Foggy Bottom Historical Encyclopedia*, created by the Special Collections Research Center.

4. Fred Brown Oral History, American Hospital Association. Interviewed by Kim M. Garber on November 6, 2015.

Frederick H. Gibbs (1902–1985) retired as a full colonel in the Army after 32 years, during which time he served as director of the Baylor-Army Program in Health Care Administration. He then became the first chair of the George Washington University Department of Health Care Administration. Forty years of healthcare administration: 1959–1999.

We learned how to present ourselves at meetings and how to present ourselves in groups, which were the consequence of our responsibilities as healthcare executives. The discipline from his military career carried over. We wore coats and ties, and we had to be at class. If you weren't in class ten minutes before the starting time, you weren't allowed in the classroom. He taught us to be responsible. He taught us to be timely."

- **Rush Jordan: University of Alabama at Birmingham.**[5] The University of Alabama at Birmingham (UAB) had one of the early graduate programs focused on healthcare administration. Jordan had already started several other graduate programs, but found a comfortable home at UAB. While there, he developed a unique annual retreat at which noted speakers were invited to share their expertise and keep his group connected. His alumni from graduate programs, residencies, and other interactions were invited to get together once a year to break bread, to share war stories, and for continuing education (at least that's what they told me).

Jordan was one of those storied personalities who was larger than life and truly authentic. Jerry Glandon, former president and CEO of the Association of University Programs in Health Administration, tells a story in which he was trying to get ahold of a prominent speaker for a conference while at UAB, but was having trouble getting a return call. He shared his frustration with Jordan in a casual conversation, and Jordan told him to use his name next time. On his next call, Glandon was leaving a message on the speaker's machine when he mentioned Jordan's name. Immediately, the speaker interrupted the message by picking up the receiver. He asked Glandon, "Rush asked you to call? What can I do for you?" Rush had quite a reach.

Some new firms were refugees from larger firms (global firms and the Big 8 accounting firms). Others were simply entrepreneurs who saw an opportunity and seized it. Not all of these new consultants were formally trained, nor were they all credible. Some disasters occurred, to be sure; it was, after all, the Wild West. Over time things calmed down, and regulation caught up with the out-of-control growth of new hospitals. Some of the unbridled growth was the result of the very generous federal (Medicare and Medicaid) method of paying hospitals on the basis of "lesser of costs or charges." The early hospital administrators quickly learned that to grow and get paid more, you simply had to spend more. During

---

5. L. R. "Rush" Jordan was assistant director of Duke University Medical Center in 1955 and went on to many significant positions, starting graduate programs in health administration (e.g., University of Florida) and running other hospitals (e.g., Miami Valley, Dayton). He was inducted into the Healthcare Hall of Fame in 2000.

this time, it did not take a lot of talent to manage the revenues, especially with an aging population that had a very attractive government insurer paying their bills.

In retrospect, it was no surprise that around this time the AAHC began to take off.[6] What began as a gathering of pioneers expanded into a juggernaut of innovators. They successfully grew their businesses and took advantage of the many new advancements that began to bring modern medicine out of the dark ages. The following sections describe some of the official tenets of AAHC.

BACKGROUND AND MISSION

[The rest of appendix A is reprinted from Prism Consulting Services, Inc. "AAHC." www.consultprism.com/aahc.htm.]

The American Association of Healthcare Consultants, a not-for-profit organization, was founded in 1949 as a professional membership society. The mission of the Association was to elevate and maintain the competence of members in recognized areas of practice, and to make this competence known to the healthcare industry by:

- Insisting upon ethical standards of performance
- Informing the healthcare industry of these established standards
- Credentialing individuals who have demonstrated proficiency in recognized areas of expertise
- Encouraging other members to actively pursue credentialed status

All members who have obtained credentialed status as a Member or Fellow in the Association were authorized and expected to use the credentials AAHC or FAAHC.

CODE

Members of the AAHC agree to adhere to the following principles:

- To exercise independence, objectivity, and integrity in all professional engagements
- To maintain client confidentiality
- To strive continuously to improve their professional skills

---

6. See the acknowledgments to learn more about some other key players who helped spawn the healthcare consulting field.

- To fully disclose to a client any interests or relationships that may affect independent judgment in a specific engagement
- To continuously enhance the professional standards of consulting
- To fully disclose to clients in advance all financial arrangements related to an engagement
- To uphold the honor and dignity of the profession
- To maintain the highest standards of personal conduct

In recognition of the public interest and their obligation to [the] profession, members and their firms agree in writing to comply with this Code.

The following is the full, verbatim, explanation of the AAHC credentials as published by the AAHC.

WHAT DOES THE AAHC CREDENTIAL MEAN?

The American Association of Healthcare Consultants has stood for consulting excellence since 1949. The credential AAHC represents documented experience, proven competence and capability, and rigid adherence to ethical and professional standards. The credential is awarded only when individuals satisfactorily meet the experience and performance requirements of the Association, and are adjudged by their peers to be worthy of such recognition.

A credentialed consultant:

- Has a minimum of five years of consulting experience
- Is experienced in project direction and coordination
- Is competent in one or more recognized areas of expertise
- Meets established professional development and maintenance of membership requirements
- Abides by the AAHC Code of Ethics

Credentialed status—Member (AAHC) and Fellow (FAAHC)—is granted only by the Association (through its Board), and is respected throughout the healthcare industry.

Hamilton's 14-Step Method of Problem-Solving

TODAY, JAMES A. HAMILTON's problem-solving method is essential to the full-time program curriculum, in which students apply it to real-world healthcare management problems. "The Minnesota Way" has been refined over the years, but its original 14-step method remains conceptually intact:

1. Define the problem by understanding the real issues of the situation and stating the problem precisely.
2. Budget the time, as well as the effort available and necessary, to arrive at an acceptable solution.
3. List the areas necessary for consideration to determine the best solution.
4. List the elements to be measured and the best means of measurement.
5. Plan, make contact, collect, and classify data.
6. Make comparisons with others, with existing standards, or with past experience.
7. Interpret results of comparisons by seeking the real reasons for variance.
8. Develop temporary conclusions.
9. Consider various solutions, and choose the best, not the first acceptable.
10. Take a fresh look at the approach to the problem and the selected solution.
11. Develop a plan of accomplishing the solution.
12. Determine recommendations, which invite action.
13. Prepare and present a report to those who make the final decision.
14. Implement the action to carry out the selected solution.

Source: University of Minnesota School of Public Health. "About the MHA Founder." www.sph. umn.edu/academics/degrees-programs/mha/master-healthcare-administration/mhafounder/.

Index

Note: Italicized page locators refer to exhibits.

Brion, Arden, 217
Bristol Group, 119
Brown, Fred, 262n4
Budgets and budgeting, 48, 51, 89
Bugbee, George, 240
Bundled payments, 231, 248
Burnout and stress, *42*, *46*, *49*, 195, 257; billable time and, 91; clinician, 5
Burns, L. R., 174
Business intelligence software, 65
Business of Paradigms, The (Barker), 218n3
Buy-in provisions, 171–72

Cambridge Health Alliance, 241
Cancer care: costs related to, 228
Capital: growth and access to, 138
Care by Volvo, 249
Career choice(s): consulting as a stepping-stone, 42; popularity of consulting among, xx; reconsidering, 257
Career consultants, xxii; work–life balance and, 3–4, 6
Career goals: progression in career path and, 39–41, *40*
"Career-limiting acts" (CLAs), 9, 29
Career tracks: financing of graduate education and, 171
Casciato, Georgia, 27
Case studies, 44, 215; capture the key exchange, 212–13; embracing different perspectives, 220–21; exceptional consultants, 179–81; fairness and getting fired, 219–20; helping people see themselves in the vision, 217–19; seeing yourself as others see you, 215–17; staying above the fray—palace intrigue, 222–23; three most important people, 211–12; when clients no longer listen, 221–22; the world's smartest—Houston, we have a problem, 214–15. *See also* Tips from the trenches
Cash flow, 138
Castling Partners, 32
Center for Healthcare Industry Performance Studies, 31

Centers for Disease Control and Prevention, 241, 242
Centers for Medicare & Medicaid Services, 77, 217n2, 235, 250
CEO Roundtable, *79*
"Certificate of need" agencies, 5n1
Certificate of Need policy, 229
Chain of command, 96
Change, 77, 205; consultants and tapestry of, 12; organic and disruptive, 241; transformational, 247
Chartis Group, 147, 154; overview comparison of, *155–56*
Chief executive officers (CEOs), 32, 103, 233; interview process and, 62; trusted advisors and, 94–95
Chief strategy officers, 95–96
CHI Systems, 148
CHS, 143
CLA (CliftonLarsonAllen), *111*
Clarity Insights, *111*
CLAs. *See* "Career-limiting acts"
Clearview Healthcare Partners, *117*
Cleveland Clinic, 217
Cleverley, Bill, 31–32
Cleverley + Associates, 31, 32
Client-centric: being, 97–98
Client experiences: authenticity and, 187
Client-initiated engagements: supplemental staffing and, 101
Client perspective: being client-centric, 97–98; defining the client, 94–97; different needs require different skills, 99; understanding, 93–106; viewing engagement as a relationship, 99–100
Client relationship, 105, 106; cutting the cord, 255–56; enduring, 200, 206–9
Client representatives, 136
Clients, 18–19; bad, 51; collaborating with, 87, 88; competition for, 18; consultant selection by, 101–3; defining, 94–97; firing, 105–6; securing, 28; who no longer listen, 221–22. *See also* Consultants; Engagements

Thieme, Carl, xv

Thinking on your feet, *36*, 38–39, 84

Third-party payment system, 229

Thought leadership: revenue growth and, 173–75; standardization and, 175, 176, 177

Time-and-expenses billing method, *141*

Time management, 190; project management and, 66; skills, 36, *36*

Timesheets, 48

Tips from the trenches: audit clients, 121; billing rates, 67; business intelligence software, 65; credit for sales, 135; decision-making framework, 215; diagnostics, 218; friends don't buy from friends, 28; keeping ego in check, 206; leadership development, 128; negotiation, 221; organization as ultimate client, 95; partnerships, 172; personal consulting brand, 26; politics of healthcare, 223; risk tolerance, 17; short-term *vs.* career considerations, 166; standardization of purchasing/contracting function, 104; steep learning curve in consulting, 9; time-and-expenses compensation model, 26. *See also* Case studies

Tolerance for risk. *See* Risk tolerance

Toomey, Robert, xiii

Touche Ross, 120, *120*

Training, *42*, 44, 137–38; formal, 53; at global firms, 116; importance of, 186; standardization and, 176

Transformational change: clear sense of the future and, 247–49; independent consultants and, xviii–xix

Transparency, 85, 247; consumerism and, 235; price, 232, 235. *See also* Accountability

Travel: aging and, *42*, 48–49; flexibility with work environment and, 73, 90; personal credit for, 126–27; seasoned consultants and, 187

Tribrook Consultants, 262

TriBrook Group, 152

Trinity Health, 28

Triple Aim, 231

Tronnes, Hans, xv

Truman, Harry, 239n1, 260n2

Trust, 12, 18, 55, 75, 93, 97, 203, 219; confidentiality and, 81; consulting engagements and, 99, 100; disclosure and, 201; earning and keeping, xvii; in enduring client relationships, 207, 208, 209; structured interviews and, 61; superior team dynamics and, 195. *See also* Empathy

Trusted advisors, 18, 94, 206

Trusted advisor status, achieving, 199–209; communication and, 200; disclosure and, 200–201; disputed resolution and, 200; enduring client relationship and, 206–9; engagement interview process, 201; falling on your sword and, 205–6; first impressions and, 202–4; muscle memory and, 204–5; reports and deliverables and, 201–2; scope of work and, 199–200

Tschetter, Bob, xiv

Tuition reimbursement, 126, 127

Turnaround engagements, 144

Turnover: dealing with, 168–70; rate for hospital CEOs, 8, *8*

Tyler, Larry, xv

Tyson, Mike, 249

Unfinished business: handling, 254–55

UnitedHealth (Optum), 142

United HealthCare, 31

United States: complexity of healthcare in, 225–26; healthcare spending as percentage of gross domestic product in, 12

University of Alabama at Birmingham, 263

University of Michigan, 262

University of Minnesota: first hospital management graduate program at, 259–60

University of Wisconsin: Population Health Institute, 236

Urgent care: reform and, 77

Urgent care centers, 231

Urgent engagements, 101

Usage-based monetization method, 141
Utility model, 230
Utilization: reduced, 246; statistics, 59

Value: shift from volume to, 247–48
Value-based care, 105, 227, 247, 248, 250
Value components: of professional consultant,
   12–14, *13*
Value equation, 247
Vault: top 20 best consulting firms for
   healthcare in 2020, 116, *117*
Verma, Seema, 235, 250
Video conferencing, 47
Virtual care, 118
Virtual firms, 68, 112, 118–19, 147–48, 153;
   accountability and, 119; flexibility in, 118
Virtual health, 47, 77, 118, 248
Virtual medicine, 231, 235
Vision, 250; business videos on, 218n3;
   corporate culture and, 163; helping people
   see themselves in, 217–19; key elements
   of, 218
Visioning: in sports, 218
Vista Equity Partners, 142
Vizient, *111*
Volatility: of healthcare management, 9
Voltaire, 73, 226
Volume to value shift, 247–48
Voluntary Hospitals of America, 143
Voyvodich, Marc, 260n1

Walgreens, 242
Wall Street Journal, 162

Walmart, 17, 242
Warrants, 45
Watson (IBM), 197
Wealth creation, *42*, 45, 174
Wegmiller, Don, xv
Welch, Jack, 26, 137
West Monroe Partners, *111*
Witalis, Roger, ix
Wivle, Earle, xv
Women: lifestyle challenges for, 47
Woodrum, David L., xv
Word of mouth: service exchange and, 19
Work environment: being flexible with,
   73, 90
Work–life balance: being on the clock and,
   48; consulting myths and, 6, *7*; seeking,
   187–88
World War II, 239
Write-downs, 143–44

Young (or new) careerists: apprenticeship
   model and, 53; consulting career path
   for, 40, *40*; exposure/experience and, 43;
   formal training for, 53; global firms and,
   116; inexperienced, 12; new learning
   experiences and, 9; nonmonetary benefits
   and, 127; small and medium specialty
   practices and, 113; solo practice and,
   112, 113

Zismer, Daniel K., 32, 162, 243
Zoom, 47, 68
ZS, *117*

About the Author

Scott A. Mason, DPA, FACHE, is an advisor to hospitals, health systems, and health-related companies as an independent consultant, board member, and serial entrepreneur. His career has spanned diverse strategy assignments with more than 400 organizations in 40 states. In addition to joining Booz Allen Hamilton and founding his own firm early in his career, he has held senior executive positions with a number of prestigious firms, including Cushman & Wakefield and ECG Management Consultants. Mason has also served in a variety of interim management positions, including as a hospital executive and president of a regional health system. After selling his consulting firm to a health technology company in 1997 (after 17 years), he helped start two other technology firms related to electronic health records.

Mason is a recognized thought leader in healthcare strategy. A trusted advisor to executive teams and boards, he has written extensively and established himself as one of the industry's prominent voices in dealing with key trends and their implications.

The focus of Mason's strategy engagements has evolved over the years from aggregating regional hospital systems (more than $20 billion in hospital mergers and 35 regional health systems formed) to conducting post-merger integration following these initial mergers. Mason was an early advocate for clinical service lines. As a Fellow and faculty member of the American College of Healthcare Executives (ACHE), he has taught a two-day seminar to senior healthcare executives for several years titled "Growth in the Reform Era." He has also served on the advisory committee of the ACHE Healthcare Consultants Forum and is proud to have been elected in past years as chairman of the American Association of Healthcare Consultants.

A popular speaker at regional meetings and board retreats, Mason has published extensively. In 2016, he received the coveted Dean Conley Award for best article of the year for his contribution to ACHE's journal *Frontiers of Health Services Management*, titled "Retail and Real Estate: The Changing Landscape of Care Delivery." Recently, his focus has shifted more toward creating "systemness" through mergers and shared clinical service lines and by improving the patient experience through adoption of retail strategies and embedding them into community-based ambulatory care and related physician practices.

Mason is a graduate of Duke University, where he majored in neuroscience (graduating with honors) and was a walk-on basketball player. He also completed a master's degree at Pennsylvania State University and a doctoral degree in health policy and administration at George Washington University.